The American
Cinema of Excess

The American Cinema of Excess

Extremes of the National Mind on Film

MIKE KING

London: Stochastic Press

Mike King, 1953-

ISBN-13 978-0995648012
ISBN-10: 0995648018

Includes bibliographical references and index.

British Library cataloguing data are available.

On the cover: Eric Bana in *The Hulk*, 2003 (Photofest)

Formerly published by
McFarland & Company, Inc., Publishers
Box 611, Jefferson, North Carolina 28640

London: Stochastic Press

For Moe

Acknowledgments

Acknowledgments are due to London Metropolitan University for my position as Reader, which has given me the time to undertake this research. Thanks also to those who read early drafts and provided encouragement and feedback, including Dana Church, Mo Dodson, Nona Ferdon, Frank McGillion, Jane Howard and Richard Milton. Above all, thanks to my beloved Heather for supporting me in this.

For this new edition I would also like to thank the staff at Mc-Farland for the original book layout which I have drawn on in the design of this edition. I would also like to thank McFarland for publishing the original work and for their co-operation in reverting the rights to me.

Table of Contents

Part Three. The American Sanity on Film

Preface

This book is about an American cinema of excess. I can trace the motivations for writing it back to the early 1970s when I walked out of a screening of Sam Peckinpah's *Straw Dogs*. It was the Magdalene Road cinema in Oxford, England, and my departure surprised my sister and friend with whom I had watched the film. I found it hard later on to describe what had prompted me to leave: I didn't think the film was a bad film, and I still don't. I just didn't want to sit through any more of the rape scene. To my later alarm, I found that this placed me in the company of what I will call "cultural conservatives"—those who object to violent or transgressive material in cultural productions. But I have made a personal and scholarly journey since the 1970s which has forced me to recognize the value of such transgressive material, and to broadly defend the avant-garde or what could be called "extreme cinema," while still owning the gritted teeth through which I experience some of this material. Hence I needed a way to contemplate extreme cinema that recognizes excess as excess, but without flinching from it and advocating its censorship, as the cultural conservatives do.

In looking at the literature on American film I found that the problem of dealing with a cinema of excess provoked in itself an extreme of response: the critics of the Right want cinema to celebrate rather than attack American culture, while the critics of the Left insist that the only function of cinema, as of all art, is to challenge or subvert the dominant paradigm. The Right wants to eliminate a cinema of excess; the Left finds its transgressional material an insufficient service to "the revolution." Neither of these extremes, I believe, is adequate to the problem of engaging with a cinema of excess; neither provides a critical framework from which to assess material like the rape scene in *Straw Dogs*. What was clear to me, however, was that a cinema of excess paints a portrait of the culture that produces it, a portrait that is not just interesting, but important. It is important for the American mind to recognize its own excesses, but just as much so for the rest of the world to know the American mind through whatever means are available.

I write as a British observer of America who has only visited a couple of

times and who personally knows only a few Americans. But I write as bil-
lions could: as a life-long consumer of American films and other cultural
productions, all of which paint a detailed portrait of the American mind.
How accurate is this portrait, constructed from mostly fictional material?
How accurate is the portrait of the American mind gone mad, constructed
from an American cinema of excess? I can never really know, but what can
be asserted with confidence is that this portrait is the shared property of
nearly every person on the planet who has access to a TV or goes to the
cinema. Of course, my particular analysis is based on my own personality,
cultural background, and my wider study of culture and history. There are so
many films made in America that one could perhaps construct *any* portrait
of the American mind through a personal selection, but I don't really believe
that. Instead, I believe that I have discovered all the major landmarks of the
American madness—that is, the American mind *in extremis*—neither leaving
out any really important variations, nor artificially highlighting some
quirk through unrepresentative cinema. George Steiner says, "I believe that
literary criticism has about it neither rigor nor proof. Where it is honest, it
is passionate, private experience seeking to persuade."[1] I suggest that extreme
cinema certainly provokes passionate, private experience—experience that
might well prompt the desire to persuade—and agree with Steiner that proof
might not be possible in criticism. But rigor surely *is* possible, and that is what
I attempt here.

An additional observation is needed: I would argue that post–9/11 the
acknowledgment of religion as a crucial cultural arena has increasingly
influenced criticism. Hence there is more discussion of religion here than has
been previously common in a book of this sort, and the term "God" is
necessarily used from time to time. Through my research into the origins of the
secular mind, I have adopted the use of quote marks when writing of "God"
not out of disrespect, but because of the hugely varying meaning attributed
to the term, not just across the secular-religious divide, but within the Western
traditions of monotheism. (A more detailed justification of this usage is
found in *Secularism: The Hidden Origins of Disbelief*.[2])

A final note on film citations: films are often introduced where they first
appear in a text with the director and year placed in parentheses, but I don't
think this is as useful for the reader in a book-length exposition as it is in an
essay. Hence I don't generally follow this convention, preferring instead to
mention director and date where appropriate, and to provide a filmography
with these details at the end of the book.

Introduction

This book essentially pursues two questions. Firstly, how can an American "cinema of excess" reveal the unique madnesses of the American mind, and its unique strengths? Secondly, what method of criticism provides an adequate engagement with a cinema of excess? The second question will be introduced first. In *A Cinema of Loneliness* Robert Kolker opens his preface with "American film begs us to leave it alone."[1] But of course, we cannot leave it alone, and the idea that criticism can leave its subject alone is absurd; Kolker is not arguing for that. Susan Sontag in *Against Interpretation* is more specific about the problem of criticism, saying, "The most celebrated and influential doctrines, those of Marx and Freud, actually amount to elaborate systems of hermeneutics, aggressive and impious theories of interpretation."[2] She is only against some systems of interpretation as "reactionary, impertinent, cowardly and stifling," while other systems pursue interpretation as a liberating act. The aim here is to eschew the impious and to discover what is liberating, to find a critical framework that celebrates its subject rather mauls it with barely disguised contempt.

The Marxist schools of criticism, as Sontag suggests, trace the structures of power that construct stereotypes in film, assuming that these stereotypes are useful to the dominant capitalist ideology of the marketplace in which films are produced and consumed.[3] Hence much analysis is conducted within the "hermeneutics of suspicion" which requires that the film—the "text"—be deconstructed to reveal its hidden conformity with dominant ideologies.[4] But a less suspicious approach is followed here, based on the notion that a complex deconstruction and extended hermeneutics often avoid the blindingly obvious, which in this case is that so many American films portray individuals and situations which are so grossly exaggerated as to be palpably insane. But, because the left-wing traditions of cultural production deploy the transgressional as a major ideological device, left-wing traditions of criticism cannot see it as such. The emetic becomes the diet.

Right-wing schools of criticism broadly agree that the transgressive is unacceptable. These schools are usefully divided into classical schools and schools of the religious right, and a useful term to cover this spectrum of thought is "cultural conservative." The classical cultural conservatives include T. S. Eliot and Allan Bloom (best known for his *The Closing of the American Mind*), while religious cultural conservatives include Jewish film critic Michael Medved and apocalyptical writer Tim LaHaye. What they share is a horror of liberal permissiveness which sanctions transgressive material in films, including vulgarity, explicit sex, explicit violence, and, above all, the promotion of values that undermine traditional culture and society.

There is much of value in both the critical traditions of the Left and of the cultural conservatives, but their responses to the transgressive make both of these traditions inadequate to a constructive critical engagement with a cinema of excess.

Film Criticism of the Left and Right

A broadly left-wing critical stance may only reveal its Marxist origins in subtleties. An interesting work that tackles the transgressive in American film, and paranoia in particular, is *Projecting Paranoia* by Ray Pratt. He quotes Frederic Jameson as saying that every film text is at some fundamental level a kind of political fantasy.[5] The subtlety here lies in the word "political"—it means in left-wing circles activism against hegemony. Christopher Sharrett, in his essay in *The End of Cinema as We Know It*, says that a cinema of postmodernity no longer believes in received myths, but "is also unable to break with these myths in favor of a historical materialist view of reality."[6] One has to have a significant acquaintance with Marxist jargon to know what a "historical materialist view" might be, and a significant investment in the tradition to imagine that it is the only alternative to received myths. Even more committed to the tradition, though this time expressing it more explicitly, Henry A. Giroux and Imre Szeman attack the film *Fight Club*, saying that it "ultimately manages to offer a critique of the social and political conditions produced by contemporary capitalism only in a way that confirms capitalism's worst excesses and legitimates its ruling narratives."[7] *Fight Club* will be one of the films examined later as portraying some key elements of the American mind in excess, a setting where a Marxist analysis simply gives no purchase. Giroux and Szeman's attack illustrates well why a "hermeneutics of suspicion" is "impious," to use Sontag's term: it brings to its subject a formulaic response, seeking only a confirmation of its own ideology. The leftwing analysis, in applying its rigid formula to each and every cultural production, is impious in the sense that cannot respect its subject. It cannot *listen* to the voice of the oracle, unless it speaks of revolution. John Davies and Paul Wells in their study of American film and politics present another example of the unchallenged assumptions of the Left: they say for example that the "deep theme of much American cinema is still the simultaneous longing to acknowledge the profound effects of late industrial capitalism,"[8] the effects of which are assumed, without any justificatory argument, to be negative. They go on to criticize much filmmaking as "apoliticized"—with "honorable exceptions" including Oliver Stone and Spike Lee; they reinforce their political assumptions when they say, "In this model, social redeemers, embodying a leftist stance, fail in the light of oppressive conservatism and hypocrisy of middle American power-broking," while insisting that films like *Seven* and *Fight Club* play out the "irrecoverable demise of the late capitalist urban infrastructure."

A key manifesto in the tradition of left-wing criticism is Adorno and Horkheimer's essay, *The Culture Industry: Enlightenment as Mass Deception*. The title sets out their stall, which is summed up in a single sentence in the text: "Amusement under late capitalism is the prolongation of work." Culture is already dismissed as mere amusement, while amusement is seen as an extension of the grinding duty of work. Most plaintive—particularly at the time they wrote this, in the early 1940s—is the term "late capitalism," expressing the forlorn hope that capitalism is in its death-throes; Davies and Wells *still* use it in 2002. Warming to the theme of amusement as work, Adorno and Horkheimer continue:

> What happens at work, in the factory, or in the office, can only be escaped from by approximation to it in one's leisure time. All amusement suffers from this incurable malady. Pleasure hardens into boredom because, if it is to remain pleasure, it must not demand any effort and therefore moves rigorously in the worn grooves of association.[9]

The sheer pessimism of this makes any constructive cultural criticism almost impossible in this tradition. All it can say is: if it doesn't serve the revolution it is irrelevant. But *Fight Club* deserves a critical engagement precisely because it does not move in the "worn grooves of association"; it is an original work, and a formulaic response cannot do it justice.

If the Left cannot approach a film like *Fight Club* constructively, then neither can the Right. The film appears to attack all civilized norms, so in the first place it fails in the requirement to celebrate American culture, but worse still is its portrayal of gross and transgressional acts. But where the Left, despite its historical fracturing into the sects of Lenin, Trotsky, Gramsci, and so on, is relatively consistent in its cultural criticism, the division of the Right between what we are calling here a classical cultural conservatism and a religious cultural conservatism creates very different critiques. At the same time we can flag an important cultural issue that will run through the later chapters: the division between the Hebraic and Hellenic in Western cultural heritage. This division may seem either blindingly obvious, or overtaken by new cultural forces, so that its use may seem terribly old-fashioned. But 9/11 changed this: we live in a time of intense scrutiny of the Hebraic religious heritage as it manifests itself in fundamentalist Judaism, Christianity and Islam. Classical cultural conservatism draws on the Hellenic—on Greek culture and civilization—while religious cultural conservatism draws on the Hebraic—on the tradition of Western monotheism.

Peter Watson, in his magisterial survey of twentieth-century thought *A Terrible Beauty*, describes the "culture wars" of the late 1980s, in which he identifies the "Great Enemy-in-Chief" of such left-wing progressive liberalism as Allan Bloom.[10] Bloom's highly successful *The Closing of the American Mind* argued for a return to the classical canon in American universities, a return to Greek thought. Watson adds that Harold Bloom of Yale was another powerful voice calling for a restoration of the classics, a resurgence of a belief in elitist culture voiced earlier in the century by T. S. Eliot and F. R. Leavis. Watson says that Eliot "is convinced ... that democracy and egalitarianism invariably threaten culture."[11] Ideas like this clearly place the classicists in confrontation with the left wing for whom egalitarianism is essential, and for whom the division between high and low culture—since Raymond Williams—is untenable. Allan Bloom has this to say in the conclusion to *The Closing of the American Mind*:

> Men may live more truly and fully in reading Plato and Shakespeare than at any
> other time, because then they are participating in essential being and are forgetting
> their accidental lives. The fact that this kind of humanity exists or existed,
> and that we can somehow still touch it with the tips of our outstretched fingers,
> makes our imperfect humanity, which we can no longer bear, tolerable. The books
> in their objective beauty are still there, and we must protect and cultivate the delicate
> tendrils reaching out towards them through the unfriendly soil of students'
> souls.[12]

Twenty years on, these sentiments seem just as hopelessly out of touch as they must have then. The idea that Plato has "objective beauty" may be argued for in aesthetic terms, but, as Sir Karl Popper argued, Plato—in particular in *The Republic*, but also in *The Laws*—can be shown to be morally ugly. The Blooms, Eliot and the other classical cultural conservatives all tend to a pessimism, as the above passage demonstrates when it suggests we cannot bear our imperfect humanity, or that our "accidental lives" are something we strive to forget. This pessimism is taken to an extreme in Christopher Lasch's *The Culture of Narcissism*, becoming another "hermeneutics of suspicion."Lasch doesn't clearly belong to either Left or Right, but he argues against the loss of traditional culture and values. He says, "With the collapse of religion, biblical references, which formerly penetrated deep into everyday awareness, have become incomprehensible, and the same thing is now happening to the literature and mythology of antiquity—indeed to the entire literary tradition of the West, which has always drawn so heavily on biblical and classical sources."[13] For the cultural conservative of either stripe, the loss of biblical and classical sources cannot be made up for by a new canon of contemporary works. We will return to Bloom when considering alienation, and return to Lasch when considering narcissism, in later sections.

Religious Cultural Conservatism

While Lasch may lament the passing of biblical reference as a common language, he has little common ground with the cultural conservatives of the religious right. His pessimism might be comparable to the "Preacher" in Ecclesiastes ("all is vanity") but he does not see religion as the remedy for the ills he catalogues—indeed he has no remedy at all. The religious right however has a very simple message: liberal humanism has destroyed the traditional values set out in Scripture and which are not open to revision. Most contemporary filmmaking, and especially extreme cinema, is at best empty titillation, and at worst corrupting of morals and society, they say. There is no argument here in favor of elite culture as it is precisely the cultural elite who appear to have corrupted the arts and cinema. The religious conservative criticism of Hollywood is that it ignores the "moral majority," allegedly pouring out a torrent of filth that interests only New York intellectuals, and is therefore unrepresentative of America, in particular its religious heritage. There may be *some* justification for this: for example David Martin at the London School of Economics has proposed a "centre–periphery" theory, which says that large cities and their universities concentrate a liberal elite which tend to atheism, while the majority living outside of these cultural centers are still religious.[14] The liberal elite write books, control TV stations, radio and filmmaking, according to this theory, ignoring religion or even actively denouncing it. From another viewpoint, it is argued that minorities "created the cultural histories of American film, radio, and television, particularly in their early years," particularly Jewish immigrant entrepreneurs.[15] How can these minorities serve an alleged majority culture?

Early in American cinema, censorship of the movies was organized around the so-called Hays Production Code, in force until 1968, a voluntary code adopted by the American film industry that embodied the necessary compromise between freedom of speech and religious sensitivity.[16] Explicit sex and violence, and attacks on religion, were self–edited from American cinema until 1968—that date so indelibly marked on the consciousness of the Left—when, as Stephen Prince puts it, "the dike burst,"[17] and an age-based system of classification came into being. "Family entertainment" was no longer the norm, but a niche market, allowing for all the darker sides of American life to be explored in adult-rated films. The defenders of family values were increasingly vocal, but at the same time were confined to the cultural margins. I would argue that the détente between a largely secular culture and a largely religious population in America (outside the cultural centers that Martin refers to) broke down after 9/11, making the voice of the cultural conservative an increasingly important one.

In the 1990s this shift was anticipated by Michael Medved's *Hollywood vs. America*, in which he put together a detailed case that "the entertainment industry has broken faith with its audience."[18] Medved is a radio talk show host, film critic and author who represents the views of religious Americans who object to the mass media. As a socially conservative critic he is aligned with more extreme religious thinkers such as best-selling American conservative evangelical Christian minister Tim LaHaye, author of the fictional series *Left Behind*, and *Mind Siege—The Battle for Truth in the New Millennium*, in which LaHaye attacks every element of contemporary American "humanism." LaHaye says, for example, "Volumes could be written on how Hollywood has devastated America's morals in the past half-century. Film moguls try to defend their exaltation of infidelity, homosexuality, violence and corruption by suggesting they are 'just supplying the public with what it wants.'"[19]

Tim LaHaye is one of the greatest promoters of apocalyptical thought in American fiction; films based on his books will be examined in chapter 7. His attack on humanism as a perverted kind of religion is so extreme as to make his work usually inadmissible to academic discourse, but anyone interested in defending humanism would do well to understand his attack on it: his best-seller status means that he influences millions of Americans. In a similar vein Medved attacks Hollywood as "The Poison Factory,"[20] pointing out what he calls the "three lies of Hollywood": (1) "it just reflects the world as it is," (2) "it just gives the public what it wants," and (3) "you don't have to watch it."[21] (These ideas were developed by Medved in an address to Greenville College in Illinois.) Medved has a case each time. Film does not reflect the world as it is; it selects elements of real life and brings out the dramatic in them: our fundamental appetite is for drama, not reality. Medved has done an analysis of box-office success, and, if we accept his findings, it turns out that warm-hearted family entertainment makes much bigger profits than the films exploring the darker sides of life.[22] Hence Hollywood largely does *not* give the public what it wants, not at least if you count purely monetary criteria. And he surely is right when he points out that it is very hard to avoid the outpourings of contemporary media: relaxing in front of the TV is a global pastime. But even if the socially conservative thinkers and those on the religious right are correct about the "three lies of Hollywood," their approach has a big problem. They simply deny the darker sides of human nature, and would deprive us of film as a shared experience that probes and questions that darkness.

In his Greenville address Medved tells us that his job as a film critic involves his personal suffering because "a normal human being will have a powerful instinct to get up out of his chair and to leave," if he had to watch a film like *Eyes Wide Shut*. One may sympathize with Medved as a religious person at odds with the mostly secular culture of his country, but he fails to grasp that Kubrick's last, great film actually stands for the same family values that American religious groups want to promote. Without going into the story details of *Eyes Wide Shut*, the film examines in a dramatic way what happens when a long-married couple suddenly get the fidelity jitters. What happens when, after many happy years of faithful marriage, the vista opens up of unbridled and unbounded sexuality, offered in a sumptuous and ritual setting? Medved presumably finds that appalling, but fails to get the psychological point, that by attending to the fact of these ideas welling up from the unconscious sexual libido, one does not *have* to indulge them. The film ends with no infidelity on either side, but with the realization that the protagonists' marriage is stronger than the "grass-is-greener" fantasies that, in reality, all honest adults experience at some time or another. And if Kubrick chooses to illustrate the point in a voluptuous, Neoplatonist setting (the infamous orgy scene), all the more poignant that the film should end with the recognition that the married pair would be mad to risk the real value of what they already had. Medved tells us that an American survey shows that married people have more sex and enjoy it more than unmarried people. Kubrick actually makes the same point, but helps us examine ourselves honestly—and entertainingly—in the process.

Medved sets out his opposition to transgressive cinema when he lambastes the notion of the serious artist as alienated from society, calling it a myth. He quotes a colleague who says, "Any art historian should know that none of the titans of the past centuries—neither Michelangelo nor Rembrandt nor El Greco nor Shakespeare—was ever free to insult and/or belittle the fundamental beliefs of his church and people."[23] That this is largely true is seen by secularists as an indictment of the past, not the present. But art historians will also know that the sculptor Brancusi's phrase "an art of our own" can be taken as the watchword for twentieth-century art: meaning an art that serves its own purposes, not that of the church, and what is more, one that belongs to the artist and is free to criticize.[24] For Medved, as for LaHaye, the twentieth century is an unwelcome intrusion into the (imagined) stable world order founded on Scripture. Medved goes on to say, "Until the revolution in the 1960s, the leaders of the popular culture served the artist's old purposes as 'celebrants of his society and all its values,' but since that time Hollywood has cast itself in an increasingly alienated role." For those who welcome the multicultural society, the notion that the artist is celebrant of culture raises the question: whose culture? The bard may celebrate his or her ethnic tradition—including white America's mythologized frontier history—but that is only a speaking to the ghetto. Yet Medved's point is crucial, in that it confronts the programmatic critiques of the left wing, the enslavement of art not to church but to revolution. It shames the Left by asking if there is nothing to celebrate. No, say the po-faced socialists, not until the revolution is total. To the extent that this is true, one must lean to the Right and say surely they are asking a vital question about art. In the survey of film in this book, despite the nature of the extreme cinema in question, the suggestion is made: perhaps the artist's role in a modern pluralistic society is to celebrate *life itself*. But the Hebraic tradition and its development within its Christian articulation are instinctively opposed to "a-Muse-ment" (the "Muse" being a Greek invention) if it does not serve explicit religious purposes. (Ironical, then, that so much early cinema was shaped by the Jewish entrepreneur.) Medved is therefore sarcastic of the notion that filmmakers are artists: he calls them entertainers.

From the Tragic to the Transgressive

If, unlike Medved, we are serious about film as art, we also need to distance ourselves from left-wing critiques which make art into politics. It makes left-wing inspired film studies into a branch of political science, and that is not what is attempted here. But in attempting to find a critical framework from which to examine an American cinema of the extreme, a thought arises: what about the classical notion of tragedy? When Lasch describes what he sees as a massive decline in American educational standards he cites a study that found amongst a class of twenty-five at Columbia not one had heard of the Oedipus complex—or Oedipus.[25] Yet the story of Oedipus includes some of the most transgressional acts possible. It is also one of the great Greek tragedies cited by Aristotle in his *Poetics*, the source also for the idea that the tragic play permits what is known as catharsis—a shared emotional experience that is cleansing.

This seems to be the missing element in critiques of both Left and Right. The idea that a community could watch a play that wrung them out emotionally and left them more peaceful, clear-headed, sober, and mutually engaged as citizens would be absurd to the Left. For Adorno and Horkheimer it would merely be a deceit practiced by the ruling classes to condition the citizens to their wretchedness, to weaken the desire for revolution. For religious cultural conservatives, tragedy has no place in their thinking as George Steiner pointed out in his *The Death of Tragedy*: "Tragedy is alien to the Judaic sense of the world."[26] He goes on to show that the case of Job, for example, is not tragic because "God has made good the havoc wrought upon His servant; he has compensated Job for his agonies. But where there is compensation there is justice, not tragedy." Interestingly, he also adds, "Marxism is characteristically Jewish in its insistence on justice and reason, and Marx repudiated the entire concept of tragedy."

What then of the classical cultural conservatives, like Lasch (to the extent that he is one) and the Blooms? Or where might Eliot and Leavis stand on this? Where do they stand on the question of the tragic and the transgressive? This can be answered by a key insight into the classical mindset: it has first and foremost an aesthetic allegiance. We saw earlier that for Allan Bloom the classics are where one lives more fully, not because of the tragic, but because they have "objective beauty." The transgressional, as in the Romantics, is wafted in and out on clouds of elegant language. A modern film, which chooses to show black ghetto violence, or suicide, rape or murder in its true sordidness, is an affront to the classical sensibility, which has been irrevocably removed from the real through Romantic-era aesthetics. Nietzsche's admiration for the "pale criminal" in the dock,[27] or Sartre's admiration for Genet as thief[28] are part of this aestheticization of the transgressive. But this is infinitely removed from the Oedipus of Sophocles, and from Aristotle's conceptionof the function of tragedy.

A Critical Framework of the Cathartic

The clarity of thought that Aristotle brings to his *Poetics* is precisely what an incisive Jewish thinker like Emmanuel Levinas objects to as unable to deal with the mysteries of life. Yet Aristotle has laid out a simple critical framework which holds out promise for adaptation to a cinema of excess. Aristotle considers tragedy to be a drama "characterized by seriousness and dignity and involving a great person who experiences a reversal of fortune." His key point about tragedy is that a tragic play must incite pity and fear in the audience. The pity is for a protagonist who undergoes suffering—or in our terms experiences the transgressive—while fear lies in the possibility that it could happen to oneself. He makes this clear: "pity is aroused by unmerited misfortune, fear by the misfortune of a man like ourselves." This immediately requires, for Aristotle, that the protagonist's character must lie "between these two extremes—that of a man who is not eminently good and just, yet whose misfortune is brought about not by vice or depravity, but by some error or frailty."[29]

His instincts for a good drama are made all the more clear when he says that "Those who employ spectacular means to create a sense not of the terrible but only of the monstrous, are strangers to the purpose of Tragedy."[30] This distinction between the terrible and the monstrous is perhaps one of the sharpest tools he bequeaths us in our examination of extreme cinema. The terrible for Aristotle has to provoke genuine pity and fear, as he defines them, while the monstrous—and here we will also use the term "grotesque"—is mere titillation. With the extraordinary special effects now available through the computer, "spectacular means" often become the only selling point of some mainstream action movies, and through Aristotle's useful distinction thus disqualify them from serious consideration here.

Aristotle's conception of tragedy is however only a starting point for our examination of extreme cinema. He is explicit for example that the protagonist must be "highly renowned and prosperous—a personage like Oedipus, Thyestes, or other illustrious men of such families." This would be both unsuitable for the modern age, and drastically cut down the number of films under consideration. The very concept of the "tragic" is also limited in terms of covering the full range of human suffering, and our much expanded ideas of personal, corporate, and state responsibility and accountability. Instead the term "transgressive"—also to be defined more carefully before long—allows us to include a much wider range of material, and even dramatic forms considered antithetical to tragedy, such as comedy.

Hence a scheme suggests itself, with its basis in Aristotle, where we can approach extreme cinema on the basis of a five-fold set of criteria, to be summed up under these terms: (a) transgressive material; (b) scenario plausibility; (c) emotional intensity; (d) aesthetic seriousness; (e) critical distance.

TRANSGRESSIVE MATERIAL: this extends Aristotle's notion of suffering to also include actions or experiences that are aggressive—for example towards mainstream assumptions or the State, that are sexually deviant, anti-religious, or "psychological" in a modern sense—to include depressive, nihilistic, mentally retarded or deviant; or that involve catastrophe whether man-made or of Nature. The viewing of this material should still invoke Aristotle'scategories of pity and fear, but perhaps in more complex or ambivalent ways than he could have anticipated.

SCENARIO PLAUSIBILITY: this requires that the transgressive be present within a framework of narrative plausibility. Aristotle understood well that a good play was forged between various competing necessities, but also wrote at a time of superstitious beliefs in the gods. Plausibility for a modern audience lives between the "central conceit" or plot device that makes for an interesting "what-if" scenario, and a development that is consistent with the internal logic that the device sets up. Aristotle thought that tragedy required that "Reversal and Recognition follow rule of probability and necessity"; that "there must be Complication and Unraveling"; and that there should be no *deus ex machina* to extricate the playwright from an ending he cannot resolve.

EMOTIONAL INTENSITY: this requires that attention to plausibility does not underplay the emotional. As Aristotle says, the action must be "serious, complete, and of a certain magnitude." The "Scene of Suffering" should therefore be neither overplayed nor underplayed in terms of emotional intensity. Another way of making this point is through the concept of "emotional bracketing" (defined by Stephen Prince in *Classical Screen Violence*[31] and discussed later), meaning a pause after a transgressional act to allow an audience to absorb its content and moral implications.

AESTHETIC SERIOUSNESS: Aristotle requires that a tragedy be "embellished with each kind of artistic ornament." The elaborate, even ornate, image that this conjures up is not necessarily appropriate to filmmaking, its history framed effectively by modernist notions of sparseness or even minimalism. However, cinema has its own aesthetic language, and there can be no doubt that the drama of a film—spelled out in bare outline in the script—is made immeasurably more memorable by acting, cinematography, editing and soundtrack of high artistic merit.

CRITICAL DISTANCE: this requires the possibility that all assumptions can be questioned, particularly the adoption in the first place of the transgressive. What purpose does it serve? As Aristotle so clearly understood, if the transgressive is merely monstrous, then the drama loses its serious purpose. But "distance" extends beyond this to cover such things as the distinction between a polemic and propaganda. A polemic argues a case, as John Stuart Mill would say, in the recognition that opposing views sharpen the polemic, whereas propaganda drowns out other voices.

Rather than give examples here of how this five-fold analysis applies to film, its application and ramification will be left to the main section of the book where some fifty films representing extreme cinema are discussed. One more aspect of Greek thought in relation to drama does need further introduction here, however: that of *catharsis*. Tragedy must inspire pity and fear, says Aristotle, but to what end? Catharsis is the answer: that state of mind which has faced its worst fears and is left wiser, more sober, perhaps. Catharsis is a purification of the mind and emotions which leaves the community which witnessed the dramatic spectacle in *better* shape to deal with the real world. In Buddhist terms, tragedy should inspire compassion, not forgetting that the word compassion meant originally to "suffer together." (The Buddha was however not interested in the arts or drama, so the idea of a tragic play inspiring compassion would not have occurred to him.)

As pointed out earlier, the Left are mostly uninterested in the dramatic arts as a cathartic experience: for the Left theatre and film are bourgeois productions designed as a palliative to numb the sense of oppression. Classical cultural conservatives have also lost sight of catharsis as a function of tragedy, being obsessed with the idea of high aesthetics and a canon under threat. The religious cultural conservatives, as Steiner points out, have no place for tragedy in their thought: for them the concept of catharsis is replaced by the concept of grace. But while the transgressive can lead to the cathartic, what happens when the transgressive becomes a habit of thought instead of the rare occasion in which a community contemplates the tragic spectacle and reflects on its impact? What happens when the emetic becomes the diet? This is a question that the Left cannot pose, and for which the Right has too simplistic an answer. The prime example of a cultural strand in which the purgative is mistaken for substance is within the group of mainly French philosophers such as Louis Althusser, Georges Bataille, and Giles Deleuze and Felix Guattari. Concepts such as the "solar anus," "assured schizophrenia," and a thousand other terms reveling in transgressional anti–capitalist ideas swamp this literature, the high point of which is perhaps Deleuze and Guattari's *Anti-Oedipus*. Any film criticism with its roots in this tradition is unable even to notice the transgressional let alone ask what purposes it serves.

Instead, the scheme proposed here will enable a middle path to be pursued, between the left-wing deployment of the transgressional as programmatic revolution, and the right-wing rejection of the transgressional as necessarily corrupting. What we could call the catharsis-value or purgative-quotient of a film can be assessed using the five-fold scheme just outlined, or to put it more simply we ask of a film: how can the transgressional lead to compassion?

A Cinema of Excess and the American Madness

Instead of a belief that Hollywood is against America, the analysis here starts with a belief that Hollywood—and independent film dealing with American issues—paints an accurate and useful portrait of the American mind particularly when it strays to the margins of its own excess. Hence filmic excess serves a valuable role in society as long as there can be a critical distance from its transgressive material. An American cinema of excess outlines the contours of a specifically American madness. More than sign-posting the specific contours of the American madness, however, it also signposts the unique contours of the American *genius*—effectively a celebration of American culture via a darker road. As various extremities of the American mind revealed in film are discussed, in most cases a rolling back of that extremity shows a valuable aspect of the American mind: for example in paranoia it will be shown that when rolled back from the brink it becomes the proper foundation of democracy, and in aggression it will be shown that when rolled back from the brink it becomes a constructive energy for change and innovation.

The unique portrait of the American madness, delivered to the whole world through film, may be consumed as mere entertainment. But there is no reason not to think that it is also received, worldwide, as a measure of the American worldview, its *Weltanschauung*. The American actress Meryl Streep makes this interesting point:

> What we do now is withhold films from most of America, which is shocking. And what do we withhold? The best films. If you live 30 miles out in mall-land, you can't see all the great movies. Same with the rest of the world: we export crap. And then we wonder why everybody hates us and has a distorted picture of what Americans are.[32]

This book to some extent explores that distorted picture of what Americans are, but in the belief that by rolling back the extremity of specific aspects of that distortion, we see the American mind more clearly—and in a better light.

It is time now to define a little more precisely some of the terms used in this book, though their meaning will become clearer as they are deployed. "American" cinema is intended to convey films that are about Americans, with largely American protagonists, even if the setting is outside America, or if the script and director are not American. A "cinema of excess" covers films dealing with extreme situations, which are treated in neither an anodyne nor sensationalist fashion. "The American madness" is a term used throughout this book to describe a set of cultural manifestations that could appear extreme or unbalanced from another cultural vantage point, and is not intended to convey anything resembling a clinical diagnosis. The term "transgressional" means here a cultural production that offends against mores or taste, dealing with such extreme matters as death, torture, rape, suicide, or which presents marginal ideas and experiences which challenge the norm. The term "cultural conservative" is defined here, ahead of any emerging consensus on its meaning, as those who object to the transgressional in art and culture, and who refer to a classical or Scriptural canon as the gold standard of taste and morality.

The book uses a number of terms borrowed from clinical psychiatry, alongside "madness," including "paranoia," "autism," and "narcissism." While

Christopher Lasch insists that "narcissism" should not become simply "the metaphor of the human condition," and that we should hone its meaning around the growing body of clinical writings on the subject,[33] the opposite strategy is taken here: to retrieve these terms from the specialist field of psychiatric medicine and deploy them in a cultural sense. The intention here is to remain broadly faithful to their technical meaning, while recognizing that they are too valuable as terms to leave them closeted within their discipline of origin.

Before looking in depth at the films representing the various categories of excess chosen here, a brief history of Western cultural influences shaping the American mind is presented. American history is unique, and it uniquely shapes the American mind, but so does Western history leading up to the birth of America, a land of immigrants. In the main section of the book two films each are considered for each of the ten major categories of excess identified in the American mind, and also a number of supporting films, perhaps covering fifty films in total. This leads to a "photofit" composite image of the American madness, an image of the American mind at the margins. Through this composite image of American madness we are none the less forewarned, but in a friendly way it is hoped. And to conclude what is something of a roller-coaster ride into darkness, it is shown how the contours of the American madness also lead us to the uniquely American sanity.

PART ONE

*Roots of the
American Madness*

1

The Hebraic
and Hellenic Sources

American culture is a variation of broader Western culture. It is unique because in some ways it is also the sum of all European cultures, these having contributed through immigration over centuries. But it is also more than the sum of the dominant ethnic influences, because there is a unique *American* history that has shaped its culture, events that no other nation has participated in. These events include the fact of immigration itself and that the motivation for much of that immigration was religious as well as economic. They include the traumatic experiences of a war of independence and a civil war, and the encounter with the native peoples of the North American continent. More recently key events include the entry of the U.S. into both world wars as the deciding party, its experience in Vietnam, and its global military and economic domination of the present era. The Cold War and its replacement with the "war on terror" are also defining events that shape contemporary American culture.

Hebraic and Hellenic Cultures

To the extent that American culture is shaped by earlier European culture, it has been forged in the tension between two powerful historical traditions: that of ancient Greece and that of ancient Israel, the Hellenic and the Hebraic. Roughly speaking the Hellenic cultural stream provides the rational, masculine and scientific, and also the arts, while the Hebraic cultural stream provides the feminine, the religious and the social. The terms "masculine" and "feminine" are used here in awareness of the gender minefield—in particular that Hitler seized on the alleged "femininity" of the Jews to justify their persecution. Otto Weininger, himself a Jew and writing at the time of Freud, had provided the detailed arguments for this stereotype,[1] and it is still a deeply contested issue in contemporary Jewish writing: for example Victor J. Seidler argues for the "recovery of traditions of heroic masculinities" in respect of the Holocaust.[2] But there are different models of masculinity[3] and what will be argued here is that the American heroic model in so many film representations is (a) Greek and (b) so extreme as to border on the insane. (Hence "feminine" here is not used to indicate weakness, but sanity.)

It ought to astonish us more that these two tiny ancient lands could have exerted so powerful an influence for two or three thousand years on the West, and that the roots of modern American culture can be so deeply understood by recourse to only these two influences. Winston Churchill thought so:

> The Greeks and the Jews are the two peoples whose worldviews have most influenced the way we think and act. Each of them from angles so different has left us with the inheritance of its genius and wisdom. No two cities have counted more with Mankind than Athens and Jerusalem. Their messages in religion, philosophy, and art have been the main guiding light in modern faith and culture.[4]

Jacques Derrida, in a philosophical conversation with Emmanuel Levinas carried out in their writings, finishes his key essay "Violence and Metaphysics" with a quote from James Joyce's *Ulysses*: "Jewgreek is greekjew. Extremes meet."[5] Derrida leads up to this by asking: "Are we Greeks? Are we Jews?" Given that both Derrida and Levinas are Jews, one might think this an odd question, but what is at stake is what it means to be a philosopher: Derrida insists that one has to *be* "Greek" to do philosophy, while Levinas insists that there must be space for something other—and we know that he means a place reserved and hidden from the light of Greek clarity, a place that can be termed Hebraic.[6]

The Hebraic element dominated European culture after the time that the Roman Empire adopted Christianity, which was at that time considered a Jewish sect. As Christianity forged its own identity over and above its parent religion of Judaism it also set itself against Greek religion, culture and science. Christianity today, and particularly in America, is deeply beholden to Judaism, retaining the Hebrew Bible as its "Old Testament." As the saying goes: "America's Bible belt is Israel's safety belt." Arab theorists who suggest that America is somehow in the grip of a Jewish conspiracy miss the point that Christianity, in particular American Protestantism, is deeply gripped by the story of the Old Testament. American culture as a whole never ceases to draw on the Old Testament for its metaphors and imagery. Historian Barbara Tuchman has traced the oscillation in English history of Christian allegiance in various periods, evidenced, amongst other things, by the choice of biblical names for children, for example: Guy, Miles, Peter and John would give way to Enoch, Amos, Obadiah, Job, Seth and Eli in a return to an Old Testament Hebraic sensibility after a more New Testament period.[7] It is arguable that America did not experience such oscillations, but remained more resolutely Old Testament in its religious impulse.

It took the works of Thomas Aquinas in the thirteenth century, then the flowering of the Renaissance, and then finally the European and American Enlightenment, to give voice again to the Hellenic roots of European culture. While the Universities of Europe and America were originally theological institutions, the increasing role of the sciences meant that all things Greek slowly crept back onto the curriculum. The very notion of the "academy" was a Greek one, and initially despised by the early Church fathers, but after the Enlightenment the modern university began to resemble again the famous Academy of Athens. The "classics" became the key cultural acquisition for educated Westerners, later defended by cultural conservatives such as Eliot and the Blooms, but we don't often remember how the advancement of Hellenic learning was resisted by the Church. Even now scholars of religion tread fastidiously around the difficult notion that the Greeks were "pagan" and "atheists."

With so many new cultural identities emerging on the world stage—at a time when revolutionary politics has been replaced by identity politics— the ancient tension between the Hellenic and the Hebraic may be downplayed. But Mel Alexenberg, professor of art and Jewish thought at the University College of Judea and Samaria, reminds us how alive the ancient polarity still is: he has subtitled a book on art in the digital age *From Hellenistic to Hebraic Consciousness*. He argues that the postmodern era represents a shift from Greek thought "honouring static, uniform, space-centred, closed systems" to Hebraic thought which "celebrates dynamic, multiform, time-centred, open systems"[8]—an echo of Emmanuel Levinas's similar insistence on the limitations of Hellenic thinking. Alexenberg's stance is chauvinistic and would have been dismissed before 9/11, but the intellectual landscape is now irrevocably changed: no critical framework can now afford to ignore the Hebraic roots of Western consciousness, particularly if it is dealing with the American cultural landscape.

There are of course other cultural influences on North America, including the religious cultures of the Native Americans, the culture of the Afro-Caribbeans, and, arguably, what could be called "Northern religion"—the religious sensibilities of the Nordic and German-speaking worlds, sometimes called Odinism or Wotanism. Both Allan Bloom and Peter Watson emphasize the more general impact on American culture with the influx of German-speaking intellectuals during and after World War II—Watson calls it "Hitler's Gift."[9] In *Pagan Resurrection*, historian Richard Rudgley argues more specifically that German Wotanism was not only the root of the Nazi experiment, but is also alive in America in "Aryan supremacy" movements such as led to the attack on the Murrah building in Oklahoma.[10] It may seem odd to catalogue minority American cultural influences as "religious," but we can see in film that Native American influence has a strongly spiritual element (e.g. *Dead Man*), that Afro-Caribbean influence is often broadly Voodoo (e.g. *Angel Heart*), and that horror and fantasy films often draw on Wotanistic symbols and elements (e.g. *Golden Compass*). Beyond this we find of course a plethora of sub–cultures. For example Spike Lee's films often deal with a triad of New York cultures: the Jewish, the Italian, and the Afro-American. What is proposed here however is that the "heavyweights"—the Hebraic and the Hellenic—should not be forgotten as the key roots of American culture.

Hellenic Genius and Insanity: The Oedipus Complex

What is the legacy of all things Greek for modern America? Where lies the Hellenic, specifically in the American greatness? We would have to answer: war, science, and the arts. This is not to say that great Jewish individuals have not made good generals, scientists and key contributors to the arts. Cinema as an art form is deeply indebted to great Jewish innovators and businessmen. But it is the Greek model of heroism and warfare, the Greek model of scientific inquiry, and the Greek model of the arts that dominate Western culture in those areas (as mediated through the Enlightenment). Even the word "amusement" is derived from the Greek *Muses*, female deities who pre-side over music, painting, poetry, sculpture and plays.[11] Hebraic culture, with its dire prohibition on "idolatry," did not provide the right setting for such a flourishing of the arts or science.

We only have to look at the American institutions of state to see that their grand buildings adopt Greek or Roman styling; we only have to look at the books studied by U.S. generals to see that they draw on Greek and Roman military genius. Science in the modern sense is an uncomfortable revelation to the three monotheistic religions of the West: Judaism, Christianity and Islam. It remains a Greek idea that has to be kept in its place, and Creation-ism—the denial of the scientific account of the world's origins—is emblematic of this long-standing antipathy between monotheistic religion and science. It represents in American society the ancient tension between the Hellenic and the Hebraic. But it is in the arts, in "a-muse-ment" that the Greek genius for the good life has become amplified into a uniquely American enjoyment, even hedonism.

But all things great in any culture have their downside, their madnesses. The unique contributions of Hellenic culture to the West also take us to the unique insanity of the Greeks, and none is more vivid than the Oedipal story. Its hero, Oedipus, is driven to despair and self–blinding by the twin accidents of his life: the unwitting killing of his father, and the unwitting marriage to his mother. This story would have remained for us just one of many great

Greek tragedies, written at the height of their cultural prowess in the field of theatre. But Freud spotted it as more than just another—perhaps improbable—story, more than the fevered product of literary talent. He decided that it was a core metaphor for the development of the human personality, for the growth of the psyche as it is shaped by the events of infancy and puberty. For Freud, a human being is defined by his (or her) complexes, psychological constructs with their roots in the unconscious, and the chief of these is the Oedipus complex: the rivalry of the male child with his father, and his desire for the mother.[12]

But was Freud correct? Or did his obsession with the Oedipus complex just represent the way his own psychology developed? After all it is known that he had a rather beautiful mother, and that he had a strong attachment to her.[13] If we look beyond the narrow confines of Western culture, do we find that the Oedipal story is common to other ancient cultures? The answer to that has to be emphatically no. Even as close to home as the Hebraic culture, we find no comparable story. In the Old Testament it is Abel and Cain, two brothers, who fight so bitterly, not father and son. Likewise in the Indian and Chinese traditions we find no comparable defining story. So was it an arbitrary selection by Freud from a multitude of dramatic Greek tragedies? To answer this question we have to consider that the Greek experience actually represented a profound turning point for Western and near-Asian culture: the dramatic shift from matriarchy to patriarchy. From this perspective we can see that the great Greek myths as they were first committed to writing were actually a revision of their earlier history: the goddesses were written out or downgraded in favor of the male gods.[14] The male warrior ideal began to replace the earlier female fertility ideal, and the new milieu was born in which male aggression and male competitiveness came into the ascendant.[15] We are so used to this idea of masculinity, that to imagine other masculinities is very hard for us now. And it is that which perhaps makes Freud's assumption of the Oedipal story valid ... for the *modern Western* context only. More ancient hunter-gatherer societies, and far-Eastern countries, although male aggression is present, involve quite other ways of being masculine.[16]

Of course aggression and competition when balanced by other human qualities are great forces for development and the fulfillment of social goals—for example, the moon landings symbolize the extraordinary vision and determination of the American mind at its best. But a very specific madness emerges when male aggression and competition go too far, and we suggest that this is a central madness of the American mind. Putting it another way: America is the most Oedipal culture on earth. This is not to suggest that American males all want to kill their fathers and marry their mothers. Rather the term "Oedipal" is used here in a less clinical way than Freud, and not really as a complex of any kind: more a way of indicating an intense competition between males. This inevitably shows as a rivalry between father and son, and we could speculate for example that George W. Bush's determination to invade Iraq was an act of Oedipal rivalry with his father, who notably failed to do so at the end of the first Gulf War. In a country where success is everything, and where the also-rans are called "losers," male rivalry and the socially elevated status of aggression are the norm. It takes a positive act of the imagination to step out of this norm and picture a father-son relationship based on a simple friendship, where the son's love of the mother is seen as a positive force by the father, and not as a threat.

Hebraic Genius and Insanity: The Apocalypse

If we are curious why two small nations, ancient Greece and Israel, had such a huge impact on Western culture, where it had literally hundreds of similar-sized cultures to choose from, then the adoption of alphabetical writing by the Jews and the Greeks may yet be the answer. It is not so much that the victor gets to write history, but that the written text assures the survival of a culture, whether victorious or condemned to victim status as a diaspora. Any civilization that leaves behind alphabetical texts for translation is immediately subject to attention from scholars and popular presses, and its legacy is perpetuated. If the writing method is hieroglyphic or cuneiform, clumsy and obscure, such as it was with the Sumerians and Egyptians, then their thought is easily consigned to the margins; and if there is merely an oral tradition of cultural transmission, then that is ignored altogether. The "Word" rules: but only if it is written down.

It is of course what the Jews call the Hebrew Bible (and Christians call the "Old Testament") that ensured the survival of the Hebraic cultural record and the continued plundering of its stories by Western culture. The dominance of these stories relied on one key accident of history however: the adoption of Christianity by the Emperor Constantine as the religion of the Roman Empire. At that time the New Testament was barely formed, but what circulated in the Christian enclaves of the empire was a form of the Old Testament known as the Septuagint.[17] When Christianity moved almost overnight from being a persecuted Jewish sect to the religion of state, the Old Testament in its Septuagint form effectively became a best seller. This might seem strange, but the fact is that the early conversion of the polytheist citizens of the Roman Empire was really a two-stage affair: firstly to the legacy of Judaism, and secondly to the new element within it that transcended race and region: the teachings of Christ.

The key figure in the early spread of Christianity, ensuring that it became a widespread underground movement across the empire, was St. Paul. It was his particularly Jewish genius that helped the cultural flow from the Hebraic peoples into the Christian world-as-underground-movement, and then to the dominant Christian cultural power in Europe and beyond. St. Paul is credited with bringing a uniquely Jewish idea—that of a welfare system— into the Roman Empire, but also a completely new element into the religious life of the West.[18] This idea is *caritas*, an emphasis on religious devotional love, a love that is also active in the world to help the poor and needy. St. Paul also perpetuated another deeply Jewish idea, that learning for its own sake, and the trickeries of science and technology, are secondary to devotion and acts of piety. In essence he stood against everything Greek, including its sciences and its arts, as a distraction from the love of "God," saying, for example, "knowledge puffeth up, but charity [religious love] edifieth" (I Corinthians 8:1). St. Augustine, although he was a deeply learned man, cemented this distrust of science and learning as the cornerstone of European religious development.[19] The so-called "Dark Ages" were in fact the flowering of the uniquely Christian development of these ideas, a turning back on the great extroversion of the Hellenic and Roman ideals. Both military expansion, and the turning to the world as the source of scientific investigation and the arts, were abandoned in favor of a deeply introverted religiosity.

But where lies the unique Hebraic madness, the inevitable counterpart to its religious and social genius, the madness transmitted down the centuries into modern America? We answer this in a single word: the *apocalyptic*. It is a unique concept in the religious history of the world, and lies at the heart of all three Abrahamic religions: Judaism, Christianity and Islam. The core idea is of the world as a fallen place, of humanity as laboring in darkness but moving towards a moment of redemption; of a coming time when "God" would sit in judgment and take the righteous up into eternal heaven. No other world religions have anything like it. Early Christianity is marked by the certainty of its adherents that the fallen world of the Roman Empire would soon be ended in a cataclysmic upheaval: the Day of Judgment would arrive and Jesus would return. The ancient Judaic idea of the apocalypse (found for example in the book of Daniel) was updated with Jesus as the promised Messiah, and the details spelt out in lurid imagery in the last book of the New Testament, The Revelation of John.[20] After the four Gospels, which give varying accounts of Jesus' life and teachings, and the various chapters detailing the efforts of St. Paul to establish the early Church, the last book of the New Testament seems to lurch back to Old Testament prophecy: it rather completes the cycle. It is not of course part of the Judaic scriptures, but it is deeply Hebraic in its thinking, and has been a source-book for much of the madness that is the darker side of American Christianity.[21]

Survivalist and fundamentalist groups in modern America, including the Branch Davidians, the Ruby Ridge family and the Heaven's Gate cult— all of which ended in bloodbaths—were fired by the ideas and imagery in the Revelation of John. The events of Waco in particular seem like a self–fulfilling prophecy: the more that David Koresh imagined himself to be the Messiah, the closer his group came to the Apocalypse, until in the end it was delivered by the misguided officers of the ATF and their reinforcements.[22] Eighty-two members of the cult died in the conflagration, and it had a profound affect, not just on guidelines for dealing with such situations, but on American culture and American cinema.

The siege of Waco can be considered a cultural echo of a traumatic event in Western consciousness, or at least in the history of the Jewish people. The Romans were capable of breathtaking brutality: it was the so-called "barbar-ians" of the North who finally ended the traditional Roman games on the basis that they were uncivilized. But the Romans did not undertake religious persecution as long as the citizens of the Empire included the Emperor amongst their prayers.[23] This worked fairly well in a world that was largely polytheistic, and, no doubt in many areas, still inclined to Nature religions. The one exception was Israel with its bizarre—to the Romans at least—insist-tence on a single "God." However with the good pragmatism required to hold any large empire together, the Romans made an exception for the odd nature of the Jews. The pragmatism was not mutual however: the Jews (quite naturally) wanted freedom from the yoke of Roman rule, especially *religious* freedom. Judaism, out of which the early Christianity so intimately sprung, became a martyr religion (as was early Christianity) when the Empire finally lost patience with the troublesome peoples of Palestine. After the destruction of the second Temple in 70 a.d. the last stand of the Jews (in terms of a pow-erful cultural image at least) was in the rock fortress of Masada. Fifteen thou-sand besieging Romans took two years to subdue the 1,000 defending Jews which included women and children. Even the Romans were horrified by what happened then: all but two women and five children committed suicide. Now, such an event is ghastly, but deaths on this scale in the ancient world were not particularly remarkable, as whole cultures were enslaved or wiped out. The Romans for example slaughtered the entire people of the king-dom of Dacia, now modern-day Romania, and replaced its inhabitants with more docile ethnic groups from around the Empire. The story of the Dacians has disappeared from Western cultural consciousness, but, one can argue, the reverberations of Masada are still powerfully felt. This is because Jewish (or Hebraic) culture became a cornerstone of Western cultural history through the spread of Christianity. And we will see the very specific image of Masada recurring in American cinema, focusing in a later chapter on the

Matrix films as one of the latest re–workings of this ancient story. The people of Jonestown and the followers of the Heaven's Gate cult committed mass suicide under the hypnotic legacy of this Judaeo-Christian tradition. In Spielberg's film *Schindler's List*, doctors in the Warsaw ghetto administer poison to help their sick Jewish patients commit suicide before the Nazis ransack the hospital: another clear filmic echo of Masada.

2

The American Madness on Film

The Uniquely American Genius

Crucial to this book is the juxtaposition of the American madness with the American sanity, the juxtaposition of the American lunacy with the American genius. For each culture has its genius, and, if it can keep the "shadow" side of it, the corresponding madness, in check, then it flourishes and becomes the envy of the world. What then can stand for the unique American genius? Clearly much that is great in America comes from the twin Western sources of the Hellenic and Hebraic. But can we take just a few figures from American history or culture, and set them up as emblematic of the rest? Any such choice is inevitably open to criticism, but two uniquely great American figures spring to mind: scientist-statesman Benjamin Franklin (1706–1790), and the poet Walt Whitman (1819–1892). Franklin represents the outward-turning American genius for science, technology, politics and the pursuit of an Enlightened social order, while Whitman represents the inward-turning, poetic, subjective celebration of the same American expansive vision. Many historians consider Benjamin Franklin to be the "First American," and he attained almost mythic status, confirmed in the famous portrait of him painted after his death by Benjamin West.[1] His polymath achievements can hardly be listed, they are so many, making him a key Enlightenment figure in his advancement of the sciences (notably electricity) and in his contribution to the founding concepts of the American nation. His sober, practical and moral approach to life attracted satire, but it represents an American sanity that had at its core a Deist vision of a just and hard-working society. As those principles became so often compromised in American history, and his Enlightenment Deism was largely discarded, it fell to Whitman to describe the American vision from the ground up: what it means to ordinary people rather than to the establishment and the powerful. Whitman's vision was expansive, democratic and inclusive in a way that no culture on earth had previously imagined.

Whitman's visionary poems were banned by the prurient Victorian censors of the time, and he lost his job as clerk in the Department of the Interior over the first publication of *Leaves of Grass*.[2] But their reputation slowly grew in America and beyond, and he became the focus of attention of a wide range of key cultural figures of the era, including Ralph Waldo Emerson, Oscar Wilde, and Bram Stoker (the author of *Dracula*). It was gradually recognized that Whitman captured the essential American expansivity of mind and attitude: a great can-do culture, big in its vision, inclusive, and above all shaped by the vast American landscape. It didn't owe anything to the reserve of the British, the fastidiousness of the French, the logic of the Germans, or the flamboyance of the Italians: it was a new spirit founded on the self-reliant pioneer and the founding principles of the legal frameworks that it created, over and above what the "Old World," with the manacles of its lengthy tradition, could aspire to. If "expansivity" is the first characteristic of Whitman's poetry (and prose), then "democracy" is the second. He was a poet who wrote (or "sang" in his own terminology) of the equality of men and women, of the greatness of ordinary people and ordinary life; a man who mingled with presidents[3] and the poorest of Manhattan's million inhabitants. His charity was boundless: he tended the Civil war sick and dying, and spent a whole winter driving a cab for a sick man, so that his family would be fed.[4]

Leonard Quart, in writing on the films of Robert Altman says: "One thinks of Whitman's catalogues of America now gone amuck; sound tracks overlap as cars crash, planes roar, marching bands perform, and TV newsmen drone on."[5] The Whitmanesque is deeply American, even if its voice is now more of a cacophony. Whitman as the bard of America is also the model for a celebrant of culture that would horrify Medved, but whose engagement with the transgressive makes him all the more relevant here.

Whitman's most obvious precursor is William Blake, but Whitman seems much saner, less apocalyptic, and less bound to the religions and traditions of the past. Whitman saw in America a country of the future: he speaks in *Song of Myself* about "jetting the stuff of far more arrogant republics."[6] The sexuality of this is as obvious as its brashness, two qualities that made him suspect for many (including D. H. Lawrence[7]). His legacy— in conventional thinking—is mixed: remembered mostly for his alleged homosexuality, and for providing the writers and poets of the beat generation with their inspiration, particularly the call of the open road. But Whitman himself, or even his poetic legacy, is not the point here. It was his ability to capture the uniquely American spirit of the time, in images that have proved prophetic of his nation, that makes him important. Above all his vision of democracy is not just of the Constitution—critical as that is in defining the American greatness—but of what makes it work, or for that matter any democracy. It is not just a system of rules imposed from above, which, in Whitman's vision, is merely the expression in legal terms of what he considers the heart of the matter: that is the reality of comradeship, of the ordinary friendship that binds communities and drives them to seek fair and just solutions to life's problems.

We may have become cynical about "democracy," because America and other Western nations have used the ideology of it to justify military adventures around the world. We have seen attempts to force it on nations in a topdown manner, forgetting the insights that Whitman had into the nature of democracy: that it must also arise in bottom-up fashion, from the consensus of camaraderie. But Whitman, though he was a truly original world-class poet, was deeply shaped by his time, and by the great thinkers who had paved the way for the experiment of American democracy. These were the visionaries of the European Enlightenment, including the English philosopher John Locke, the French writer Voltaire, and Englishman Thomas Paine. It was Paine above all who helped unshackle Western society from the power of the Church and return it to the ordinary individual. Paine met Benjamin Franklin in London, who advised him to go to America to seek his fortune. Paine did so, but via France at the time of its revolution, and his experiences there forged his democratic convictions. Once in America he wrote pamphlets against slavery and in favor of independence from Britain. It was his call for freedom from colonial rule that made him a household name in America, and allowed his wider ideas of egalitarianism to take hold, favoring education for all, and the rights of the ordinary man and woman. These ideas were published in his widely-read *Rights of Man*. Unfortunately for his later reputation, his ideas of emancipation from religion went too far for the deeply religious American sensibility of the time and he was later vilified as "that filthy little atheist" by Theodore Roosevelt. But such was his legacy in America that the French writer Alexis de Tocqueville went to study American democracy at first hand, returning to France to publish his highly influential *Democracy in America*. What had started in France was returned to it in a new form: the American egalitarianism.

To take two American figures from earlier in its history as representing its founding sanities raises the question of whether they are relevant today. In David Riesman's seminal and highly influential *The Lonely Crowd*, he suggests that modern America is undergoing a transition from what he calls the "inner-directed" person to the "other-directed" person. The inner-directed person—of which Franklin and Whitman are great examples—has shaken off tradition and embodies expansive principles of self-reliance, exploration and entrepreneurship: Riesman's metaphor here is of the gyroscope.[8] In contrast the other-directed person "lacks the inner-directed person's capacity to go it alone," relying on signals from a complex social environment to guide behavior. The metaphor here is radar, and the shift to this type of personality is partly the result of urbanization and the loss of the expansive vision associated with the "frontier." Riesman's analysis will be useful in the section on film and narcissism, because this is an essential characteristic of the other-directed person. Whitman may say that while others dispute he would rather "go bathe and admire himself"—which sounds narcissistic—but the point is he doesn't require the opinions of others, the continual feedback to establish who he is, which is the essential anxiety of the other-directed person. If Riesman's thesis is true, it is still the case that he is talking about a development in American society, and this does not change its roots in the innerdirected person. Hence Franklin and Whitman can perhaps still be regarded as indicators of the American sanity, if other-directedness is pulled back from its extreme.

Paranoia and the American Madness

For Riesman the inner-directed person's pathology hinges around *guilt*: the inner voice that drives him or her onwards can become relentlessly self-critical. The other-directed person's pathology hinges on *anxiety*: the pervasive concern that in a highly complex social environment he has misread the signals—that he may become a "nobody," a "loser." Allan Bloom, though apparently contemptuous of Riesman's ideas, nevertheless finds the term "other-directed" perfect to describe Woody Allen's personality in general, and the protagonist of his film *Zelig* in particular.[9] (More of this in chapter 9 on narcissism.) But when this anxiety gets pushed a little further it may appear as *paranoia*, and it is through the concept of paranoia that we begin our examination of the American madness. Why should the revolution of democracy in America, the end-product of the European Enlightenment, cemented in place by the founders of the American constitution and evolving over time to progressively emancipate the blacks and women, creating the conditions for the greatest prosperity ever known on the planet, why should this slowly but inevitably produce paranoia? It is of course not just any old paranoia, but the specific paranoia of a nation that is successful, rich, and dominant.

In answering this question, much hinges on what is meant by "paranoia." Freud defined it as an aspect of narcissism, related to general anxieties about self-importance,[10] and included it amongst the neuroses of defense. As popularly understood, paranoia is the unjustified belief that "they" are out to get you, and which reads signs of this intent into even the most innocent of events (Freud had much to say about this as an ego-defense strategy). In the non-clinical sense it can be taken as merely a misplaced self-importance, an idea that the whole world revolves around you. It is the desperate attempt to extract self-worth out of the barrage of otherwise indifferent signs that impinge on one; a means in the negative where the positive seems to have failed. Much New Age "psychobabble" can be understood in this way, as we shall see.

While whole nations in ancient times could act in a paranoid way, it was perhaps understandable: the fragile nation of Israel for example was beset on all sides by enemies, and its experience, as recounted in the Old Testament, is of a seemingly endless series of inundations by hostile forces (and it is here we discover the intimate relationship between paranoia and apocalypticism). But the paranoia of modern America is a paranoia intimately bound up with the democratic possibilities handed to the individual. The ancient religious systems of power that bound the ordinary man or woman into society were deeply hierarchical, and there was nothing voluntary about the "contract" between the individual and the state or feudal kingdom or tribe. With democracy came the right to question all man-made systems of power, and the possibility for an endemic suspicion of authority. No religious authority now confers the divine right to rule on democratically elected counselors and politicians; instead we can question every step of their rise to power. Hence the first entry for paranoia in the American soul is the suspicion towards its own democratic process, and this is particularly reserved for anything *federal*.

The American Civil war must surely be the starting point for the widespread reservations that American citizens feel about government at the national or federal level. Part of it must also be the perceived geographical remoteness of federal government for many regions of America, though this must be more keenly felt in the South than elsewhere. But there is ambivalence here: the Americans are also deeply proud of their nation, and its Federal government is the symbol of that.

After the War of Independence, the American Civil War ensured a more inward focus. Having dealt with the old colonial power, Britain, which was at that time the most powerful military force on the planet, America really had no external enemies, and could afford to virtually ignore the rest of the world, other than to exploit its markets. But with the rise of Russia as the world's only other superpower after World War II, America had an enemy to fear again. And it was not just a straightforward military rivalry, which forced all other countries to choose allegiance to one or the other, but it was also an ideological rival. "Communism" was as direct an end-product of the French Revolution as was American democracy, but its ideology was polarized during the Cold War years into anti-capitalist rhetoric as powerful as America's anti-communist rhetoric. Because this was now a war of ideas, a cold struggle rather than a hot one, each American citizen was now under suspicion from the state: "Are you, or have you ever been, a member of the Communist party?"

Cold War paranoia reached its height with the House Un-American Activities Committee, which ran from 1938 to 1975, and with the parallel anti-communist crusade of Senator Joseph McCarthy. Leading public figures including novelists, playwrights, actors and cinema moguls came under suspicion, including Charlie Chaplin, who left the U.S. as a result (his entry permit was revoked while he was visiting Britain). More than 300 Hollywood directors, radio commentators, actors and screenwriters were boycotted by the studios as a result of the anti-communist sentiment that gripped America.[11] (More recently a similar wave of suspicion has surrounded Hollywood stars who came out against the second Gulf War, and has been satirized in the film *Team America: World Police*.) The end of the Cold War in the 1980s and 1990s has meant that communism has receded as cause of American paranoia, only to be replaced by "terrorism"—a blanket term that includes any small group seeking to fight with non-conventional weapons, resulting in so-called "asymmetrical warfare."

If American paranoia has these two historical elements: suspicion of all things Federal and all things communist, it has a third: the specific anxiety of the rich that the poor will take their wealth from them. This is perhaps illustrated in the way that Federal agencies handled the aftermath of Hurricane Katrina in New Orleans. Watching events unfold on television, it seemed extraordinary that the relief effort stalled interminably on the outskirts of the city, because of the "security" situation. Heavily armed troops and police were afraid to enter because of alleged lawlessness and shootings, all of which turned out to be highly exaggerated. It was simply the fear held by the rich and powerful—and white—regarding the poor and supposedly lawless blacks. In another incident a British interviewer flew with a Black Hawk helicopter pilot patrolling the Mexican border. The TV journalist asked him if they had stepped up their vigilance since increased emphasis on anti-terrorist measures in the wake of 9/11, to which he replied, "I think all immigrants are terrorists." The journalist was taken aback, and asked him why he thought that. "They terrorize me, at least," he said, and shrugged his shoulders. One can only imagine that the pilot felt "terrorized" by their poverty, perhaps partly because he couldn't bear to think of living like that himself, and partly because their influx might lower his standards of living (though actually they perform the lowest-paid work that Americans shun, and hence *increase* his standards of living). His was the unthinking and natural paranoia of the rich. Actually, the Mexican border is apparently the daily site of a very American contrast: between vigilantes with guns "helping" the authorities keep out the

Hispanic influx, and groups who patrol the desert with drinking water to prevent would-be immigrants dying of thirst. It is a very American conundrum too : which of these groups more accurately represents American Christianity?

An important factor in the American paranoia, we suggest, is the wealth and leisure of the bulk of its citizens. Of course, average citizens do not easily notice their own wealth and leisure, as their eyes are rather naturally on those with more wealth and leisure, not less, such as those in third-world countries. This wealth not only gives grounds for the inevitable fear of losing it, but gives the time and resources to cultivate and refine paranoia through *psychotherapy*, despite its supposed aim of curing such an affliction. One can say that America is the most Oedipal nation on earth, but another way to say it is that it is the most Freudian, or to say that American culture is a "shrink culture." Christopher Lasch bemoans this move from the political to the therapeutic :

> Having displaced religion as the organizing framework of American culture, the therapeutic outlook threatens to displace politics as well, the last refuge of ideology. Bureaucracy transforms collective grievances into person problems amenable to therapeutic intervention; in clarifying this process, the trivialization of political conflict, the new left made one of its most important contributions to political understanding. In the seventies, however, many former radicals have themselves embraced the therapeutic sensibility.[12]

"Freudian" is of course a term that indicates a tradition in which many of Freud's ideas may have been extensively revised or even overturned. Peter Watson gives a useful summary of the various attacks on Freud's psychoanalytical theories including those of Jeffrey Masson and Ernest Gellner.[13] But none of this changes the centrality of what Lasch calls the "therapeutic sensibility" in American cultural life, and more specifically, in film.

The irony of course is that psychotherapy is meant to cure the patient of neuroses, including paranoia, but the fact is that so much time spent in the company of a professional paid to listen to one's every real or imagined problem, must often—though not always—generate the very thing it is trying to eradicate. In other words American paranoia is the luxury of the self-absorbed rich. If democracy places the individual at the centre, then how could the individual fail to become self-absorbed? It is exactly what the philosophy of the communist regimes around the world were determined to eradicate, and to this extent their critique of the capitalist West had some merit.

But there is another analysis of paranoia, an analysis that itself may be paranoid, drawing on the "hermeneutics of suspicion." In this version, pursued for example in respect of film by Ray Pratt, paranoia is a *legitimate* fear justified by consistent misuse of power by the State. Pratt discusses the issue of McCarthyism, U.S. state surveillance, covert operations and the Waco debacle, and concludes:

> In these and thousands of other cases, one could easily conclude that paranoia concerning perceived conspiracy by government agencies was not delusional, given the actual experiences of victims and documented lies and deceptions of the government. Such deceptions—perhaps endemic to centralized government—will continue to breed suspicion, contempt of authority, and, ultimately, a popular paranoia that, while commonly deprecated, is in many ways an understandable response to government deceit and secrecy.[14]

Pratt is pursuing a leftist analysis, in which he regards films projecting Americans' paranoia about their own country as a legitimate response to oppression. This analysis assumes a gradual degeneracy of the Enlightenment ideals of Franklin and the founding fathers of the American Constitution, resulting in an ever-worsening curtailment of individual freedom. Certainly the Patriot Act, introduced after 9/11, might be argued to represent just another step in this direction. The growing paranoia visible in American filmmaking, starting with "film noir" classics, should then be read as a documenting a legitimate rise in fear regarding government conspiracy. But Pratt's use of the term "paranoia" has distanced itself further from the clinical definition than is really useful, because paranoia in most definitions implies *unfounded* fears. If the fears are really unfounded, then Pratt's Marxist analysis of power must be flawed; conversely, if the fears have a basis in proven historical fact, then it is hardly paranoia.

Furthermore, the argument that American paranoia is legitimate has several flaws. Whatever the level of state conspiracy and surveillance in the U.S.— including during the McCarthy era—it has never reached the historical level of any Marxist state, or even that of most Arab states. In addition, the very fact that the U.S. state permits the making of films—such as Oliver Stone's *JFK*—which accuse government agencies of conspiracy, shows that Americans are a great deal more free than citizens of, for example, the Islamic world. All that a Marxist analysis can show is that, *relative to a utopian state*, things could be better: hardly a justification for paranoia.

So, if we reject the idea that the paranoia in American film is the result of increasingly oppressive government, how is it that the expansive and positive vision of Benjamin Franklin and Walt Whitman should have degenerated into such dark fantasies? Marita Sturken, drawing on the work of Lauren Burlent, suggests instead that "paranoia can be seen as the direct outcome of the daily infantilization of citizenship."[15] This can be understood as a progressive withdrawal of the citizen—originally epitomized by such as Benjamin Franklin—from the public sphere to the private consumption of entertainment, and an increasing suspicion of government due to an increasing ignorance of its workings. Riesman's thesis of a transition from innerdirected to other-directed perceptions of society supports this idea, as the other-directed person is less likely to show the leadership necessary to take on roles of power. Pratt considers this infantilization as a result of the manipulation of the media, so for him it is part of a greater conspiracy: he does not consider the citizen's role or responsibility in the resulting retreat from enfranchisement.[16] However, this alone may not complete the explanation for the dark and apocalyptic nature of the imaginings in American film. The missing element turns out to be *millenarianism*, and so we now consider the progress of millennial ideas in America from it foundation to the present day.

In *An Angel Directs the Storm*, Michael Northcott, no less a leftist in instinct than Pratt, exposes this rather subterranean progression in American thought: the shift from an optimistic millenarianism to a pessimistic one. At the time of Franklin, says Northcott, many Americans believed that "America was the new Canaan, and on this land would emerge the fabled millennium of peace foretold in the Book of Revelation."[17] Northcott usefully explains that "millennium" is not an event that must happen in the year 2000, 3000, and so on (though it might), but that it refers to the "thousand-year reign of the saints" the so-called fifth kingdom. These ideas were part of early Christian beliefs in the first and second centuries after Christ (though this is denied by Northcott), emerging again in the Middle Ages with Joachim of Fiore.[18] Isaac Newton exemplified the millenarian instincts of his age, when he fell in with the general fever surrounding the date 1666.[19] America, founded on deeply Abrahamic religious principles, had in its own prophets, like Cotton Mather (writing around 1700) and Jonathan Edwards (middle eighteenth century): a vision of America as not just a democratic paradise for all, but as a New Jerusalem, a "City Upon a Hill," all of which ideas were incorporated into the doctrine of Manifest Destiny. Northcott explains that these early visionaries were *post*millennialists, meaning that they were building the millennial rule of the saints *after* which Christ would return, whereas the majority of millennialists in 21st century America are now *pre*millennialists, meaning that Christ's return, and the last judgment, would occur *before* the new order.[20] This might seem like a hair-splitting theological nicety, but the practical implications are profound: the premillennialists have given up any hope of a just society, and seek everywhere instead for signs of the immanent Apocalypse. And instead of building the New Jerusalem in America, the focus has increasingly been on the return of the Jews to the ancient land of Israel, an idea that had no support at all during the time of Benjamin Franklin. It remains an open question then: has premillennialism influenced post-war U.S. Middle East policy?

Premillennialism is a doctrine that the underprivileged and undereducated in America might be easily drawn to, receiving little share of America's massive prosperity. However it may have just as big an appeal for the rich, whose prosperity in many cases has led to no lasting happiness, instead creating the strata of the middle-class "worried well" whose recourse, if it is not to religion, is to therapy or Prozac.[21] Apocalyptic cinema seems to have a broad appeal in America, across the income divide. In *Visions of the Apocalypse—Spectacles of Destruction in American Cinema*, Wheeler Winston Dixon suggests that "there is, after all, something comforting in the thought of imminent destruction. All bets are off, all duties executed, all responsibilities abandoned." [22] But while the Hellenic secularist may comprehend this as a merely nihilist analysis, the Abrahamic religionist—particularly when in premillennialist mode—is confident of something more: that the Day of Judgment is at hand. Northcott traces the path of premillennialism as an extreme worldview from its heartland of Christian fundamentalism all the way into the levers of power via the Neocons in the White House (Reagan was deeply influenced for example by a best-selling premillennialist tract *The Late Great Planet Earth*[23]). In this journey we discover the natural relationship between millenarianism and paranoia: every negative interpretation of events is proof of the coming desired apocalypse.

Pratt's thesis, that paranoia is legitimate, rests on whether the citizen is insane to subscribe to conspiracy theories (in which case Pratt is wrong), or whether the citizen is sane to do so because the administration is mad. Peter Knight, in *Conspiracy Culture: From Kennedy to the X Files*, supports Pratt's analysis by going more deeply into the realm of conspiracy theory itself. Starting from the consideration of "American demonology," that is the array of enemies that the U.S. feared from its foundation, such as Jews, Freemasons, Catholics and Communists, he says "traditionally these countersubversive fears have been regarded as little more than the delusional rantings of those on the fringes of society, a persistent but marginal feature of American political life. Since the 1960s, however, conspiracy theories have become far more prominent, no longer the favored rhetoric of backwater scaremongers, but the lingua franca of many ordinary Americans."[24]

Whether one favors the view of Pratt and Knight that paranoia is a sane response to the contemporary situation because the situation is mad, or whether paranoia is always in itself, as Freud insisted, a pathological condition, is all grist to the mill at hand. This is because *either way* we can treat specific paranoias—whether framed by premillennialism or anti–Federal anxieties—as an essential American madness, which the rest of the world has cause to worry about. If at one extreme American government agencies are so gripped by paranoia that they persecute their entirely reasonable citizens, or if, at the other extreme of interpretation, American citizens are genuinely paranoid and elect governments that reflect it, then either way the collective action of America on the world stage will be irrational. More likely in fact is that American government agencies are part of a general culture of paranoia, along with American citizens. On this basis we can fruitfully examine American cinema as an expression of that collective mood, which at times at least *borders* on the insane.

It was mentioned in the Introduction that the terms such as "paranoid" or "Oedipal" are not used in this book in the clinical sense, despite the reference to Freud's usage of the terms. For example it is quite possible that the incidence of clinically diagnosed paranoia and paranoid schizophrenia is higher amongst the American poor than the American rich, but at the same time a cultural paranoia may exist that crosses this divide. Instead, the terms are used in a more colloquial sense as is widespread in contemporary culture. In a famous 1964 essay published in *Harper's Magazine*, titled "The Paranoid Style in American Politics," historian Richard Hofstadter traced a widespread American tendency to paranoid thinking right back to the late 18th century. He says:

> I have neither the competence nor the desire to classify any figures of the past or present as certifiable lunatics. In fact, the idea of the paranoid style as a force in politics would have little contemporary relevance or historical value if it were applied only to men with profoundly disturbed minds. It is the use of paranoid modes of expression by more or less normal people that makes the phenomenon significant.[25]

He makes clear that he is not using the term "paranoid" in a clinical sense, as he considers himself not qualified to make such a judgment. Instead he has borrowed the term, and uses it to convey a form of expression that "more or less normal" people are often inclined to: a mild and pervasive skepticism. Knight refers to it as "popular paranoia" in reference to Hofstadter's ideas, and gives a detailed account of similar and more detailed studies in this tradition.[26] Hofstadter himself gives an indication of how the clinical and cultural uses of the term could be distinguished: the clinically paranoid suffers the delusion of persecution as directed to himself or herself, while the culturally paranoid suffers delusions of persecution as directed against "a nation, a culture, a way of life whose fate affects not himself alone but millions of others."[27] Reactions by Muslims against perceived insults to their religion are of this second type perhaps, but we are interested here in American culture. Hofstadter points out how the Stalin purge trials were a "wildly imaginative and devastating exercise in the paranoid style," reinforcing the point that the paranoid style does not belong to America alone, but that it takes on a particular shape in each culture.

The paranoia of the rich is very different to the paranoia of the poor, and this applies even more so to whole nations. But why chose paranoia as the core pathology of the American mind, the central American madness? Because it is a stance that indicates a failure of trust, and when that failure of trust is projected onto the world stage with seemingly unlimited economic and military resources, then we are all in trouble. The rich are rarely sane, because to acquire their wealth requires a single-mindedness that easily tips into obsession and a disregard for others and the natural world. The rich also have the leisure in which all their demons can multiply, and the cash to pay for others to take an interest in those demons.

The Complete American Madness on Film

Pratt suggests that an "exploration of visionary paranoia in American movies might begin with the body of films known as *film noir*, a collective style or mood in which urban America is depicted as dangerous, dark, and insecure place—usually photographed in black and white—characterized by paranoia, menace, violence, personal betrayal, greed, lust and the corrosive effects of a society based on the pursuit of money."[28] Paul Schrader, screenwriter for *Taxi Driver* and director of many films with a paranoid mood, denied that *film noir* was a genre as such, "more a question of subtle tone and mood," and of post-war disillusionment.[29] Michael Stephens, in his comprehensive reference work on *film noir*, is certain that it is a genre.[30] Nicholas Christopher's loving treatment of *film noir* in his book *Somewhere in the Night* suggests more simply that it is a form of escapism and aesthetic nihilism.[31] Certainly, period *noirs* such as *Chinatown* (Roman Polanski, 1974) and *Angel Heart* (Alan Parker, 1987) are essentially escapist costume dramas of great artistry, the latter adding to its titillation through Afro-American voodoo. But whatever the merit of starting with genre as a way into the darker aspects of the American mind, and of *film noir* as the entry point for paranoia in particular, a different approach is adopted here.

We have touched on several key madnesses of the American mind so far: its paranoia, its Oedipal competitiveness and aggression, and its apocalypticism. Dana Polan considers that, in the context of post-war films of the 1940s and 1950s, "paranoia is literally the underpinning of aggressivity."[32] Barely mentioned so far but also important in the American psyche is its collective guilt over the destruction of the Native American peoples and their culture, a guilt that appears to have more visible expression in film than any guilt over slavery. Other very visible aspects of the American madness include sexual obsession, New Age beliefs, nihilism, and what could be called "cultural autism," a trend in favor of the intellect and science over the emotional and intuitive. Finally the ability of a wealthy nation to indulge in the most fantastical escapism cannot be overlooked.

The Marxists say: "historicize, always historicize." One could say instead, with Aristotle: "taxonomize, always taxonomize." Along with the five-fold method of approaching the transgressive in film outlined in the Introduction, a taxonomy of the American madness on film is constructed here as a second tool to approach this subject. In all, ten categories have been chosen deriving from a consideration of American film itself, attempting to find reservoirs of approximately equal significance:

1. Paranoia / Conspiracy Theories
2. Aggression / Serial Killers
3. Oedipal / Freudian
4. Sexual Obsession
5. The Apocalypse and Armageddon
6. Native Americans and Cultural Genocide
7. The New Age and Narcissism
8. Nihilism, Alienation and Self-Destruction
9. The Intellect and Cultural Autism
10. Virtual Reality and Saccharine Fantasies

These ten manifestations of American madness have suggested themselves as useful and distinct categories through a survey of uniquely American films. British and French cinema, just to take two other examples, would throw up a different set of concerns, highlighting quite different cultural margins at which the perverse, the transgressional, and the truly mad are encountered.

Given that we have a chapter devoted to Native Americans on film, why not an equivalent chapter on the place in American film of black culture? After all, African Americans form a larger part of the population than Native Americans. The answer is to do with film: there is no equivalent to the revisionist Western in filmmaking that is by blacks or deals with black culture. There is nothing to "revise:" blacks began their American life in subjugation, whereas Native Americans began it as ferocious warriors of resistance, demonized and deemed fit only for extermination. Mainstream African American actors and directors are largely involved with films that are framed by white culture; their achievement has been to succeed in a white man's world, for example Sidney Poitier with *Stir Crazy*. There are exceptions, e.g. Spike Lee, but his films *Do the Right Thing* and *Jungle Fever* portray African Americans as conforming to stereotypical behaviour (*Smoke Signals* does same thing for Native Americans). Julie Dash's *Daughters of the Dust* also accepts white literate culture as the framing "gold standard," perhaps symbolized by high-Victorian clothing and artifacts, whatever the sense of loss of black oral culture. Revisionist films involving Native Americans that portray them sympathetically present a complete culture that was targeted by white settlers; in contrast, the culture of African Americans was ignored, left behind, or Christianized (as for example in *The Last Supper*). For the typically American forceful character, a form of boldness which will be discussed as "aggression" (whether black or white) has cultural sanction, whereas racism does not (even if it might be systemic in American institutions, as alleged by African Americans). This is not to diminish the importance of race relations in the U.S. and its relation to culture. To explore this through film would be an interesting project, but for another book.

PART TWO

Filmic Journeys into the American Madness

3

Paranoia and Conspiracy Theories

KEY FILMS: *Dr. Strangelove, The X-Files*
ADDITIONAL FILMS: *Conspiracy Theory, JFK,*
The Conversation, Enemy of the State

We have suggested that if America suffers from "popular paranoia" (as opposed to the clinical variety) then it is the paranoia of the rich and powerful, rather than the paranoia of the poor. It constructs enemies such as "communism" and "terrorism" from without, and from within it appears as a deep mistrust of anything Federal, leading to conspiracy theories, e.g. around 9/11. Before 2001 the key American conspiracy theory concerned the assassination of President Kennedy, although a number of other lesser conspiracies have been mooted. Perhaps the most amusing is "moon landing denial" which accuses NASA and the American officials of faking the whole Apollo moon mission series (no doubt given impetus by the film *Capricorn One*). Others delve into the world of science fiction, such as the belief that an alien spacecraft landed at Roswell and that officials covered up the subsequent autopsy of the dead aliens. Conspiracy theories around 9/11 dominated the Internet in the years following the attack, and became part of a movement to discredit American foreign policy. Much spurious "scientific" evidence is bandied about to support, for example, the idea that the Twin Towers were brought down by controlled demolition. Theologian David Griffin leads this campaign in a series of books leveling the most serious accusations against government agencies: the fact that these are published at all might suggest to the non-paranoid that America is still a highly open society.[1] One example of the scientific debate is the suggestion that the substance thermite was responsible for the molten metal in the basements of the buildings, pointing to controlled demolition: but thermite cannot be used in controlled demolition according to industry experts.[2] Of more interest however is the wider social context of distrust in government: statistics in both the U.S. and the U.K. show a growing proportion of the population losing faith in government.[3]

Robert Kolker considers that "paranoia films" are the "reverse side of the heroic venture."[4] Even in action-hero films setting out to deny the apparently universal sense of anxiety and loss of community, the heroes are often "as repulsive as the villains," and we will certainly see this in some of the films examined here, looking ahead for example to Travis Bickle in *Taxi Driver*. But the films we look at here are less subtle. Stanley Kubrick's *Dr. Strangelove* is chosen here as the first film through which to explore paranoia and conspiracy theories, even though the Cold War basis of it is now only a distant memory. It is a good reminder how the American mind could seize on "communism" as no mere philosophical construct with which to debate rationally, but as an insidious threat to the very fabric of American life ... not to mention one's "precious bodily fluids." *Dr. Strangelove* is a comedy that confronts head-on the insanity of the nuclear threat of M.A.D. (Mutual Assured Destruction) that the post-war generation grew up with. The second film chosen to explore this topic is the film version of the *X-Files* TV series, representing a more modern paranoia focused on Federal agencies, including the FBI and FEMA (the Federal Emergency Management Agency).

Dr. Strangelove

Kubrick's marvelous *Dr. Strangelove* is both a period piece and a timeless comedy. The target of its satire is the American paranoia about the principal constructed "other" of the Cold War age: communism. Peter Sellers plays a number of parts in the film, including President Muffley, and revealing in that case a sadly neglected talent for the straight role. Otherwise he plays the British officer Mandrake seconded to the mad Colonel Jack Ripper, and also the title role of Dr. Strangelove, an ex-Nazi scientist advisor to the President. The film gets into its stride when Mandrake discovers that Ripper has committed his nuclear bomber wing to an attack on the U.S.S.R. To start with Mandrake assumes it is an exercise, and then some kind of mistake, but reality slowly dawns on him as Ripper locks him into his office, resists all demands to issue the recall code, and then shows that he is prepared to shoot Mandrake if he gets in the way of his deranged plans. We see Colonel Jack Ripper, filmed from below, beautifully lit in black and white, calmly smoking a cigar (Robert Kolker compares this with a shot of Norman Bates in Hitchcock's *Psycho*[5]):

> RIPPER: Mandrake, I suppose it never occurred to you that while we're chatting
> here so enjoyably, a decision is being made by the President and the Joint
> Chiefs in the war room at the Pentagon. And when they realize there is no pos-
> sibility of recalling the wing, there will be only one course of action open: total
> commitment. Mandrake, do you recall what Clemenceau once said about war?
> MANDRAKE: No. I don't think I do sir, no.

RIPPER: He said war was too important to be left to the generals. When he said that, fifty years ago, he might have been right. But today, war is too important to be left to politicians. They have neither the time, the training, nor the inclination for strategic thought. I can no longer sit back and allow Communist infiltration, Communist indoctrination, Communist subversion, and the international Communist conspiracy to sap and impurify all of our precious bodily fluids.

We are being prepared here for the true extent of Ripper's madness, but his paranoia about his "bodily fluids" will be shown to have apparently just cause. Ripper has to be stopped of course, and President Muffley has gathered his staff in the war room at the Pentagon to consider their next move. Fellow military man General Turgidson, while accepting that Ripper may have exceeded his authority, cannot hide his glee at the forthcoming battle. He gives the President likely figures on the millions of casualties, clearly oblivious to the real meaning of those deaths. But there is no simple possibility of recall: both the inexorable military procedures of the U.S. and of the Soviet Union mean that there may be no avoiding planetary destruction. The race is on for Muffley to do what he can, which means overriding his war-hungry generals and cooperating with the Russians. Horror! The American paranoia about those dirty commies is only matched by the caricature presented to us of the Russian ambassador, who attempts to photograph everything of military interest in the war room with—of course—a period piece miniature camera. It is only the obsequious pleadings of Muffley with the Russian premiere, calling him "Dimitri," that halt any immediate retaliation.

But while the paranoia about communism is relatively easy to understand, Ripper's obsession with his bodily fluids needs some elaboration. Ripper tells Mandrake: "Do you realize that fluoridation is the most monstrously conceived and dangerous communist plot we have ever had to face?" But why on earth should fluoridation be a communist plot? Is this just the scriptwriter's fancy, to make Ripper look mad? The answer is no; it is in fact a widely held anxiety, if not quite a conspiracy theory in its own right, that fluoridation is foisted on citizens for less than benevolent motives. Knight considers that at the time of making *Dr. Strangelove* (1964) the issue of fluoride was little more than a rhetorical device in the film, but that by the 1990s "anxiety about precious bodily fluids became quite literal."[6] This is interesting because it says a lot about modern technological societies and the scope that citizens have to either understand the sciences underpinning their lifestyles or the decision-making processes involved. Both are equally arcane and remote from the average citizen. Even someone trained in the sciences would have to work quite hard to pursue the evidence for and against the use of fluoridation to strengthen the teeth, if that wasn't her immediate field of expertise. And without training in political science or governance, it is an even harder job figuring out just what kind of Government committees make the original recommendation, and how that eventually passes into law. What kind of people get to shape these decisions? How much do the politicians actually understand of the science? A trained researcher might eventually get a reasonable grasp of these complex issues with a bit of patience and time. But how can one expect the ordinary citizen to have either the patience for such research, the aptitude for it, or the time and willingness to do it? It is much easier to read the tabloids and listen to the man in the pub. Or taxi.

Which takes us to the opening scene of the film *Conspiracy Theory*, featuring Mel Gibson as Jerry Fletcher, a New York cabbie. Knight regards this film as an example of how conspiracy culture builds a self-conscious element into its own discourse, evident in the very title of the film, which invites one not to dismiss it because it names upfront its very basis.[7] Fletcher harangues his passengers with an endless series of conspiracy theories including this one:

> You know what they put in the water, don't you? Fluoride. Yeah, fluoride. On the pretext that it strengthens your *teeth*. That's ridiculous. You know what that stuff does to you? It actually weakens your will, takes away the capacity for free and creative thought and makes you a slave to the state.

As the sentence ends the music peaks and the film's title appears: *Conspiracy Theory*. The premise is a promising one: that an amiable idiot who continually spouts off about conspiracy theories actually stumbles into a real one. More interesting is the potential for the exploration of why perfectly intelligent people do succumb to such views, but the film fails in this because it turns out that Fletcher is no ordinary cabbie, but an assassin whose training through mind-control has gone wrong. The "self-conscious" element of such films turns out to be a special pleading, rather than any real critical distance. Nevertheless, the film runs through just about every angle on conspiracy theory (apart from 9/11 because it was made before that event). Here are Fletcher's next lines:

> You ever wonder about all these militia groups? Survivalist-type gooks on the right wing sites? They say they are defending the country from the UN troops. These guys are yelling so loud that my theory is that this is a conspiracy, pal, that they *are* the UN troops, and that they are in place, that the infrastructure is ready, and that when the time comes we'll all be killed.

This idea is mystifying to most Europeans: that some Americans think that the UN is a hostile army poised to invade the U.S. Joel Silver, the film's producer, is quoted as saying: "What a weird idea to believe these might be bar codes on the back of Federal road signs that are secret instruction for the UN army planning a takeover. It shows the persistence of paranoia."[8] A U.K.

television documentary once explained how this issue went to law in one American state, pitting the conspiracy theory against the official version that the bar codes made it quicker to order replacement parts. Whatever the outcome of the case, it is inconceivable that similar allegations could ever reach court in Europe. (Later we will see that for some Americans the Secretary General of the United Nations is nothing less than the Antichrist.)

But in the meantime, what is happening to Mandrake and Ripper? Army units from outside Ripper's base are fighting their way in, and things look bad for the mad Colonel. But in a lull in the fighting Ripper wants to justify himself to Mandrake and returns to his fluoridation theme, telling him there are studies underway to fluoridate salt, flour, fruit juices, soup, sugar, milk, and ice cream. Ripper concludes: "A foreign substance is introduced into our precious bodily fluids without the knowledge of the individual, and certainly without any choice." The fighting grows more intense, and Ripper makes for the bathroom, where he shoots himself. It is left to Mandrake to explain himself to the wonderfully-named Colonel Batguano, who calls Mandrake a "deviated pervert" for the obvious crime of being British. Batguano represents everything *normally* paranoid about the military: he is deeply suspicious of Mandrake's claim to have the possible recall codes that could bring back the nuclear bombers. He only reluctantly allows Mandrake to call the president.

We'll leave the drama there with just a comment about Kubrick's intentions. Pratt tells us that he began work on the screenplay with the idea of a "serious military suspense thriller" but eventually decided that the only way to tell the story was as a black comedy.[9] Kolker considers it an application of the specific literary form of eighteenth century satire.[10] The target of Kubrick's satire is the ignorant paranoia that drives Ripper to take the world to the edge of destruction, but we are not expected to share the prejudice against either communists or fluoridated drinking water. The fact that *Dr. Strangelove* is a comedy in no way softens the real polemic here, which is anti-war. Hence the film both accurately delineates a key American madness, and at the same time is itself deeply sane. In contrast a more recent film, *Team America: World Police*, satirizes terrorism—the replacement threat to communism—but fails to show any redeeming sanity in its critique. It is also meant as a comedy, but its producers (creators of the *South Park* cartoon TV show) have not included any sane characters at all, everything being grist to its mill of crass and vulgar satire. Kubrick's *Strangelove* is a true indictment of American madness, where *Team America* mostly succumbs to it, displaying only the consciousness of those totally alienated from the political process, and offering instead only universal cynicism. *Team America* could well be an example of what Kolker refers to when he says "Film ... has either forgotten satire or replaced it with parody or lampoon."[11]

Charles Maland writes: "Taken as a whole, *Dr. Strangelove* fundamentally challenges the Ideology of Liberal Consensus by attacking anti–Communist paranoia."[12] So the film might be said to satisfy the ideological requirements of the Left, while obviously attacking those of the Right. But does its transgressional material evoke catharsis, or a response of compassion? It is a comedy, but is there a tragic figure in it? Clearly a film like this meets none of Aristotle's requirements for a tragedy, but in terms of the five requirements laid out here it certainly has transgressional elements; its scenario is frighteningly plausible (there is great attention to military procedural detail); its emotion is intense; it is beautifully made (nothing less than a cinematic masterpiece); and it has critical distance because of its equal treatment of the characters: the Russians are no less absurd than the Americans. It remains to consider whether Ripper is perhaps a tragic figure, or whether his character strays into what Aristotle called the "monstrous" or what we call here the "grotesque." The situation is certainly terrible in Aristotle's sense, and the point of the film is to grapple with incomprehensible possibility of nuclear annihilation. To the extent that a thermonuclear world war was—and remains—both technically and politically possible, it makes the situation terrible rather than a monstrous or grotesque construction of the human imagination. And Ripper's character, to the extent that we believe it psychologically possible in context and because nuclear weapons are science fact not science fiction, must also be considered terrible, or even tragic, rather than monstrous or grotesque. It is perhaps here that Kubrick's decision to film *Dr. Strangelove* as comedy pays off: Mandrake as the comic foil to Ripper's insanity makes it more believable rather than less. The film evokes fear because Ripper is, in his own terms, an honorable soul with the courage to act upon his beliefs, and we provide the cultural context which furnishes him with those beliefs. It doesn't let us off the hook, unless we are foolish enough to believe that his madness is not to some extent ours.

The X-Files

The X-Files as a TV series, and in the film, exposes a uniquely American paranoia: the suspicion directed against all things federal. This is intimately bound up, in science-fiction genres at least, with aliens from outer space as the evil and aggressive "other," one that takes the place of the Communists or the Terrorists. But the *X-Files* does more than this in terms of letting us examine a uniquely American preoccupation: it allows, along with horror films, for a presumed secular audience to grapple with the supernatural. It stands in the noble American tradition of science fiction as a means to explore contemporary issues, replacing for a younger audience the *Star Trek* role, providing unfamiliar settings for familiar human problems.

The heroes of the *X-Files* are two FBI agents called Fox Mulder (David Duchovny) and Dana Scully (Gillian Anderson). They present an interesting comparison with *Star Trek*'s Captain Kirk and Spock, because in both pairings one of them is intuitive and the other rational. Kirk usually triumphs through his ability to draw on the emotional as well as the logical, whereas Spock, confined to the more rigid world of his undeniably superior intellect, is usually confounded. In the *X-Files* it is Mulder, the male, who is the intuitive one, and Scully, the female, who is the logical one. As a barometer of our times this is actually worth commenting upon, because no writer of drama a hundred years ago could possibly have countenanced such apparent role-reversal of gender.[13] As Knight puts it, the caption "I want to believe" on Mulder's UFO office poster "expresses his atavistic desire for something beyond the logical strictures of orthodox science initially represented by Agent Scully."[14]

The *X-Files* film starts a little like *2001: A Space Odyssey* with reference to Stone Age man and a freak encounter with aliens. It then fast-forwards to the present day and a chance discovery by local boys—in a direct reference to the Lascaux caves discovery—who are attacked by the same aliens. We are soon treated to a sudden influx of white trucks and boffins: it is an archetypal U.S. film scene depicting the moment where Federal agencies move in. The obligatory "good old boy" local fire captain is bewildered by it all. But anyone who is aware of the Roswell incident understands the references: the Federal agents are going to remove the evidence and prevent any access to it by the public and its independent researchers. This is all background however, because we first meet Mulder and Scully dealing with a bomb alert in a city setting. True to their temperaments, it is Mulder who gets to the bomb first, following a hunch, and calls in his FBI bomb-disposal teammates. Bomb disposal agent Michaud orders the rest of the FBI staff to leave—then simply sits and watches the bomb until it goes off. It is no surprise to Mulder and Scully: they are deeply aware of how the FBI is compromised from within—after all it isn't called the *Federal* Bureau of Investigation for nothing, and we all know what *Federal* implies. (One might have a bone to pick with the scriptwriters here: Agent Michaud, as a Federal agent not named Mulder or Scully, is obviously capable of anything heinous—but not suicide. Surely that is un–American? Isn't that what separates Americans from Islamists?) What the scene establishes for its audience however is the comfortable fiction of the FBI as part of the problem, not the solution.

The film of the *X-Files* was released in 1998, so it is odd that the Oklahoma bombing of the Murrah Federal Building in April 19, 1995, is not mentioned. There are plenty of conspiracy theories around the lone figure of Timothy McVeigh who was found guilty of that crime. His confession, and the admission that he carried it out in revenge for the Waco siege, is dismissed by conspiracy theorists as surely as the notion that Lee Harvey Oswald shot President Kennedy. But the building in the *X-Files* turns out to be the building opposite the Federal building, so what is going on? Actually, it turns out that the Feds wanted to hide some dead bodies—the ones infected with alien gloop—and so they bombed their smaller operation next door.

Although paranoia is collective as a cultural phenomenon in America, it is the lone individual, standing against the faceless organization—"them"—that counts. After failing to prevent the explosion, a morose Mulder gets drunk in a bar and confides to the barmaid:

> I'm the key figure in an on-going government charade, the plot to conceal the truth about the existence of extraterrestrials. It's a global conspiracy, actually, with key players in the highest levels of power, that reaches down into the lives of every man, woman, and child on this planet.

The shadowy figure of Dr. Kurtzweil, an old friend of Mulder's father, then confronts Mulder. He tells him that the Federal Emergency Management Agency (FEMA) had offices in the destroyed building. In real life FEMA was the one meant to deal with the aftermath of Hurricane Katrina, for example, and its widely-perceived failure to act quickly led to the resignation of its boss. FEMA also drew up the first report on the 9/11 destruction of the World Trade Center, and has consequently drawn endless criticism from conspiracy theorists who believe that the buildings were demolished by controlled explosions. Burning jet fuel can't possibly melt steel, they cry, though FEMA never claimed it did.[15] But where the *X-Files* would have the average European baffled is the idea that FEMA is going to take over the government of America. What exactly would it do? An agency that couldn't even get relief supplies to the flooded-out citizens of New Orleans is apparently going to perpetrate some massive coordinated evil on the American public? Will it gather its forces on the edge of U.S. cities and wait weeks for the alleged crime-rate to drop? But Dr. Kurtzweil explains further:

> KURTZWEIL: The plague to end all plagues, Agent Mulder. A silent weapon for a quiet war. The systematic release of an indiscriminate organism for which the men who will bring it on still have no cure! They've been working on this for fifty years! While the rest of the world has been fighting gooks and commies, these men have been secretly negotiating a planned Armageddon!
> MULDER: Negotiating with whom?
> KURTZWEIL: I think you know. The timetable has been set. It will happen on a holiday, when people are away from their homes. The president will declare a state of emergency, at which time all government, all federal agencies, will come

under the power of the Federal Emergency Management Agency. FEMA, the secret government.

MULDER: And they call me paranoid.

Yes, they do, Mulder. But the paranoid folk of America are not content to imagine that it is just the agencies of their own government that are in on the plot (the most amusing aspect of this being that it would take place when people are on holiday). Sinister individuals from sinister countries—like Britain for example—are helping to make this a global conspiracy. Meet the "Syndicate," who are gathered in an elegant library near the Albert Hall in London: their plans are going awry. The conspirators themselves are the victims of a conspiracy by aliens. It gives these men gravitas to be meeting in oak-paneled rooms in the United Kingdom, the source of all those aristocratic villains of early horror movies.

Meanwhile Mulder and Scully are out in the desert tracking down the original archaeological dig. "Unmarked tanker trucks. What are archaeologists hauling out in tanker trucks?" says Mulder. Suspicion about agribusiness and its "fluids" is another rather natural paranoia of the developed world: why is it that farms seem to have these strange tanks with "God"-knowswhat chemical gloop in them, when they are supposed to be producing "farmfresh" meat and vegetables for us? Or "barn-fresh" or "natural" or any of a thousand other marketing lies? But back to the X-Files. Mulder and Scully enter fields and then a vast covered area in which transgenic crops are growing (strangely, the American public aren't particularly suspicious of genetically modified food, at least not compared to the Europeans). They are discovered and only just escape, but by now Mulder despairs of being able to convince the authorities of the alien conspiracy. Scully is about to give up as well, and they have a heart-to-heart talk with the tantalizing possibility, as usual, that it could get romantic. Their intimate moment is interrupted, however, because Scully gets stung by a transgenic bee with an alien death-virus implant. She is going to die unless Mulder can save her from the evil attack by the Syndicate—they have targeted her, so as to distract him.

But they get the break they need: one of the Syndicate betrays his organization by giving Mulder the vaccine necessary to save Scully's life. Like Agent Michaud this bit-part is expendable, so he gets blown up in the standard exploding car fireball (though not before he shoots the equally expendable driver). Before he dies he gives Mulder a rather unnecessary piece of advice: "Trust no one, Mr. Mulder." Scully meanwhile is being fermented in a vat, or to give it the proper name a "cryopod." These are reminiscent of the *Aliens* films, and return us to the opening premise of a black goo that travels subcutaneously up to the eyes and makes them big and black, like the Roswell aliens. Naturally Mulder rescues her, blows up the facility and puts an end to the threat, at least for the time being. But of course no-one is going to believe him.

At the end of the film the FBI conduct an internal hearing, which is in reality some kind of disciplinary procedure against agents Scully and Mulder. The chairwoman does finally admit that "there is now direct evidence that a federal agent may have been involved in the bombing." How casual! But they won't accept the fact of an alien conspiracy. As Mulder says: "They'll never believe you, not unless your story can be programmed, categorized, or easily referenced." So, it seems that an FBI agent as a suicide bomber is easily programmed, categorized and referenced, whereas aliens are not. Perhaps the *X-Files*, by dramatizing such preposterously absurd ideas, actually makes the FBI *more* likely to be trusted by most Americans. For the harmless few who take it seriously, there is little one can do.

If we return to Knight's point about conspiracy culture incorporating a self-conscious element into its polemic, we can ask again: does it suggest a critical distance in the *X-Files*? It is self-conscious in certain ways, but this might just be a cultivated image. Its real problem is that the material is transgressional enough, but it fails our test with scenario plausibility. Michaud's suicide bombing, to pick just one small element, is utterly ludicrous, as is the response to it. What on earth would motivate a Federal agent to sacrifice his life in a non-combat situation? Why not use a remote control, or any other device of science fact or fiction? The arbitrariness of his act is typical of the remove from real life of the entire film and series. But it raises for us an interesting question: can science fiction, even if its material is transgressive, actually deliver anything cathartic? The apparent knowing, self-conscious image of the *X-Files* hides its inability to deal with the real: if there is critical distance within the production team, it is only marketing cynicism. And without critical distance a film cannot evoke the response of compassion. Yet Pratt, as a left-leaning theorist, can say "the series presented a serious, though sometimes playful, examination of the unexplained or repressed aspects of U.S. politics and culture during the past half century." In a similar vein Knight says: "In the conspiracy culture typified by *The X-Files*, belief in a conspiracy is no longer necessarily a sign of gullible paranoia, as it was for Hofstadter, and as it still is for mainstream critics." Michaud's actions alone are evidence against such assertions.

Conspiracy Theory and *JFK*

Going back to the film *Conspiracy Theory*, Jerry Fletcher, the New York taxi driver, naturally makes reference to the "big one" prior to 9/11—the assassination of President Kennedy. This is still during the opening of the film, where Fletcher harangues his passengers in his cab: "Oswald, he said, 'I'm just a patsy,' right, that means he didn't do it, right?"

The conspiracy theory around the Kennedy assassination in 1963 is the subject of Oliver Stone's film *JFK*. This is a three-hour epic following the case that New Orleans District Attorney Jim Garrison constructed to prove that there was a conspiracy—involving the FBI, the CIA, the Mafia, and others— to murder the President because he was soft on Communism and hard on organized crime. Knight suggests that the "Kennedy assassination has become synonymous with conspiracy theory, weaving its way into the cultural fabric of everyday [American] life."[16] Pratt considers *JFK* the "pre-eminent embodiment of the political film and, in a more limited sense, is also the finest 'conspiracy thriller' of recent decades."[17] Kolker is interested in it as a film in which sentimentality is contained, if not eradicated,[18] but this is doubtful: we are clearly meant to identify with Garrison at every emotional level, and, critically, to take on the heavy load of assumption that there really was a conspiracy against Kennedy. How can this not be sentimental at some level? The film certainly provoked strong reactions. Leonard Quart offers this from conservative *Washington Post* journalist George Will, describing *JFK* as an "act of execrable history and contemptible citizenry, by a man of technical skill, scant education, and negligible conscience," and this from Norman Mailer, that "Stone 'has the integrity of a brute.'"[19]

A key issue in this apparently persuasive thesis of a film is that of the bullet that had to follow an almost "impossible" trajectory, if it had in fact been fired by Oswald. But a considerable background in physics would be required to decide it one way or the other, as is the case for 9/11. It is significant that a film like *JFK* can be so apparently convincing when in reality it revolves around highly technical questions of ballistics that the average citizen has no chance of disentangling. It only takes a few minor factual inaccuracies or uncertainties to remain unchallenged for them to become the cornerstone of a grand conspiracy. The problem with *JFK* is that Stone has already made up his mind; he does not leave it for the viewer to decide. When he brings in the science of it, he doesn't point out that science always starts from a "don't know" position, and he certainly doesn't point out that nearly half a century later it still doesn't know. Paranoia cannot bear uncertainty, and in this case it also cannot bear the idea that the most powerful man in the world could be killed by a lone sociopath, and that a lone vigilante should then decide to kill the killer. The concept of personal agency, so crucial in the psychoses of ego-defense, as Freud says, is paramount: if Kennedy, the most powerful man in the world, is killed, then it must have been by a group at least as powerful. If he was killed by a loner, with no more backing than I have, then what chance do I stand, the average citizen? It is *safer* to believe in the conspiracy.

That the conspiracy theory might ultimately be proved untrue doesn't change this.

Given all this, when Jerry Fletcher takes home the love interest in the *Conspiracy Theory* film (Justice Department Attorney Alice Sutton, played by Julia Roberts) it is inevitable that the subject turns to Oliver Stone. Fletcher's flat is everything one can imagine of the conspiracy theorist's hideout: locks and security devices everywhere, including on the coffee jar in the fridge. (In fact Fletcher is so flustered at finally having the lovely Alice in his apartment that he forgets the combination to the coffee and has to offer her orange juice instead.) Alice spots a printout which includes "The Truth About UFOs" and "The Oliver Stone-George Bush Connection." "Oliver Stone?" she queries. "Oh sure," replies Fletcher, "He's their spokesman. Do you think that if anyone had the information he had, and the national podium to shout it from, they'd let him do it? No, it's quite clear he's a disinformation junkie for them." Alice just stares at him. "The fact that he is still alive says it all," concludes Fletcher. He is of course simply doing what comes naturally to conspiracy theorists: to distrust even other conspiracy theorists. Alice asks him if he can prove any of this. "No, absolutely not," he says. "A good conspiracy theory is an unprovable one."

It might be of interest then to see how Oliver Stone's film about 9/11—called *World Trade Center*—treads regarding alleged conspiracies. It turns out in fact that he has avoided them altogether, playing the film straight and without any political or conspiracy agenda. This should give the Fletchers of this world further proof—as if it were needed—that Stone really is a government agent.

The Citizen and Paranoia

Is Pratt right to say that "basic to the notion of infantilization is the view that U.S. citizens have been treated as less than adults, denied full information, deceived, controlled, manipulated, spied upon, and lied to for much of the [twentieth] century"?[20] Marita Sturken gives a different inflection to this by saying that paranoia "is the result of the bitter shock that comes from having been naïve about power."[21] If we disregard the denouement of *Conspiracy Theory*, and take Fletcher as he first appears, then does he represent—as an ordinary citizen—a victim of this manipulation, or has he colluded with it by insisting on maintaining his naivety about power? In real life no adherent to a conspiracy theory would admit, as Fletcher does, that a good conspiracy theory is an unprovable one. Instead, what is fundamental in their arguments is that "they"—whichever government, group, or criminal hierarchy they believe in—have sufficient *agency* to carry through the plot. But

Freud insisted that paranoia was inextricably linked to the narcissism of defending the ego and creating self-importance: perhaps the key to the paranoid outlook is that by ascribing sufficient agency to the outside body, it gives the self a reflected importance. It would be infinitely worse to regard one's woes as the result of exterior incompetence, because this would make one's life so much more accidental and meaningless. On this basis the "shit-happens theorist" has actually a more balanced and sanguine temperament, able to withstand neglect and incompetence from authority. But is it *more fun* to be one of the Fletchers of this world? To collude with infantilization, to revel in paranoia? This is a question that the entire Marxist tradition and its hermeneutics of suspicion dare not pose.

Both Pratt and Polan[22] conceive of popular paranoia as a legitimate "social practice." Pratt says: "Paranoia thus becomes a reasonable kind of social practice as a response to unreasonable, manipulative, deceitful political power, demanding a responsive strategy not simply of skepticism or the attenuated attention which characterizes cynicism but a more total orientation toward power."[23] This "total orientation to power" is a Marxist idea, and is Foucauldian in its ramification for Polan. Knight points out that Sir Karl Popper has raised objections to this conception of power and to the corresponding valorization of paranoia.[24] The relevant passage in Popper's *The Open Society and its Enemies* runs: "This view [the conspiracy theory of society] of the aims of the social sciences arises, of course, from the mistaken theory that, whatever happens in society—especially happenings such as war, unemployment, poverty, shortages, which people as a rule dislike—is the direct design by some powerful individuals and groups."[25] In Popper's analysis neither individuals nor groups have sufficient agency in a complex world to *design* such events. But, as Knight adds, the conspiracy theorist is not likely to have faith in such sophisticated analyses of history. More than this, one can point out, the very complexity of the modern world, and perhaps physical existence itself, inclines any but the prodigiously determined towards the "attenuated attention" of cynicism. It is extremely difficult to follow the ballistic evidence regarding the bullet that killed Kennedy. It is extremely difficult to weigh the immunological evidence regarding the fluoridation of drinking water. It requires considerable dedication to begin to understand how government works and makes its decisions, to *actively* shed one's naivety about power. And it is almost impossible to penetrate the inferno of the Twin Towers to decide whether the impacts of the jets and subsequent fires could have brought them down without additional planned demolition. Benjamin Franklin was one who might have mastered such detail, and who understood power intimately, while Walt Whitman was perhaps one of the least infantilized men in American history ("bearded, sun-burnt, gray-neck'd, forbidding" as he describes himself in "Starting from Paumanok"[26]). Sadly, the ordinary citizen is more likely to fall in with madness of Fletcher than with the sanity of Franklin or Whitman.

The Conversation and *Enemy of the State*

Two more films, dealing this time with the surveillance side of paranoia, are worth considering. *The Conversation* is a dark, existentialist and despairing examination of surveillance, while *Enemy of the State* is an action adventure with an implausibly happy ending, both for its protagonists and for the state of American democracy.

Gene Hackman appears in similar roles in both films, but *Enemy of the State* is a Will Smith film, not a Gene Hackman film, and hence it is a cartoon, involving implausible scripts, implausible stunts, and implausible endings. But, usefully, at the beginning of *Enemy of the State* congressman Phillip Hammersly is told: "... this is the richest, most powerful nation on earth, and therefore the most hated, and you and I know what the average citizen does not, that we are at war twenty-four hours of every day." This is a reminder of the paranoia of the rich, and of the justification that it gives to law-makers and security services to deploy a ubiquitous surveillance regime against their own citizens.

Unfortunately, *Enemy of the State* so exaggerates the capabilities of the technology that, as in any cartoon, we fail to take it seriously. However it might also unwittingly demonstrate that the level of human resources required to successfully track an individual means that the average citizen is unlikely to warrant such attention: it is and always will be far too expensive in human labor and technology. *The Conversation*, with much more plausible Cold War technologies, reinforces the point: even to catch a half-hour conversation of a couple in a park requires a team of highly skilled professionals with the latest equipment. Pratt says of the two films: "Both illustrate the potential, all-pervasive nature of government power, demonstrating how data about you could be used against you, how your slightest suspicions could be actual clues...."[27] Yet his own observation, that an entire satellite was devoted to tracking Will Smith in *Enemy of the State*, fails to suggest to him that the average citizen is in fact remarkably safe from such intrusion. *The Conversation* is particularly interesting because, while a Foucauldian reading of it is possible, it can also be understood as an essay in nihilism (and so is discussed again later in the chapter on nihilism, alienation and self-destruction). Its central character is by no means an infantalized citizen, but an expert in surveillance who falls victim to his own profession and who lands up in a state of "desperate, methodological, paranoia."[28] In this sense the film is a much darker and more anguished exploration of paranoia than anything offered by *The X-Files*. But whatever interpretations we wish to place on paranoia in American life and in its films, commentators seem to be agreed that it is a key feature of the American mind when driven to excess.

4

Aggression and Serial Killers

KEY FILMS: *Rambo: First Blood,*
Silence of the Lambs
ADDITIONAL FILMS: *Copycat, Seven,*
Natural Born Killers

In a great and powerful nation like America, paranoia does not lead to a cowering self-effacing existence; it leads instead to *aggression*. On the world stage it has led to the new American doctrine: the right of First Strike, the principle that led to the 2003 U.S.-led invasion of Iraq, and is poised in principle at least to act against Iran and North Korea. On the domestic front the centrality of aggression in the American psyche is epitomized by the private ownership of guns and the powerful influence on legislation wielded by the gun lobby.

At an individual level there exists a very typical male American aggression, a stereotype that even some liberated women follow. One could characterize this as an *armored, pumped-up* aggression, a stance that is pervasive in the personality rather than a response in the moment to a genuine threat. The word "armored" comes from the psychotherapeutic world, and means the development of the musculature in such a way as to apparently protect the body, though in reality it is an emotional protection. The goal of much therapy is to break down this armoring, and may even involve such techniques as Rolfing, which is a deep tissue manipulation. Of course the point is not to leave the individual physically and emotionally defenseless, but to prevent the defensive stance becoming the default response to every eventuality. Such a permanent state of aggressive defensiveness rules out much of normal human discourse and tends to invite aggression from others, becoming a self-fulfilling dynamic. It is also a deeply distrustful stance, a mistrust at the root of most paranoia.

"Pumped-up" means here an aggression deliberately cultivated, using the machinery of the gym, or even performance-enhancing drugs such as steroids. It is partly mind over matter: the perfect body representing the triumph of the human will over the weakness of the flesh. It is also technology over nature, as the shining pump-action machines in the gym and the laboratory-produced stimulants testify. And the shining pump-action *gun* is the preferred designer accessory for this constructed American persona. The term "hard-body" is even applied to a fit woman, to mean attractive and, presumeably, able to participate in athletic sexual activity for prolonged periods. All of these images come together in the film *American Psycho*, where the protagonist works out and works himself up to predatory sexual encounters that lead to sadistic violence and murder.

In his *Culture of Narcissism* Christopher Lasch devotes a chapter to "The Degradation of Sport" in which he says: "People today associate rivalry with boundless aggression and find it difficult to conceive of competition that does not lead directly to thoughts of murder."[1] He goes on to cite a study of students at Columbia which showed that "they could conceive of no competition that did not result in someone's annihilation." But we pointed out earlier that Lasch drew heavily on sources in clinical psychology or rather psychopathology, which makes his assertions probably only true of an extreme in American society. While we use the term "aggression" here to cover such an extreme, it is also used here in a non-clinical sense to cover the ordinary forcefulness that is part of the American character and which can very often be admirable. To use Reisman's terminology, this boldness, appearing at times and to some people as aggression, is a natural part of the independence of mind that goes with the inner-directed personality. For the other-directed personality, a more pathological aggression emerges perhaps out of paranoia, out of a sense of being overwhelmed by hard-to-read signals that may appear hostile.

The widespread ownership and use of small arms on the streets of America, so emblematic of the American aggression, gives rise to another cultural paranoia: the fear of the serial killer. One could argue that the serial killer has effectively taken the place of "God" in secular American society: he is apparently omnipotent, omniscient, and omnipresent. If I am a weak individual, gripped by a sense of personal insignificance and prey to paranoia, the idea that a serial killer might choose *me* as the next target is perversely satisfying. Hence the serial killer is raised to the status of a cultural icon, and we find in a number of films that he is often highly educated (preferably with an English accent) and culturally sophisticated.

To explore the unique American aggression and the fascination with serial killers, two films are chosen to start with: *Rambo: First Blood* and *Silence of the Lambs*. The runaway success of the *Rambo* films made the name synonymous with American violence: Sylvester Stallone appears the perfect image of the man with the pumped-up body and the pumped-up weaponry, an invincible hero. We will see that the first *Rambo* film, rather than the sequels, actually holds more subtle insights into this uniquely American aggression than the comic-book reputation might suggest. For an image that represents the American serial killer, then the obvious choice had to be Hannibal Lecter in *Silence of the Lambs*, a film that won five Oscars. Rambo is an all–American hero, whose violence is overt, shiny, and necessary, whereas Hannibal Lecter is the vilest of American villains, whose violence is introverted, dark, and—in an inversion of all values— also necessary.

Rambo: First Blood

The first of the *Rambo* trilogy is often dismissed with the other two as mindless violence, but in fact the film has much merit. It represents two faces of American violence: firstly the violence of its most disastrous war, Vietnam, and secondly the violence between individual Americans across the divide of mainstream and counter-culture. Then-president Ronald Reagan set off a minor controversy when he admitted he admired the second *Rambo* film. Leonard Quart says: "For Reagan, Rambo was a symbol of American machismo and patriotism, and the film's crude Russophobia and narcissistic camerawork worship of its star Sylvester Stallone's glistening, Nautilus-crafted body provided perfect fodder for Reagan's Hollywood brand of populism."[2]

In fact there is much to sympathize with in Rambo's predicament, even if his violence is comic-book and ultimately out of proportion. *Rambo: First Blood* opens as John Rambo attempts to track down a fellow Vietnam vet, only to learn he had died of cancer from the "orange stuff " they sprayed. The local sheriff advises him that he shouldn't hang around, particularly as he wears the American flag on his jacket. That wouldn't go down well in that area, and his appearance in other respects identifies him as a drifter. Rambo is obviously poor, and he also lacks the first possession that defines entry into American economic credibility, a car. The sheriff drives Rambo out of town, across the river bridge that serves as the city limits. But Rambo just walks back in, and the sheriff, furious at this quiet insubordination, arrests him. America is a vast, sparsely-populated country compared to Britain or Holland (America has one-twelfth the population density of Britain), and its small rural towns appear over and again in American films as isolated communities who distrust outsiders.

What exactly the American flag denotes here is uncertain, but the hostility shown to Rambo by the local police must represent a paranoia hard to imagine in Europe: he is not, after all, a foreigner. He is taciturn and unco-operative, but the contempt shown for him by the police officers seems out of proportion, especially after they find out that he is a decorated Vietnam veteran. He in turn eventually reacts disproportionately in his bid for freedom, escaping across the bridge seen earlier and up into the mountains. The scenery of the film is beautiful: it was an inspired move to locate the drama in a part of rural America providing snow-capped mountains in the background and hills, forests and ravines to allow Rambo to prove his survival training. America is the land of the lone individual succeeding against the odds, and more importantly, the system. The lone individual is decent, long-suffering, humane; but when pushed too far, beware! As the title of the film "First Blood" suggests, Rambo only gets really violent after the police show their intent to kill him. The moral basis for all his escalating violence is that they, the police, the state, the officials, started it. Now there will be no quarter, or sanity. He first kills the tracker dogs sent after him, and then disables his pursuers, one by one, but clearly does not intend to kill them. It is only after he is deliberately shot from a helicopter that he resumes his state of mind as a soldier pitted against the Vietcong and sets out firstly to kill his pursuers, and secondly to take revenge on the whole town that seems so against him.

Rambo epitomizes the Armed Forces that the U.S. is proud of, an aggression of mythical proportions. He is trained to kill using million dollar machines, or just a knife. And he is "trained to ignore pain and the weather, and to eat things a billy-goat would puke up," says Colonel Trautman, his mentor, proudly. Trautman appears along with Federal forces once it is clear that the situation has got out of hand. Of course the sheriff doesn't want interference from State forces, and hasn't a good word for Trautman either. When the colonel makes it clear that he hasn't come to protect his boy from the police, but to protect them from his boy, the sheriff is outraged.

The story has unique American features, but so far the level of violence is perhaps universal and believable. Any European nation could produce a Special Forces kind of soldier trained to survive in harsh conditions and act alone behind enemy lines. Such a soldier could, in theory, take on the local police and militia and outwit them at every turn, even though he was in unknown and hostile terrain. What makes *Rambo* the film, and "Rambo" as a piece of terminology, is what happens next: John Rambo takes the initiative, captures a truck bringing up a heavy machine gun, and drives it into town, across the now symbolic river bridge. While the official forces are still mostly running around the hills, Rambo is pursuing a sensible military strategy: cut off the head of the organization, the sheriff. He does this in the most spectacular fashion by blowing up a gas station and then a general store, which also serves as a gun shop. Once he has the biggest, most macho weapon in it (used against rhinos? elephants?) he lays siege to the police station, where his enemy is hiding. It is the completely out-of-proportion violence in this last scene that helped define "Rambo" as the epitome of a uniquely American violence: you don't have to be American to want to blow everything up, but it helps. The truly effective ending of this film, John Rambo's tirade and break-down in tears, is made possible by the stark contrast with his mute or monosyllabic delivery up to that point. Having destroyed almost everything in his path and wounded his enemy the Sheriff, he stands over him to deliver the finishing shot. Trautman enters at just this point and confronts him, desperate to talk him out of the final act of murder.

> TRAUTMAN: It's over, Johnny. It's over!
> RAMBO: Nothing is over! Nothing! You can't just switch it off! It wasn't my war. You asked me, I didn't ask you! I did everything to win, but someone didn't let us win. And at home at the airport those maggots were protesting. They spat at me, called me a baby murderer and shit like that! Why protest against me, when they weren't there, didn't experience it?
> TRAUTMAN: It was hard, but it's in the past.
> RAMBO: For you! Civilian life means nothing to me. There we had a code of honor.
> You watch my back, I watch yours. Here there's nothing!
> TRAUTMAN: You're the last of an elite troop, don't end it like this.
> RAMBO: There I flew helicopters, drove tanks, had equipment worth millions. Here I can't even work parking! Where is everybody? I had a friend who was there for us. There were all these guys. There were all these great guys! My friends! Here there's nothing! D'you remember Dan Forest? He wore a black headband. He had found magic markers, that he sent to Las Vegas, because we'd always talked about that. About the Chevy Convertible we wanted to drive until the tires fell off. In one of these barns a kid came to us with a kind of shoe cleaning box. "Shine?" He kept on asking. Joe said yes. I went to get a couple of beers. The box was wired. He opened it.... There were body parts flying everywhere. He lay there and screamed.... I have all these pieces of him on me! Just like that. I try to get him off me, my friend! I'm covered with him! Blood everywhere and so ... I try to hold him together, but the entrails keep coming out! And nobody would help! He just said: "I want to go home!" And called my name. "I want to go home, Johnny! I want to drive my Chevy!" But I couldn't find his legs. "I can't find your legs!" I can't get it out of my head. It's seven years ago. I see it every day. Sometimes I wake up and don't know where I am. I don't talk to anyone. Sometimes all day long. Sometimes a week. I can't get it out of my head.

Rambo's speech is absolutely to the point for right-wing Americans: they think it was a disgrace that the U.S. pulled out of Vietnam when they could have stayed and "won," and it was a disgrace that veterans like John Rambo should return to a country so divided over the issue that the return was not at all the hero's welcome they deserved. Yet it is conservative right-wing America that also turned its back on the traumatized vets like Rambo, as do most

Western nations when their troops return with unanswerable questions as to the point of all that horror and destruction. Indeed the developed world is only just putting in place counseling and mechanisms for recognizing post-traumatic stress disorder for those returning from war. But in the macho world that the term "Rambo" came to represent, such things are inconsistent with the tough image of the heroic soldier.

Rambo is the first of our protagonists who could qualify as a tragic figure in the Aristotelian sense. The film as a whole certainly has transgressive elements to it; it is plausible as a scenario up to the final conflagration; it has emotional intensity (particularly in Rambo's final monologue); is artistically serious (if one excuses the finale); and, perhaps surprisingly, it has a certain critical distance. Although it can be read as supporting the Vietnam War, one could equally read it as a critique of that war and all wars. In fact the film does not give that much purchase to the critiques of either Left or Right, beyond suggesting to the Left that authority is corrupt, and suggesting to the Right that the film is unpatriotic (as Medved does in pointing out that Vietnam vets later protested that such films promote "Post Celluloid Stress Disorder"[3]). But John Rambo is an honorable character whose misfortune, as Aristotle requires, "is brought about not by vice or depravity, but by some error or frailty." Frailty certainly not, but perhaps error. He is certainly not grotesque, if one allows for a little narrative exaggeration, and so his situation properly arouses pity and fear in the audience, that is, if they can accept the premise of his training in ultimate violence.

Silence of the Lambs

Rambo's image, of oiled muscles and oiled phallic weapons of ludicrous proportions, is the "positive" stereotype of American aggression: it is merely the destination of a vector that begins in self-reliant boldness. The serial killer represents the negative stereotype. *Silence of the Lambs* is the archetypal serial-killer film, which shows how the serial killer is elevated—in a pathological sense—to the status of the deity, and how this individual becomes an antihero far removed from the sordid reality of real murderers. By having Anthony Hopkins in the lead role of Hannibal Lecter, and endowing him with a formidable intellect and cultural sophistication (he is a psychiatrist), the American public are led down the road of worshipping insidious violence. Not sordid, everyday, spontaneous violence, but exquisitely planned violence, almost as an art form, and taken to the extreme of cannibalism. Hopkins has a delicious tinge of an English accent, as far as an American audience is concerned, and it is to England we turn to look at the first exemplar of an educated serial killer: the Victorian Jack the Ripper. (There is still uncertainty as to his exact identity, but most theories place him as an upper-middle class professional, or even a member of the aristocracy.) Pratt says: "Like Jack the Ripper, Dr. Lecter now seems a pop-culture immortal, perhaps riding on a wave of human self-loathing that seems increasingly evident at the dawn of the twenty-first century."[4]

Silence of the Lambs opens by introducing the ambitious trainee agent, Clarice Starling, played superbly by Jodie Foster. The character's name is well-chosen, suggesting a slight, nervous figure who is clearly going to undergo an ordeal that will test her to the limits. Special Agent Crawford is her tutor and boss, and has chosen her for a job for which he can't spare a graduate agent. Crawford says to her, "Be very careful with Hannibal Lecter. Dr. Chilton at the asylum will go over the physical procedures used with him. Do not deviate from them, for any reason. You tell him nothing personal, Starling. Believe me, you don't want Hannibal Lecter inside your head. Just do your job, but never forget what he is."

Starling arrives at the asylum and its director, Dr. Frederick Chilton, prepares her for the interview. He tells her: "Lecter carved up nine people— that we're sure of—and cooked his favorite bits. We've tried to study him, of course—but he's much too sophisticated for the standard tests." The interview is almost designed as an ordeal for the trainee agent: she has to run the gauntlet of the other inmates as she passes their cells. She is unnerved by this, and by her initial discussion with Lecter, who establishes his control from the outset by asking to see her credentials. Lecter quickly realizes that Jack Crawford has only sent a trainee to him, the great serial killer; this is a slight to his self-esteem. He gets her to sit down, again establishing the superior position, and asks what the inmate next door had hissed to her as she had passed his cell. She hesitates, and then tells him, straight-faced: "'I can smell your cunt.'" He responds, sniffing the air, "I see. I myself cannot. You use Evyan skin cream, and sometimes you wear L'Air du Temps, but not today." His sophistication, which includes also the explicitly sexual, is established not so much by his keen sense of smell but by the fact that he knows his cosmetics and perfumes.

As an agent Starling is surely absolutely compromised by now, with no chance of getting the upper hand. This of course is the central device of the film, that Starling, forgetting Crawford's advice and yielding up all kinds of personal information, in fact gets Lecter interested in helping her in a way that a male agent, following procedure, may never have done. In the following conversation Lecter establishes her lower social status:

> DR. LECTER: You're sooo ambitious, aren't you? You know what you look like to me, with your good bag and your cheap shoes? You look like a rube. A well-scrubbed, hustling rube with a little taste. Good nutrition has given you some

length of bone, but you're not more than one generation from poor white trash, are you, Officer Starling? That accent you're trying so desperately to shed—pure West Virginia. What was your father, dear? Was he a coal miner? Did he stink of the lamp? And oh, how quickly the boys found you! All those tedious, sticky fumblings, in the back seats of cars, while you could only dream of getting out. Getting anywhere—yes? Getting all the way—to the F ... B ... I.
CLARICE: You see a lot, Dr. Lecter. But are you strong enough to point that high-powered perception at yourself ? How about it...? Look at yourself and write down the truth. Or maybe you're afraid to.

Clarice hits back most pointedly, but we are left in no doubt that the serial killer is the sophisticate, not her. And on the return journey past the other inmates a masturbating prisoner flings at her a sample of that precious bodily fluid so prized—we assume—by Colonel Jack Ripper: semen. Inmates scream at her, and Lecter calls to her. She is nearly overwhelmed. Hesitating, she returns to his cell, and he apologizes to her for the discourtesy shown to her. Seizing her chance she asks if he will complete her questionnaire. He refuses, but offers her a lead in the current murder investigation. By this stage in the film we have been asked to accept a far more implausible scenario than the Rambo one, but that is the point: a soldier, a Vietnam vet, and violent outdoor combat are "realistic" in many senses. But the serial killer is a *mythical* creature in American culture because he operates in the dark. Rambo's psychology is straightforward: he is the decent man driven to breaking point. But the serial killer is unfathomable, and because of that is much more potent in the imagination. Rambo's orgy of violence will inevitably meet violence on a greater scale that will stop him in his tracks (he lands up breaking rocks in a State penitentiary). But the serial killer's violence is incomprehensible and cannot be opposed by State or Federal armies. Because he operates seemingly beyond all the usual policing of society he is also sometimes attributed with the mind of that other feared individual in American society: the intellectual.

But Lecter has what Starling wants: the leads to Buffalo Bill, the serial killer taking woman after woman after woman. She is sent back to Lecter with a deal: information on Buffalo Bill in return for a room with a view and a week every year on a beach. But Lecter still has the upper hand, as he knows time is running out for the latest victim, a senator's daughter called Catherine. He demands that Starling tell him more about herself—he questions her as if he were a paid psychiatrist interested in a client. Betraying again her instinct and instructions, she is forced to tell him about the death of her father. Lecter demands further personal details before he will give her more, but he provides her with a vital clue in the end.

After bungling attempts by the FBI to outsmart Lecter, Starling manages to interview him again. He can't resist playing the experienced tutor to her rookie psychiatry, and leads her step by step through the mind of Buffalo Bill. Quoting Marcus Aurelius, he gets her to see that the murderer *covets*. But he won't continue, insisting on his original bargain with her, the bargain that continually reduces her to an object—not a sexual object, but the object of his analysis. He is a brilliant psychiatrist, and it is only when that role is restored to him that he gets what *he* truly covets. She pleads with him that time is short, but has to give in, telling him now about the slaughter of lambs on her grandparents' ranch when she was ten, scenes which gave her nightmares. He pursues her analysis as if she were on the couch, and she gives it all to him. Who knows? Perhaps it will help her, as well as achieve his cooperation. After all, as is suggested here, America is the most Freudian culture in the world, and Starling is a human being searching for her personal truth like everyone else. Lecter gets to the core of her being, her personality, her motivation:

> Do you think if you saved Catherine, you could make them stop? Do you think, if Catherine lives, you won't wake up in the dark, ever again, to that awful screaming of the lambs? Do you?

"I don't know ... I don't know," she says, but for Lecter it is enough: he has penetrated her more satisfyingly than if he had sex with her. She is no longer any old "rube," an anonymous girl with ambitions from a white-trash background, but a solved case. His face softens, he thanks her, and she knows that she has given him something more precious than any official can bestow. "Tell me his name Doctor," she urges. But at that exact moment Dr. Chilton has arrived with the guards to expel her, and all she retrieves from the situation is the case file. As Lecter hands it to her through the bars, his finger strokes hers. And we know that Lecter is besotted with her, as the next day the camera pans over a new drawing he has made: it is of Clarice holding a lamb. The cannibal Lecter has a doctorate in psychiatry, can spout Marcus Aurelius, knows his cosmetics ... and is a master draftsman. Ridiculous. When he now manages to escape after atrocious violence to the guards, he walks free to the sounds of Bach: again we have an association between high culture and murder.

Against all the odds, it is Starling, not the male agents, who kills the serial killer. Her final ordeal has her pitted against Buffalo Bill in the dark, relying on her instinct against his night-vision goggles. After the fatal shot the camera slowly pans up from his dead body and rests on a pretty lampshade decorated with butterflies. Lecter remains free.

Silence of the Lambs is undoubtedly a milestone in transgressive cinema, but its huge critical success means that the shock-value of cannibalism and garment-making-from-human-skin, never mind the general issue of serial killing, requires attention. The film is not a tragedy, because Lecter is not a noble person brought low by "frailty or error"—rather he is just the monstrous character of "vice and depravity" that Aristotle thought foreign to tragedy. To the extent that his character, the combination of high culture and extreme depravity, makes him grotesque (one could argue) the less plausible the entire scenario. But the film is a useful testing of our five-fold scheme, because it raises the question of plot device, the central conceit of a film, as *beyond* plausibility. We are prepared to suspend disbelief regarding one element—as in science fiction—if other elements follow the resulting logic dictated by that one element. And Clarice Starling is made at every turn to be highly believable. She evokes pity and fear, not because she is tragic, but because she has to deal with the monstrous. Lecter is not required to be believable—and this is what the label "pure evil" intends—as long as his character sets up an interesting "what-if " scenario within which the protagonist does battle. This gives our requirement for "scenario plausibility" more flexibility than Aristotle's scheme. So, we have extreme transgressive content, scenario plausibility of nuanced kind, and intense emotion: we are drawn again and again to Starling's "rite-of-passage" graduation in policing, the stakes of which are ramped up by knowledge of the latest victim's grim situation. The film certainly embodies aesthetic values, though they do raise the disturbing question of the relationship between high culture and extreme depravity. Finally, we ask, does the film have critical distance? Despite what could be called a merely titillatory or gratuitous use of the cannibalism motif ? Are we led—catharsis-like—through our pity and fear for the protagonist to a point of emotional discharge and compassion? The answer is yes, because Starling is a woman.

Much critical discourse around the film centers on its feminist credentials, Pratt for example showing skepticism to this stance, saying "it is not Clarice who has been liberated from her fear but Lecter...."[5] The "hero's journey" analysis of the film by the Jungian John Izod appears much better able to tackle the gender issues, being one step removed from mainstream Marxist or feminist thought.[6] For the Left, whose feminism is so advanced, it is demeaning to say that a woman has done as well or better than a man in a man's world, because for them the project of making the world gender-free has already been completed. In reality such completion is merely an intellectual fantasy, and *Silence of the Lambs* was amongst the first to show women in successful roles in violent or dangerous male-dominated professions. Starling's triumph is still extraordinary, and her submission to Lecter, which Pratt sees as "psychic rape," can instead be construed as a positive strategy that a man would be less likely to adopt. For right-wing critics such as Medved, the mere presence of the transgressional material—admittedly more extreme than most of what preceded it—writes off the film from the start. He quotes fellow film critic Stephen Farber: "... but the question remains, why make it at all? ... We know that these kinds of madmen exist, but the film offers no insight into what makes them tick.... The criminals are so bizarre and extreme in their sadistic pleasures that they are more ridiculous than frightening....."[7] Medved and Farber follow Aristotle here, but they are focusing on the wrong element: the film is about Starling, not Lecter. It is Starling's journey that demonstrates the critical distance in the film, because her eventual success hangs on her vulnerability, which at all times threatens to engulf her: there is no certain outcome. We are left with no insight into Lecter, because it is not needed.

Lecter knows everything: he is grotesque in this too. But we have to look beyond *Silence of the Lambs* to find films that show serial killers truly demonstrating all three characteristics of "God," which are omniscience, omnipotence, and omnipresence. Lecter appeals to one of them at least, omniscience, but cannot be omnipotent and omnipresent until his escape from jail. Lecter is the genius of criminal psychology, the master analyzer of human emotions, the suave and erudite professor Starling must look up to. But who is potentially superior to the serial killer? Why, of course, the criminologist or agent who outwits him. Lecter remains supreme, but Starling reaches out for that ultimate role and succeeds, at least where Buffalo Bill is concerned. We are drawn to her character, because she is a woman, slight and unsure of herself, and so much the greater is her (partial) triumph.

Copycat, Seven, Natural Born Killers, and American Psycho

In the film *Copycat* it is down to women again to defeat a serial killer who really does appear omniscient, omnipresent and omnipotent. He seems to know everything about his planned victims; he seems to be everywhere (and nowhere); and he seems able to strike at will, unimpeded even by a 24-hour police guard. But he has one weakness: he is not original, choosing instead to murder each victim in the style of serial killers he admires (hence "copycat"). This time we have again a relatively inexperienced female law enforcement officer, M. J. Monahan, in pursuit of the killer, joining forces with a female criminologist who becomes the victim of an unsuccessful attempt by the killer. In a stroke of casting genius, it is Sigourney Weaver who plays Helen Hudson, the criminologist brought low by the criminal. We are familiar with Weaver in her "über-bitch" role from the *Aliens* series, in which she largely adopts the masculine Rambo-style aggression normally reserved for males, so that her vulnerability in *Copycat* is all the more effective. At the start of the film she comes over as the confident academic, used to speaking to large audiences on the subject of her research: serial killers. What is more, she makes a point of showing that half her audience—all the males—are suspect. But when she is nearly killed by Peter Foley—one of those who had attended her lecture—she has a breakdown of confidence and becomes agoraphobic. Foley is not an erudite man like Lecter, but plays very much on his ability to know everything about Helen Hudson, his power—ultimately—to kill her, and the fact that he is everywhere, and nowhere. Her paranoia grows as we come to understand the killer's "God"-like abilities.

It is in the film *Seven* (also spelt *"Se7en"*) that we find the ultimate serial killer: he has both the "God"-like characteristics of Foley and the erudition of Lecter. As in *Copycat* we have a team of two attempting to track down a serial killer. This one has concocted an aesthetic triumph of a crime: seven murders based on the seven deadly sins. Pitted against him are sophisticated and reserved Detective Lt. William Somerset (Morgan Freeman), and a second officer, Mills (Brad Pitt). Somerset knows his Milton, his Bible, and is generally cultured in a way that we do not expect from a homicide officer. But he is matched against a serial killer equally erudite and sophisticated. In the library Somerset looks up Dante's *Divine Comedy* to the strains of Bach, while his sidekick Mills looks at photos of the murder victim ... to the same music. Somerset is convinced that the serial killer, having taken already so much trouble to dramatize the killing of his first two victims around the themes of gluttony and greed, will follow the sequence of the seven deadly sins as unfolded in the illustrated plan of Dante's *Inferno*. But the cultural references roam more broadly, across *Canterbury Tales*, to Shakespeare, and to Ernest Hemingway. It "does Mills's head in." Somerset drinks wine, Mills drinks beer. *Seven* provides us with another example of the rational / emotional pairing that Spock and Kirk illustrate, as do Scully and Mulder. At one point, when a bad-tempered Mills kicks out an annoying photographer, Somerset says to him: "It is impressive to see a man feeding off his emotions." At another point they discuss the killer: Mills calls him a "nutbag" but Somerset won't dismiss him so easily. "This guy is methodical, exacting, and worst of all, patient." Qualities that he admires, it seems. Although Mills has no interest in culture, he reads up on the references, determined not to be outshone by Somerset.

But as fast as Mills tries to close the culture gap, the killer steams ahead: he is also witty. By hanging a piece of modern art upside down, he leads the detectives to information he wants them to have: a lead to the wrong suspect. Why is he wrong? Because he is clearly not a man of learning. Nevertheless we enjoy watching the less clued-up officers hunt down the wrong man (in quintessential pumped-up American style, maximum force): we are in on the "culture" thing, and the ordinary cops are not. Their quarry turns out to be the third victim (rather than the perpetrator), having suffered "about as much as anyone, give or take." The extreme and lengthy suffering of each victim (this one perishes from the diseases born of sloth) makes the film more sickening than most. But our fascination is morally lubricated by the obvious status of the film as great "art," and by the device of making us feel deeply cultured.

It is fitting therefore that the library becomes the focal point of their investigation (this film was made before erudition could be obtained so easily via the Internet). We learn that the FBI monitors reading habits, for example books on nuclear power, *Mein Kampf* and so on. "How can this be legal?" asks Mills. "Legal, illegal, it doesn't apply," says Somerset. Which is just by way of reinforcing the observation that anything Federal is suspect, and beyond the law. At the same time we are in thrall to the power of this investigative machine, and, lo and behold, the FBI computer analysis takes them to the perpetrator's flat. Religious icons abound, though fingerprints mysteriously do not. The murderer calls them while they are subjecting his flat to intense forensic investigation. They tape his phone call, and Mills is forced to concede: "You were right. He's a preacher." "Yeah," responds Somerset, "His murders are his sermons to us." The next sermon is on the theme of lust, and the sexual violence within it could barely be more appalling. Like Hannibal Lecter, the serial killer in this film now makes a bargain with the police. He is known only as John Doe (moodily played by Kevin Spacey), and the denouement involves them escorting him to the place of his choosing, in order for him to reveal the whereabouts of the last two victims, already—in principle—dead. En route Doe explains to them: "Wanting people to listen, you can't just tap them on the shoulder any more, you have to hit them with a sledgehammer. And then you'll notice you've got their strict attention." This is the moment that John Doe helps us all to excuse the film itself, by claiming that his brutal torture and murder of his victims was deserved because they were guilty of the specific sin in question. Doe's inverted morality eventually gets to Mills, whose emotional nature cannot take the baiting. Somerset broods at the wheel, but his forensic intelligence has not worked out the logic of the last two deaths. Mill's emotionality plays into Doe's hands, ensuring that his exquisitely planned project succeeds: victim six is Mill's wife, and victim seven—despite all of Somerset's pleadings— is John Doe at the hands of Mill.

John Doe is as grotesque and unexplained as Lecter, providing the scenario for Somerset and Mills's trial of strength. However the emotional intensity of *Silence of the Lambs* is missing because we are not greatly identified with the suffering of either officer, until right at the end when Mills learns of his wife's murder: pity and fear are evoked too late in the film. Instead we are engaged with the film's *cleverness*. *Seven* is a disturbing film because the highbrow culture it parades is not a necessary device, but borrowed: a trophy erudition, like a trophy wife. So *Seven* is transgressional enough; its scenario is plausible enough in the response of the officers to an implausible killer; it fails on emotional intensity; it's shot and acted well enough, though its high aesthetics are merely a fashion accessory; but what about its critical distance? Here too we must argue that it fails, on the ground that it makes an unquestioning assumption about the relationship between high culture and sophistication, where that sophistication may be owned by both the serial killer and the police detective. While Doe and Lecter are cultured to make them more grotesque, where is Somerset's cultural prowess justified? It serves only to suggest a moral equivalence between killer and policeman. Hence, despite some surface similarities between *Silence of the Lambs* and *Seven*, Aristotle's distinctions help us understand why the former has much greater cathartic power than the latter. Rather than leaving shaken at the precarious victory of the protagonist in the former, one leaves queasy at the spectacle of aesthetics serving voyeuristic morbidity in the latter.

The cultural conservatives would find nothing to like in the film: the religious right would be particularly offended by the notion of serial killing as "sermonizing," while the classical cultural conservatives would object to their precious canon in the service of popular culture. The Left is perhaps summed up by this predictable response from Philip John Davies and Paul Wells in their introduction to *American Film and Politics*: "*Seven* plays out theological tropes as metaphors for not merely spiritual collapse but the irrecoverable demise of the late capitalist infrastructure." By classing John Doe, with Aristotle, as grotesque, we make the point that we have no access to his "spiritual collapse" or any other insight into his serial killer mentality, while it is impossible to understand why this confection of a transgressional figure should say anything about either the demise or the prospering of "late capitalist infrastructure." Indeed, most of the "capitalist" infrastructure in the film looks to be in perfectly fine form. All this aside, the film helps make the point that the elevation of the serial killer to the position of vengeful omnipotence marks out a unique characteristic of the American mind.

In *Natural Born Killers* Oliver Stone gives us a rather different kind of serial killer. The young couple who go on a killing spree in the film are neither erudite nor "God"-like; their murders have no reason and they know nothing ... about anything. They are "low-life white-trash psychopaths" as one commentator put it. On its release Stone received considerable criticism, even the charge that so-called copy-cat killings in the U.S. were the result of his film. *Natural Born Killers* was originally written by Quentin Tarantino, who largely disowned it later on. It was, according to *Entertainment Weekly*, the eighth most controversial film ever. For Stone the movie is metaphoric and satiric, targeting the media presentation of serial killers, rather than the killers themselves. As one critic explains, Stone's message seems to be that we should ban TV; ironic, as that is what Stone is deeply part of, the media that purvey to us apparently endless sex and violence. Attempts were made to ban the film in the U.K., but Stone, in a U.K. TV interview, was adamant that it is not the media that creates violence: it is society, domestic arms sales, urban deprivation and the like. He had been disturbed by its depiction in the media, and his film was a "vomiting up" of his own distress. He argued that his role was to be a mirror, a "grotesque, fun-house" mirror to what he saw. When pressed as to why the killers get away without being brought to justice in the end, Stone said that "it was all Jell-O" in the nineties, there was no morality anymore, no-one cared anymore. Everyone got away with it in the nineties. Perhaps Stone had been over-influenced by postmodern ideas on the relativism of values, but he is adamant: don't blame me. It is grotesque, but that is what he saw, and his job was to depict it. When pressed about the alleged "copycat" killings Stone made the point that all the juveniles involved had a history of crime; the film was not the cause of that history.

Marsha Kinder suggests, in her essay on film violence, that *Natural Born Killers* references three key earlier films: *The Wild Bunch, Bonnie and Clyde,* and *A Clockwork Orange.*[8] In Stephen Prince's examination of film violence he agrees that "Sam Peckinpah was the key filmmaker who popularized ultra-violence in the years following the onset of the Code and Rating Administration system in 1968."[9] He also cites *The Wild Bunch* as a key film for its portrayal of violence after the transition. One of Prince's really interesting contributions however is his classification of methods used by pre–1968 filmmakers to suggest violence without actually showing it, though his scheme could be applied to any transgressive behavior. As mentioned in the Introduction it is the method of "emotional bracketing" that is most relevant here to our concept of emotional intensity. He defines it as a method that works by "opening a space inside the narrative where the viewer can recover" and expands on this by saying that in employing this device "a filmmaker is acknowledging that the violence on-screen is intended to have an emotional impact on viewers and that these viewers have the prerogative to recover from that impact." Furthermore, "By contrast, the absence of emotional bracketing can suggest that a filmmaker is staging violence without a corresponding moral perspective."[10] We will look at films by Woody Allen and Paul Schrader that seem to fail in respect to emotional bracketing, but in the context of serial killers such as John Doe, Lecter, and the Stone's "natural born killers" Mickey and Mallory as grotesque characters, the lack of emotional bracketing simply flags up their moral emptiness. In *Henry: Portrait of a Serial Killer*, where Henry's character is formed like Mickey's and Mallory's through abuse in childhood, he calmly eats French fries after murdering two prostitutes.

However illuminating the serial killers so far discussed, one might suggest that the ultimate American psychopath is the protagonist of the film *American Psycho*, directed by Mary Harron. Based on the novel by Brett Easton Ellis, the central character is called Patrick Bateman, perhaps a nod to a much earlier American killer, Norman Bates. In the intervening time between Hitchcock's *Psycho* and Harron's *American Psycho* much has happened, particularly the Thatcher/Reagan commercial revolution of the 1980s. Patrick Bateman lives in the American dream of corporate expansion and champagne lifestyles, and although the film was released in 2000, it is deliberately placed in the 1980s—mobile phones the size of a house-brick make that clear. The film shows us the two sides of Bateman: slick, erudite, successful and terminally stylish on the one hand, and devoted to the killing and horrible mutilation, mainly of women, on the other.

The film opens with Bateman telling us of his morning routine, which involves a regime of health-care, exercise and self-pampering more appropriate perhaps to Cleopatra. But, he tells us, "there is no real me, ... I am simply not there." His life is hollow, an existential sham, and his growing need for extreme violence fills that vacuum. After killing a tramp in an alley-way he is shown receiving an expensive massage the next day: there is no emotional bracketing. He tells us: "I have all the characteristics of a human being—flesh, blood, skin, hair—but not a single, clear, identifiable emotion, except for greed and disgust. Something horrible is happening inside of me, and I don't know why." His downward trajectory is brutal and disgusting, covered up all the time by his high-life sophistication. His erudition is now truly American: it owes nothing to the great cultural history of the West, but involves a fastidious and encyclopedic knowledge of the things that money can buy: restaurants and their most gourmet creations, the whole world of popular American music, and mineral water. (Actually the film leaves this out, but in the novel Bateman could waxes lyrical for pages about different mineral waters: his palate is so sophisticated that he can distinguish between a dozen of them blindfolded.) He uses this acuity to maintain his social superiority, while in fact he is sliding into the deepest and bloodiest sadism.

Bateman's violence is pumped up, for example, by the violent stomach presses that he performs, while incidentally on the TV behind him plays a scene from *The Texas Chainsaw Massacre*. He does drugs to take up his adrenalin level, and has violent and narcissistic sexual encounters with pairs of women, tape-recording their intercourse and also watching himself perform in the mirror. He is the least likeable creation ever to take the role of "hero" in a film. Before slashing away at his latest female victim he tells her: "Since, Elizabeth, it's impossible in this world we live in to empathize with others, we can always empathize with ourselves." He lives hermetically sealed in his own vanity, and the only thing that can reach him is extreme violence. So he stands, naked and covered with Elizabeth's blood, holding a screaming chainsaw as his next victim runs any which way through his apartment to escape.

But slowly the cracks appear in this story. The apartment he uses to carry out his attacks doesn't appear to bear any trace of his existence. Its owner, who he is supposed to have killed with an axe, has dinner with a colleague of Bateman's in London. Police cars explode after he shoots some officers: the stereotype comic-book fantasy of an explosion forces even Bateman to look at his gun in suspicion. (If only *The X-Files* could embody this level of self-awareness.) And slowly we get it: he is not a serial *killer*, he is a serial *fantasist*. None of it took place at all, except in his mind. His final speech to us reflects on his predicament:

> There are no more barriers to cross. All I have in common with the uncontrollable and the insane, the vicious and the evil, all the mayhem I have caused, and my utter indifference toward it, I have now surpassed. My pain is constant and sharp, and I do not hope for a better world for anyone. In fact, I want my pain to be inflicted on others. I want no one to escape. But even after admitting this, there is no catharsis. My punishment continues to elude me, and I gain no deeper knowledge of myself. No new knowledge can be extracted from my telling. This confession has meant ... nothing.

Bateman is the loneliest of serial killers because he only imagined it: there will be no punishment, no catharsis, no hope of redemption. The film ends with no hope or resolution, and it also made little mark on the film critics and juries, picking up only two minor awards, compared with five Oscars and thirty-four minor awards for *Silence of the Lambs*. But it is a quintessential glimpse into the dark corners of the American mind, for a number of reasons.

Firstly it depicts a Freudian honesty of self-examination, *taken halfway*. The good-looking, fit, sophisticated, rich, and successful American moneyman, working in mergers and acquisitions, has an infinity of reasons to be happy, but isn't; his inner demons, welling up from the subconscious, are overwhelming him with frightful demands. It is a tragedy with its roots in ancient Greece, only instead of the gods taunting this apparently successful man, it is his own unconscious. Instead of clamping the lid shut on this festering cauldron, he is facing it, though only with the increasingly failing device of his perverted imagination. Secondly, the film adds to horror of this tormented man by revealing that it is all a *sham*. Everything in his artificial meaningless world is ersatz, including his one attempt to bring into it some meaning. That which could be the only real thing he could cling to, his potentially Nietzschean obedience to his vilest instincts, turns out to be unreal as well, and hence there is no catharsis in it. He is trapped in the bubble of his own vanity, in the construction that is Patrick Bateman, and his apparently monstrous rage is impotent to prick it. It offers no hope. The shallowness of the American dream when predicated solely on material gain and social climbing doesn't permit the admission of weakness, that he needs help. Although in one sense there is an honesty, that Bateman is facing his demons, he is hamstrung as far as any follow-through goes. His self-image within the group of competitive alpha males he is surrounded by would not permit the truly American recourse to psychotherapy. This psycho badly needs analysis, but he won't get it.

5

Oedipal / Freudian

KEY FILMS: *The Devil's Advocate*, *The Hulk*
ADDITIONAL FILMS: *Star Wars*, *Affliction*

The American mind, gifted with warmth, humor and an expansive vision of life, may in its darker corners fall prey to paranoia, and to aggression. But the American mind may also be deeply self-absorbed, and has taken the insights and methods of Freud as the starting point for its journey of self-discovery. Everyone, darling, is in analysis, or at least in therapy of some kind. In contrast, as E. Ann Kaplan points out, "psychoanalysis has tradition-ally been marginalized in British intellectual and cultural life."[1] Kaplan also makes the useful point that Freud's legacy can be considered under three headings: psychoanalysis as a science, psychoanalysis as a therapeutic inter-vention, and psychoanalysis as a tool for examining cultural productions. Psychotherapy as a science is mostly disregarded, while its therapeutic value is disputed, but its cultural relevance appears perennial. Peter Watson says, "After some early hesitation, America proved a more hospitable host to psy-choanalytic ideas than, say, Britain, France, or Italy."[2] We saw earlier that Peter Watson documents the various attacks on Freud's scientific ideas and clinical practice, but what is more interesting is his speculation that, if Freud was so wrong in those aspects of his legacy, does it not rob "Freudian" art of most of its meaning?[3] Are paintings, novels, plays and films that have a Freudian basis now only to be considered as period pieces? Definitely not, one could argue, based on the films examined in this chapter, three of which were made in the late twentieth century and one of which was made early in the twenty-first.

One could argue that American culture is perhaps the most deeply Oedi-pal in the world, which shows on the one hand in an immature psychology, and on the other in a rage against the father. When not outright pathological it shows as an intense competitiveness between father and son: could the two Presidents Bush be an example? American film is deeply Freudian, both in the way that the characters are motivated, and also in explicit references to psychological complexes and to people undergoing analysis or therapy. Alfred Hitchcock was the master of the "psychological" thriller, and deeply aware of Freudian ideas; for example Norman Bates in *Psycho* can be understood in Oedipal terms. Nicholas Haeffner tells us that the censors wanted to take out lines in the film which made explicit reference to Bates's Oedipal relationship with his mother: "A boy's best friend is his mother," and "A son is a poor substitute for a lover."[4] In Hitchcock's *The Birds* Lydia Brenner is possessive of her son Mitch, and while his former girlfriend explicitly denies that it is Oedipal, clearly it is. The film revolves around Lydia's almost psychotic personality, perhaps the inward image of the external disturbance that manifests outwardly in the birds' frenzied attacks. Hitchcock, like other non–American directors considered here (such as Sam Mendes and Ang Lee) seems to have an eye for the American madness.

Although one can make quite a list of films alongside *Psycho* where the Oedipal shows itself as love for the mother, it is films showing the aggressive competitiveness with the father, and then by extension to all other males, which are more telling of the American mind. This competitiveness may well have a sexual origin in the first place, as American men strive to attain the status of alpha male in their search for sexual fulfillment. But it spills out into every other arena, including science, politics, the arts, and religion. Hence the term "Oedipal" is being used here in the rather specific sense of fatherson rivalry.

Sigmund Freud was the first to establish the intensely "psychological" conception of human motivation (with its core idea of the irrational unconscious) as a cornerstone of modern Western culture. Carl Gustav Jung, his first pupil and co-worker, has also greatly influenced Western culture, perhaps more vividly in American film-making than anywhere else. Jung placed less emphasis on the Oedipal and more on the "archetypes," which are role models in the psyche such as mother, hero, trickster, and so on. It is the archetype of the hero that most influenced Hollywood, through the work of Joseph Campbell, who was deeply influenced by Jung and also his own research into mythical stories from around the world. Campbell spotted a pattern of heroic behavior that he termed the "monomyth,"[5] and which became the prototype for some American cinematic drama, often through another writer called Vogler, whose book, *The Writer's Journey*, is geared as a manual for directors and scriptwriters.[6] More directly, Campbell influenced George Lucas in the making of *Star Wars*. Such films convey a Greek idea of the hero, but now an intrinsic part of American culture. Campbell's Greek monomyth is, on the face of it, an admirable struggle of the individual to conquerlife's difficulties and return as a mature "individuated" adult to society.

(Note that "individuation" is Jung's term for the goal of psychotherapy, a state of independent maturity.)

But when Campbell's monomyth becomes the sole model for how an individual, whether male or female, is supposed to relate to society, then this becomes problematic. This is because the hero's journey over-emphasizes the individual; it elevates achievement to the highest goal; and it forces a deeply competitive mindset. In short it inevitably leads to a male, armored, pumped-up aggression, instead of a balanced, co-operative, social mindset. Instead of a network of social relations, and relations to the essential forces of Nature such as the earth and its plants and its animals, it narrows down these relations to power-relations: only those individuals who can assist on the heroic quest are of importance, and only those elements of Nature that can be exploited are of importance. The wise man or martial arts teacher is used as a source of instruction, while the weaker man or woman is used as a tool to reach the goal, or as a trophy of conquest. Forests are used for profit instead of being seen as sacred places, instead of treating the trees and the animals as equals, as part of a network of mutually-enhancing relationships. The linear is elevated over the network, over the web of life where co-operation keeps competition within proportionate boundaries.

In Greek mythology there is actually a better understanding of the problematic nature of the hero: both the myth of Prometheus, who was punished for his ambition to acquire fire, and Icarus, who flew too near the sun and fell back into the sea and drowned, illustrate the point. The Greeks saw the heroic as inevitably *hubristic*, a word meaning the failure resulting from over-ambition, specifically through an arrogant challenge to the gods. In American culture the person who fails is a "loser." The more aggressively competitive the culture, the more "losers" there are going to be, who will form a resentful underclass and who will mill threateningly outside the gated communities of the rich and successful. This is as true outside America as it is inside: the resentment of the Islamic world outside of America perhaps mirrors the resentment of the American underclasses within America.

In this chapter we look at American competitiveness in terms of the father-son relationship, a relationship that appears skewed in the heated environment of American male aggression. To reinforce the point: the term "Oedipal" is used here to emphasize that competition begins between father and son, and to highlight the Greek origins of its supposedly heroic dimension. The first two films discussed here involve sons who do not know their fathers at the outset but engage in a life-or-death struggle with them, making the parallel with the Oedipal story all the stronger (though both films lack the other Freudian element: the desire for the mother). The first is *The Devil's Advocate*, which is set in a quintessentially aggressive American context: the legal profession. The second is *The Hulk*, a recent film adaptation of the comic book story where an "ordinary" man is transformed into a fearsome green giant when his peculiar body chemistry is triggered by the onset of rage.

The Devil's Advocate

In *The Devil's Advocate* the casting is perfect: Al Pacino as the father-figure John Milton, and Keanu Reeves as the fresh-eyed but successful young lawyer Kevin Lomax. The film opens with Lomax possibly facing his first lost case as a rising provincial lawyer in Alachua County. He is taunted by a colleague in the men's room, and he regains his determination to win at all costs. He turns his case around with a dubious use of evidence, and retires to celebrate his undefeated run of defense cases. During the party he is offered a job in New York to select a jury, a process depicted in such a way as to cast doubt about the judicial system itself. Once in New York Lomax displays his prodigious intuition in selecting a jury, and the scene is set to test his judgment. The accused is acquitted, and we are left to wonder at one of the prime moral issues in America: how lawyers can defend the indefensible and win. To help us in our doubts various special effects make New York and the offices of Lomax's new firm appear just a shade spooky ... or should that be diabolical? So we are led to meet his new boss, John Milton, who reminds us that the defense lawyer who sets clients free earns way more than the prosecutor who locks them up. In a scene perhaps designed to remind us of the temptation of Christ, Lomax is taken to the roof of a skyscraper and effectively offered the world. Actually, just a job, for now. The salary is great, the apartment is the envy of other employees, and his wife can now dream of a baby.

But Lomax's first case is a dark one: ostensibly a public health issue, it is really about defending a group that seems to practice voodoo or animal sacrifice. Somewhat unrealistically Lomax has to visit the man he is to defend, Moyez, in his underground shrine. "I'm here about the animals," says Lomax. "We have an investment in blood," replies Moyez cryptically, "Think of it as spiritual currency." He then proceeds to unwrap a piece of meat that we are led to believe is the tongue of a large animal, and strews it with nails. We are in no doubt: voodoo is to be practiced, and the target will be prosecutor Merto, who is Lomax's legal adversary in the coming court case. When it comes to the trial Lomax presents us with some critically American reference points regarding its founding principles:

> Men kill animals and eat their flesh. Phillipe Moyez killed a goat. He killed a goat. And he did it at home in a manner consistent with his religious beliefs. Now, Mr. Merto may find that bizarre. It's certainly not a religious practice performed by everyone. It's not as common as, say, circumcision. It's not as common as the

belief that wine transforms into blood. Some people handle poisonous snakes to prove their faith. Some people walk on fire. Phillipe Moyez killed a goat. And he did it while observing his constitutionally protected religious beliefs.

The reference to Moyez's right to pursue his religion, any religion, as constitutionally protected goes deep into the history of America's unique origins as the haven for non-conformist Christians, but also deep into its difficulty over extending that constitutional right to non–Christians. This is because Christianity has defined itself from its origins as "other" and against earlier practices such as idol-worship, polytheism, and the practices of nature religions. All of these were vilified as "pagan," "heathen," and even, ultimately as "satanic." Lomax's defense goes well however, as the judge is Jewish and is naturally sympathetic to the idea that Moyez practiced something comparable to Kosher butchery. But the clincher is unfolded as prosecutor Merto is strangely unable to argue his side of the case when he has a coughing fit, which progressively worsens as he clutches his throat. The voodoo works, and it's a walk-over for Lomax.

Milton congratulates him, and offers him a murder case that is a big as it gets in New York. Later on his mother turns up and lectures him: "Wide is the gate and broad is the way that leadeth to temptation," but he has no time for scripture, as by now his case is going badly. Kevin is more than just preoccupied, he is being drawn into Milton's New York lifestyle. As a metaphor this serves us well, as what is on offer here is basically the American dream, the high life, the seduction into American values heard as a sirensong all over the world, and which comes, of course, at a price. Lomax's wife Mary Ann is getting left behind, and is increasingly prone to nightmares, and the daytime nightmare of her recent medical diagnosis: "non-specific ovarian failure." Milton now gives Lomax a clear choice: his wife or the case. Far from pushing Lomax to serve the firm, Milton argues with him that his duty is to his wife, but Lomax's ambition is greater. He won't take the proffered way out, and we know that he is now heading the wrong way, into the darkness.

We saw earlier that if the serial killer seems to hold for the dark recesses of the American mind some of the key attributes of "God," then the criminal investigator is the one being that can usurp that place. Lomax as the criminal lawyer is gilded with that aura: part mythical being, and part university professor gifted with implacable forensic logic. We are mere rabbits in his unnervingly focused gaze, as is the chief defense witness (interestingly named Melissa Black) during his rehearsal with her of likely prosecution questions. But has Lomax overreached himself? Black snaps out of his hypnotic hold over her and tells him to get lost: the questions are too personal. The real problem for Lomax is only just coming into focus though: he has realized that Melissa Black is lying, and he has to face the possible guilt of his client. It is also now that we begin to get into the father / son aspect of the Milton / Lomax relationship. Yes, Milton has offered him top place in the firm; yes, Milton has given him an older man's advice on Mary Ann. But we now see that Milton is putting the pressure on, though oh so gently at first. Again he offers Lomax a way out: "follow your gut, make the decision, I'll back you either way." But he slips in the poison: "Maybe it's your time to lose. Think I haven't lost before?" Lomax stares at him: he has never lost a case yet, and will not accept the possibility.

The case reaches its climax, and, as if playing "God," Lomax looks at the jury, and at the court. The judge has called him to present his case, and the wait is agonizing as Lomax deliberates. But in the end he pronounces the words that will free his client, and which condemn him: "call Melissa Black." The prosecution fails to press her as hard as he did, so her lies are believed— as we must guess at least—because the next scene tells us that Lomax won the case. The descent into darkness begins in earnest now, as Mary Ann kills herself in the hospital ward witnessed by a frantic Kevin trying to batter down the door that separates them. But this dreadful event has interrupted his mother's painful confession that, yes, she had once been to New York, and that she had been so kindly spoken to by a man who knew every word of the Bible, ... she falters. "Say it!" Lomax screams at her, "Say it!" She sobs: "Milton, ... he's your father, he's your father." And Kevin realizes that Milton was always there, watching over his career.

In the surreal finale, Kevin has to confront his father, in the great American-Oedipal moment. "What did you do to Mary Ann?" he screams at his father, and when Milton boasts of how he "got it on" with her at a modest score of seven out of ten for depravity, Kevin pulls out a gun and shoots him repeatedly. But Milton isn't human, and the bullets just go through him: he merely shouts his approval at the boy's fury. For an American father is fulfilled, it seems, when his son descends into unchecked rage. Quite naturally Kevin asks "Who are you?" to which comes the rejoinder, "And who are *you?*" A lawyer who never lost a case? What did that make Kevin? And why did he blame Milton for Mary Ann, when Kevin could have saved her at any moment with some show of love? He is now close to the truth about Milton: "*What* are you," Kevin finally demands, "... Satan?" Milton merely responds: "Aw, I have so many names.... Call me Dad."

And now the real argument begins, on that ancient question of free will. Milton reminds him that at each turn there was a way out, a way back, but Kevin won't take the blame, insisting that it was Satan, his father, who set him up, that it was entrapment. To some extent *The Devil's Advocate* can be understood as a modern telling of *Faust*, the Romantic novel by German cultural hero Goethe. In the finale of *The Devil's Advocate*, its hero Lomax is redeemed, having seen where his pact with the devil takes him. In that sense it is more moral than Goethe's story, which is closer to *Natural Born Killers*, in that its hero "gets away with it." Al Pacino as Milton is ideal in the role because he comes over as genuinely paternal and kindly towards his son. Even the temptations he puts in his way, and the "infernal" skills he gives him to achieve his ambitions, are tempered by his continual warnings and offers of a way out. One could argue that these offers were a sham, but the fact is that at the very least the audience is clearly presented with what should have been Lomax's overriding concern: the welfare of his wife.

Milton—despite of, or perhaps because of, his humanity—becomes the grotesque foil for the protagonist Lomax: once we accept Satan here as a plot device, the scenario is realistic, and the emotion genuinely intense. Because ultimately we understand Milton to be a psychic reflection of Lomax's personality, the film can make a genuine claim to critical distance: nothing more is assumed than the Freudian or Jungian concept of the unconscious as an active agent. The film as a whole is therefore to be understood as an *indictment* of Oedipal male competitiveness, and an indictment of the force of ambition which sacrifices the natural balance of the world, and of married love, on the altar of personal greed. In the next film, *The Hulk*, we are presented with a father bearing almost no redeeming features, one who does not so much test his son as attempt to exploit him as a laboratory animal.

The Hulk

The Hulk is a film adaptation of the comic-book hero by Taiwanese-born director Ang Lee. He has worked in America since his film studies days at New York University, but his early work reflected his Taiwanese background and concerns with far-Asian culture.[7] His later films however are finely attuned to American audiences, and it is intriguing to see the extent to which Lee has incorporated Oedipal issues into *The Hulk*. Lee's status as an intellectual ensures that *The Hulk* has depths beyond the comic book, but also made audiences unsure about the film, and it was no great commercial success.

The Hulk opens as U.S. Army research scientist David Banner is told by his commanding officer that his work on modifying the immune system is stupid and dangerous, and must not be applied to any human subjects. But Banner is a man of great vision—and ambition—and when his own son Bruce is born we can practically see him thinking about the opportunity this presents him. We get an early indication of Bruce's own psychology: he does not fight back when another kid hits him, and doesn't "make a peep" when the band-aid is applied. His mother says: "That's Bruce. He's like that. He's just so ... bottled up." And so is every one else. When Banner's superior officer discovers human blood in his lab he doesn't just initiate a disciplinary hearing, he smashes Banner's microscope. The two men act out the American aggression at full tilt: Banner is off the project, just like that. But Banner won't stand idle as his life's work goes down the drain: he blows up part of the military complex in which he both works and lives.

Bruce as a four-year-old overhears his parents arguing in the next room and acts out this perceived aggression with his toy animals. The shouting grows louder, and little Bruce's attempts to block out or act out his distress fail: he stands bewildered, listening. The shouts grow into screams, and suddenly we cut to a teenage Bruce being woken by his foster mother from yet another nightmare. It is a special day: Bruce is off to college to train as a scientist, and his foster mother is convinced that he will make a great contribution to the world. He lands a job in a lab where his co-worker and romantic interest, Betty, presses him on his birth parents: we learn that Bruce believes them to be dead.

Ang Lee piles on the Freudian: we already know that Bruce's childhood must contain powerful suppressed memories that make him "emotionally distant" as Betty puts it. Bruce's nightmares intensify. Next, we follow a mysterious "janitor" home with his dogs, and watch him analyze Bruce's DNA. He has newspaper cuttings on his wall following all stages of Bruce's development, and in particular his progress as a scientist. "My Bruce," the old man mutters *sotto voce*—we realize that this is his father, David Banner (played by Nick Nolte). The inevitable and key event now happens: the experiment Bruce and Betty have been working on goes wrong and Bruce gets full exposure to the rays from their massive machine as he tries to save a colleague. We know that the process has killed everything else it has been tried on, illustrated earlier by exploding frogs. So how come Bruce Banner not only survives, but feels great? Betty cannot understand it: she thought she was going to have to watch him die. "Betty," he reassures her from his hospital bed, "I am not going to explode. I have never felt better."

He wakes up in the night to find the janitor and his dogs by his bedside. It is his father, who wants to help him understand his new predicament. If Bruce will let him. If Bruce will forgive him. It is a classical scene where the son meets his father for the first time, and these are no ordinary circumstances. David Banner tells his son: "Of course, you're my flesh and blood. But then, you're something else too, aren't you? My physical son, but the child of my mind too." We also get a glimpse of the father's rage: he was imprisoned for thirty years for his act of sabotage on the base. He has been prevented from knowing his son, and prevented from continuing his work. "You see, everything your extraordinary mind has been seeking all these years ... it's been inside you. Now we will understand it." But Bruce won't accept the story and gets angry. "Get out! Get out!" he shouts. The old man moves to the door with his dogs. His parting shot is: "We're going to have to watch that temper of yours."

Bruce begins investigating his own DNA now, and hears his father's voice repeating the line about his extraordinary mind. He is getting worked up: events are crowding into his mind and he is getting angrier and angrier. The first of his body-transforming rages is upon him, and he transmutes from a normal man into the green muscle-bound giant of the comic book. He destroys the lab that made him what he is, charging through walls and equipment until he reaches the big machine, which he hurls through the outer walls, crushing a police car. His father looks on.

The green giant now confronts his father in the universal Oedipal moment. David reaches out to his son Bruce, wanting to both comfort him and to exult in the triumph of his scientific endeavor. But dimly lit memories well up from Bruce's unconscious of the key moment in his childhood: he cannot understand them and his rage returns. He punches his way out of the research complex, leaving his father covered in rubble, shaking. "My Bruce, my Bruce," he says. Bruce disappears into the night and is discovered the next day, back to his normal physique, collapsed on his bed.

Soon another testosterone-fuelled encounter takes place, this time between Bruce and General Ross, Betty's father. No understanding develops here either. The general is mad at Bruce, glaring at him, and, with raised voice, demanding how Bruce, as a four-year-old, could have missed what happened on that fateful day. Bruce genuinely doesn't know, and the general has enough shrink-speak to lean back and say sarcastically: "Oh, some more repressed memories." Bewildered, Banner asks: "Just tell me." Stony-faced but perhaps with just a glimmer of feeling, the general replies: "I'm sorry, son. You're an even more screwed-up mess than I thought you'd be." He tells Banner that he won't ever work on any research project more exciting than the next generation of herbal hair gel. And then, mutual aggression building, he leans into Bruce's face and says: "One more thing. If you ever come within a thousand yards of my daughter again, I'll put you away for the rest of your natural life."

Banner Sr. now reveals the full extent of his mad bid for power. He sees Betty and her father, the one who put him away for thirty years, as obstacles to his dream, and has used Bruce's own DNA to turn his dogs into the very weapon of her destruction. They will follow the scent of her scarf.... But the key element in the old man's twisted ambitions is the knowledge that Bruce won't be able to destroy the part of himself that liberates his rage; won't want to, he loves the rage too much. But how will Bruce react to the knowledge that the same part of himself is now directed to a target he loves more than anything in the world, Betty? Bruce at this point doesn't know how to trigger his transformation, but most conveniently the deeply aggressive Glen Talbot, a business rival, turns up and gives him hell for "cutting him out" of a laboratory deal. Bruce is only concerned to save Betty, while Talbot just wants to beat the crap out of him. Banner just says: "Talbot." "Yeah?" comes Talbot's reply as he glares into his opponent's face, poised to smash his fist down on Bruce.

"You're making me angry," says Bruce.

Don't we all identify with Bruce in this moment? Don't we want all our opponents to hesitate, uncomprehending, and then cower, terrified, as the transformation takes place? Bruce "goes green" again and has a better idea now of his power. Sending Talbot and sofa through the window, he punches his way out to freedom. Machine-gun fire just fuels his rage, and he is off. After saving Betty from his father's genetically modified dogs Bruce tells her: "You know what scares me the most? When it happens, when it comes over me, and I totally lose control, I like it."

This observation captures the essence of how Freud's work has entered into mainstream culture. The emotions in Banner, as in all of us, well up from the irrational unconscious, a scary invisible place, unlike the physical body which is finite and can be patched up mechanically. Hence the fear that rage can be boundless in its destruction—even to the point of a chain reaction in which the whole world will be consumed. Christopher Lasch suggests that "as authority figures in modern society lose their 'credibility,' the superego in individuals increasingly derives from the child's primitive fantasies about his parents—fantasies charged with sadistic rage—rather than from internalized ego ideals formed by later experience with loved and respected models of social conduct."[8] Later on he adds: "The fury with which the superego punishes the ego's failures suggests that it derives most its energy from aggressive drives in the id...."[9] The id is then unleashed in stressful or regressive situations. In a much earlier and equally Freudian science-fiction film, *Forbidden Planet* (1956), Dr. Morbius has tapped into the technology of an advanced civilization which had destroyed itself by unwittingly harnessing the power of the unconscious. Their huge machines were designed to materialize anything they could think of, but they had forgotten the "monsters of the id," which now emerge from Dr. Morbius's unconscious and threaten to destroy him and his research station. *The Hulk* visualizes the eruption of the id in equally memorable imagery.

Bruce returns to the original military base that he and Betty grew up in; they look up his old house, the very place where the traumatic moment as a four-year-old set his life onto its present course, physically and psychologically. Betty acts as therapist: she wants him to unlock his predicament through the recovery of the repressed memories. He can't face the locked room; he trembles. What had he seen as child? But he pulls back from the brink. Next, the general is himself in a rage: control of the project has been handed over to the company headed by the vengeful Talbot. But Talbot takes the "scientific" route and places Bruce in an isolation tank, wired up and regressing into his unconscious mind.

Banner Sr. now seeks out Betty and wants to set up a deal with her father, but it is too late of course. He then attempts to justify himself to Betty when she blames him for Bruce's condition.

> And what have I done to my son, Miss Ross? Nothing. I tried to improve on the limits within myself. Myself, not him. Can you understand? To improve on nature. To improve on oneself. It's the only path to the truth, to give man the power to go beyond God's boundaries.

(Note how Banner is recapitulating for us the essence of the Greek idea of "hubris" as a challenge to the gods.) David Banner now accounts for the fateful day that changed his son's life, or rather as we now begin to understand, spared his life. The furious argument between his parents had an outcome that Bruce had blocked from his conscious mind all his life. Intercutting with Bruce floating in his tank, his father reveals the awful sequence of events. All his work at the lab had been in order to save his son from becoming the monster that he knew he would otherwise become, and when Betty's father had thrown him out of his lab, there was only one course of action: to kill the boy, out of compassion. But he had not reckoned on his wife's determination to save her son, and in the struggle the knife intended for the child mortally wounds the woman he loves. As she staggers dying into the desert the lab explodes, visible as a small mushroom cloud in the distance, and we understand that in addition to his intention to kill his son, Banner had determined to destroy his research as well.

"Bingo," says Talbot. At exactly that moment they have probed into Bruce's mind, uncovering the awful memory, and Talbot is within reach of his goal: to extract Bruce's morphing DNA. But the green-machine-thing process is too fast, so Talbot is reduced to watching as Bruce bursts free from his tank. Now he is really mad. He gets past everything, even the demented Talbot determined to extract that DNA sample. Bullets just fall off him (and clink to the ground *Matrix*-fashion). Bruce as the big green giant pauses outside his childhood home on the base. The memories come back: his mother killed, his father arrested and bundled out in a straight-jacket, the hand on the young Bruce's shoulder. It was the hand of General Ross in his younger days, about to send the boy to foster care. Fittingly the house now blows up and secondary blasts send him hurtling to the ground. The general is bombing him. Despite the massive leap he now takes, he cannot immediately escape the general: the desert is a target range in which the full arsenal of military hardware is unleashed, and Bruce is the specified target.

He is of course invincible, as is anyone in a true psychotic rage. Ang Lee gives us some reflective moments during the "boy's toys" parade of military hardware deployed to destroy Bruce: at one point Bruce contemplates the trees, rocks and lichen of the tundra. We too are involved in this reflection: how nature's DNA is now in our hands to modify at our will, to break the boundaries set by "God." But it is now a showdown between two pumped-up male egos, both with narrowed eyes and furrowed brows. "Make it into a parking lot," is the general's order—in other words to bomb the beauty of the ancient rock formations hiding the green monster of the id, to bomb the natural world and its untamed monsters into submission. Eventually Bruce is captured.

For some obscure reason Ross now places father and son face-to-face with each other within some large machine. "I should have killed you," says Bruce. "I should have killed *you*," says his father. "I wish you had," is Bruce's reply. He breaks down. "It's all right, son, go ahead and cry." But Bruce won't accept his father's embrace. David's gloves are now off, after this rejection. "I didn't come here to see you. I came here to see my son. My real son. The one inside of you. You're nothing but a superficial shell, a husk of flimsy consciousness, ready to be torn off at a moment's notice." But what David really wants is Bruce's raw energy. Whereas Bruce is stable in his transformation, David is not, and he wants to bio-engineer himself through his son. "I gave you life," he snarls at him, "and now you *must* give it back to me!" Nick Nolte now delivers a superbly deranged rant about the military fools holding them captive; he wants his energy back a thousand times more powerful, more radiant, as it is in his son. Together they could make all the governments, the flags, the anthems, the military might of the world disappear in a flash! What do you say? "I'd rather die!" growls Bruce. "Stop your bawling, you weak little speck of human trash," says the thwarted David.

But he won't take this sitting down. In a scene that is perhaps a direct reference to *Forbidden Planet*, Banner Sr. grabs a power cable, bites off its insulation and begins to absorb the high voltage. He grows and glows, becoming the perfect Freudian monster of the id. Bruce meanwhile also transforms and soon catches up with Dad in size, fury and power. The two behemoths ascend into the lightning-torn skies in an apocalyptic scene from which they tumble to the ground, still bathed in electric discharge. They are now in a primeval setting in which their mutual atavistic rage batters and grunts to destruction.

His father takes on the characteristics of the elements, first rocks and then water, taunting him: "the more you fight, the more I take." They are extracting all the ambient energy of the natural surroundings to fuel their titanic struggle, but it is David who finally traps Bruce in the ice he has created. "Sleep my little Bruce, and forget for ever," comes his father's soothing tones, as we see the face of the infant superimposed on the Hulk (absolutely Oedipal, all of this). "Struggle no more, and give me all of your power." Bruce in fact wants to give all his rage to his father, and breaks free. Banner Sr. then gets more energy than he bargained for as General Ross drops a nuclear device on the pair of them. The American solution.

The Hulk is a film about rage: a primeval aggression that bursts the banks of all civilized control. This rage is anger taken to an extreme, where anger is a natural counterpart to fear, and fear is also the motivation for paranoia. But here this is all in the context of the father-son relationship, one that has as its original basis one of nurturing and protection, with competition merely as part of play, as part of the spur to explore and develop. When competition between father and son outweighs all other motivations, then tragedy is bound to follow. Al Pacino's diabolical Milton nurtures his son Lomax, imbuing him with perhaps an above-average ambition, but is otherwise protective. His only real crime, it seems, is to place his son onto the horns of a moral dilemma, an almost impossible moral testing. But David Banner seems to be utterly uninterested in his own son's development, moral or otherwise: what he is after is his own vindication and glorification through his son. Bruce Banner is merely an instrument for his father in his insane lust for power. Here is another element of the Oedipal story that is not actually present in the Greek original, or in Freud's adoption of it: the sadness and alienation that a sons (or daughters) must feel when they realize that they only represent a means to an end for their father (or mother). In a world gone mad on success and competition, sons and daughters are mere trophies, and the natural response is rage. "You were never there for me, Dad," is the repeated cry of the son or daughter neglected in favor of the father's ambition: a deeply American accusation.

Star Wars and Affliction

In Star Wars, written by George Lucas with close attention paid to the "monomyth" of his friend and author Joseph Campbell, the protagonist, Luke Skywalker, is again ignorant of who his real father is. Like Lomax in The Devil's Advocate and Bruce Banner in The Hulk, he encounters a powerful figure that he must oppose. This time it is Darth Vader. Like Lomax and Banner, young Luke eventually has to come to terms with the nature of his father, and ultimately resist the offer from the older man to "join the firm." The only choice remains after that: a fight to the death. This is a twist on the hero's journey of Campbell: in the struggle against evil which allows the young warrior to prove himself, there is the temptation, not of the sirens of feminine allure, but of going over to the "dark side" of the Force. This is made doubly poignant—and very Oedipal—when the older man turns out to be the younger man's father.

Leaving the realms of fantasy and science fiction, we now turn to a more gritty realism in Paul Schrader's *Affliction* (1997). This time Nick Nolte plays the son, Wade Whitehouse, rather than the father in a struggle to the death. In Marita Sturken's telling analysis of the film, she relates the Oedipal struggle back to the typical paranoia of the American male: "When this paranoid citizen gets angry he does something to up the ante, to be noticed forever—sending mail bombs, bombing a federal building ... or gunning down schoolmates."[10] Wade occupies rather lowly positions in his community, which obviously weigh on him as potentially labeling him the "loser" his father always taunts him for being—his favorite abuse of his sons is to call them "candyasses." Wade's pent-up rage against his father finds an odd outlet when he suspects a colleague of murder: it allows him to construct an identity as the only one smart enough to work out the truth. Sturken shows that the film works because we assume that Wade's theory might be right, and the recognition that it would bring would be his redemption. But it turns out to be nothing more than an empty conspiracy theory: he is "empowered by his paranoid narrative" for a while, but as it and he unravel he is brought into the ultimate conflict with his father. He kills him with a blow from his rifle butt and burns the barn down around him; he then goes to shoot dead the innocent man he believes guilty of murder. He then disappears, prompting Sturken's comment: "This is inevitably the paranoid person's ultimate nightmare, that their story will not be noticed and finally have no effect."

The mutual rage between Wade and his father, just ordinary Americans, ought to be more convincing than the father-son pairings in the previous fantasy films. Schrader depicts daily American life as it is for the less successful in stark terms: the outcome of being a "loser" is Oedipal rage and paranoia, leading to murder. But *Affliction* is also the least convincing of these four Oedipal films because of a Schrader trademark: the clumsy use or omission of *emotional bracketing*. At one point in the film Wade's mother dies of cold, but there is a completely inappropriate response from everyone, not just the emotionally damaged father and son. Hence, while the transgressive is present in patricide and murder and while the scenario is plausible—neither are grotesque figures—the emotional intensity is missing due to poor emotional bracketing. Similar flaws are present in Schrader's *Light Sleeper* (1992), a reworking of the *Taxi Driver* motif of vigilante-killing-as-redemption (more on this later). Nonetheless, *Affliction* ends with a soliloquy, quoted by Sturken, which captures the deeply American tragedy of masculinity-gone-mad:

> Our stories, Wade's and mine, describe the lives of boys and men for thousands of years, boys who were beaten by their fathers, boys whose capacity for love and trust was crippled almost at birth. Men, whose best hope for connection with other human beings lay in detachment, as if life were over. It's how we keep from destroying in turn our own children and terrorizing the women who have the misfortune to love us. How we absent ourselves from the tradition of male violence, how we decline the seduction of revenge.

One cannot help feeling that this is Schrader's own story, and that the "detachment" he speaks of here inhabits his films as well.

We can see that the original play *Oedipus Rex*, one of the Theban Plays by Sophocles, is a tragedy in which the hero is punished despite the fact that his crimes are unintended accidents. He has offended against the gods, or against human moral codes (it does not matter which), and must suffer the consequences, regardless. But it is not fair: "hubris" means to defy the gods, resulting in punishment, whereas Oedipus did not, or at least, did not do so intentionally. In comparison to many far-Eastern cultures the West can reasonably be accused of possessing the mind of the drama queen. The self-blinding and subsequent exile of Oedipus is surely an over-reaction, an over-dramatic, typically theatrical Greek story for an audience that wanted to experience the deep catharsis of witnessing a crime punished. America appears to have inherited that Hellenic thirst for the dramatic in general and the Oedipal in particular. In turn it took the deeply Hebraic mind of Freud to turn the Oedipal story into the archetype for American masculinity.

6

Sexual Obsession

KEY FILMS: *American Beauty, Happiness*
ADDITIONAL FILMS: *American Psycho, Blue Velvet*

Walt Whitman shocked the Victorian age in the U.S. with his exuberant celebration of the body, and since that time the U.S. has led the world in the sexual revolution. At the same time this shift was fiercely resisted by Christian conservatives through a range of movements. Susan Jacoby suggests that Protestant America took its lead from the Catholic minority, which had an influence far beyond its size because its activism was so well organized.[1] Its flagship campaign was always its anti-abortion activism, and this became a defining issue in the broad resistance to the sexual revolution. But the legacy of Freud and countless other innovators in the growing field psychology ensured the broad cultural propagation of the idea that the sexual impulse is a healing and creative force, the repression of which leads to a stifling of positive human energies. The truly American story of immigrant Wilhelm Reich and his "orgone accumulators" is bizarre, but typical of the sexual experimentation of leading psychiatrists in the early and middle twentieth century.[2] The sexual revolution—usually considered as a phenomenon of the 1960s and 1970s—was the end-result of academic thought manifest through hippie and other youth movements and affecting millions. When the "dike" of the Hays Production Code burst in the late sixties, American filmmaking was free to portray explicit sexuality as well as explicit violence.

It is an obsession with sex, and in particular the widespread assumption that the sexual and romantic provide the secular world with its highest values, that is also deeply American, despite the powerful presence of the religious right. In a culture that is deeply and aggressively competitive, then the sexual sphere becomes one of conquest, and a site of further paranoia that one might be a "loser" here too. The films *American Beauty* and *Happiness* have been chosen too explore this side of the American madness, both comedies of a sort, and which show sexual competitiveness reaching down to school age. *American Psycho* is re-examined here along with some aspects of *Blue Velvet* and *Basic Instinct*, all of which assert a necessary relationship between sex and violence.

American Beauty

American Beauty was directed by Sam Mendes and written by Alan Ball, who also created the American TV series *Six Feet Under*. This shares many values, both cultural and aesthetic, with *American Beauty*. One might also include *Nip/Tuck*, *Desperate Housewives*, and perhaps also *Sex and the City* among TV shows that emerge from the same cultural stable and share the same sexual values. *American Beauty* opens with a teenage girl, Jane, saying: "I need a father who's a role model, not some horny geek-boy who's gonna spray his shorts whenever I bring a girlfriend home from school." She is referring to the film's protagonist Lester Burnham, played by Kevin Spacey, who tells us early in the film: "Look at me, jerking off in the shower. This will be the high point of my day. It's all downhill from here." He both appears in the film and narrates it, from a disembodied existence floating over his neighborhood. In the opening scenes we learn that he is dissatisfied with his job and family life, and that new neighbors are moving in. These include a young boy who videotapes life rather than living it. Lester's wife Carolyn runs the perfect suburban American home with clinical precision; even the handles on her pruning shears are color-coordinated with her gardening clogs.

Carolyn insists that Lester and she attend the school games, where Jane is part of "Rockwell High's award-winning Dancing Spartanettes," entertaining the audience in the interval. Dad looks on hoping that they can leave after this, but is suddenly captivated by one of the girls, the lead dancer. In his imagination she becomes detached from the rest of the cheerleaders, appearing in a glow of her own and revealing a tantalizing glimpse of breast. The sequence ends but instead of clapping he just gawks from the stands. To his absolute delight it turns out that the lead dancer, named Angela, is his daughter's best friend. He almost drools as he offers the girls a lift home, to no avail of course, as Angela has a car of her own (this is affluent suburban America, after all). Jane, mortified, says: "Could he be any more pathetic?" to which Angela replies: "I think it's sweet. And I think he and your mother have not had sex in a long time." That night Lester lies in bed fantasizing about a naked Angela, covered in rose petals. Angela is confident of her sex appeal, in contrast to Jane's self-doubts. Later, the two girls are smoking pot in Angela's car, where Angela talks about being the subject of adult male attention at the age of twelve. She claims to like it because "if people I don't even know look at me and want to fuck me, it means I really have a shot at being a model. Which is great, because there's nothing worse in life than being ordinary."

We now switch to the new neighbors: teenage Ricky, his father Colonel Fitts (a loud-mouthed homophobic disciplinarian), and mother Barbara. There is a ring at the door and two smiling men, Jim and Jim, present the Colonel with a basket of garden produce and fresh pasta, a gift to welcome them to their new neighborhood. After a little confusion the Colonel gets it: they are a gay couple. Ricky meets Jane at school, and has to justify why he was filming her the previous night: he finds her interesting. "Thanks, but I really don't need to have some psycho obsessing about me right now," is Jane's response, but she is, like, interested too. Angela has her doubts about Ricky though: "I don't believe him. I mean, he didn't even like, look at me once." How is that possible? A girl destined to be a model, and he doesn't want to jerk off over her?

Lester nearly has a fit when he discovers that Jane has invited her best friend Angela home. He fantasizes in real time as Angela reaches past him for a root beer from the fridge, and goes into overdrive when he later overhears their conversation in Jane's bedroom in which Angela says that he is cute. "If he built up his chest and arms, I would totally fuck him." Naturally, Lester turns to bodybuilding. But Ricky has a little surprise of his own for Jane, her name in burning candles on the lawn. The film now gets into its stride with Angela posing provocatively at the window for "weirdo" Ricky to capture on video. He isn't interested in her however, having found Jane's thoughtful face in a small mirror; his viewfinder then moves down the exterior of the house to find Lester stripped to his waist and pumping iron in the garage. It gets worse: Lester strips off completely to examine his waistline in the reflection in his garage window.

Lester's mid-life crisis has provoked his fantasy about Angela, which has liberated him to talk back to his wife, smoke pot with Ricky, and to quit his job in a manner which would be the envy of millions of Americans. *American Beauty* sets out to document the emptiness of the American middle-class lifestyle, but in doing so creates cameos of considerable beauty. It also has many little asides that add texture to the broad-brush strokes of the otherwise archetypal American stereotypes. Jane offers Ricky a lift home in Angela's car, but he declines, saying that he will walk. Jane offers to walk with him, to which Angela responds with this immortal line: "What? Jane, that's like, almost a mile."

Lester in the meantime has applied for a job flipping burgers—the archetypal employment indicator of the "loser"—while Ricky and Jane are now watching one of Ricky's videos, perhaps the most widely remembered non-acting scene in the film. It is of an empty plastic bag, swirling with autumn leaves by a wall. Is it saying to us: *this* is American Beauty? Who knows. But Ricky is quite sure, telling Jane that it is the most beautiful thing he has ever filmed. We are now getting to the secret of Ricky's poise, a self-confidence that has unnerved Angela (along with his lack of sexual interest in her), and has drawn Jane to him. As they watch the fragile white plastic bag animated by the eddying wind, he says:

> It was one of those days when it's a minute away from snowing. And there's this electricity in the air, you can almost hear it, right? And this bag was just ... dancing with me. Like a little kid begging me to play with it. For fifteen minutes. That's the day I realized that there was this entire life behind things, and this incredibly benevolent force that wanted me to know there was no reason to be afraid. Ever.

But Jane has to rush back for supper at which Lester's mid-life crisis builds and his marriage unravels further. Lester may be enacting the dream for millions of hen-pecked husbands in re-asserting his authority over his wife, but it is done with no regard for Jane, who is forced to sit there and watch the degenerating behavior of her parents. After dinner Ricky videotapes her from his house. Jane plays to the camera, removing her top to stand framed by the window in her bra, and then slowly removes that too. Ricky's loving act of recording her vulnerability is rudely shattered when his father bursts into the room and shouts at him: "You little bastard!" and knocks him down. Colonel Fitts had discovered Ricky's act of break-in earlier, when he had shown Jane a Nazi plate his father kept locked in a cabinet. But when the Colonel discovers that his son had picked the lock yet stolen nothing, and that Ricky's explanation is that he wanted to show the item to his girlfriend, he is shamed. In all the degeneracy of modern American life that swirled around him, here was a sign of dependable normalcy: his son had a girlfriend!

But of course, nothing is as it seems. Later on Colonel Fitts returns to Ricky's room, when the boy is out. He starts to watch the tapes that Ricky has made, and comes across the shot of Lester stripped naked and working out. He is mesmerized. Meantime Carolyn turns up with her lover at the Smileyburger drive-through where Lester is now working, and her infidelity is exposed. But Lester doesn't mind, simply asking them if they want Smileysauce with their burgers.

Colonel Fitts watches from the window and sees his son enter Lester's garage, where Lester is stripped to the waist again for his workout. The windows frame what appears to the Colonel as a gay encounter, which he observes with fascination. In fact Ricky and Lester are merely sharing a joint which is hastily abandoned as Angela and Jane drive up. Lester is now fit and confident as Angela enters the kitchen, and she is irresistibly drawn over to touch his now bulging biceps. "You like ... muscles?" asks Lester suggestively. We cut to Ricky's room where his dad's fury has built up after watching what he has taken to be absolute proof of his son's homosexuality. He hits Ricky again: "I'd rather you were dead than be a fucking faggot!" Sprawled on the floor, Ricky has finally had enough. He gets up and taunts his father that he is a gay prostitute, going into lurid detail, provoking the breakup he has always wanted. It is clear: he now has to leave the family home. He says goodbye to his mother and joins Jane in her room, much to the disgust of Angela who still insists on calling him "psycho-boy." The dramatic threads now accelerate to the finish: the Colonel knocks on Lester's garage; Carolyn draws a gun from the glove compartment in her car; and Ricky asks Jane to come to New York with him. Angela gives up on them and storms out. Lester tells the Colonel that he has no idea where his wife is, probably being unfaithful, but he doesn't care. He acts kindly to the older man until he realizes what the colonel wants: gay sex. Colonel Fitts attempts to kiss Lester, to which he responds by pushing him away. "Whoa, whoa, whoa. I'm sorry. You got the wrong idea." The poor Colonel retreats in confusion in the pouring rain.

Back in the kitchen Lester has grabbed a beer from the fridge as Angela comes in, distressed at the parting scene with Ricky and Jane. While a number of other themes in the film reach their inevitable and intertwined conclusion it is the scene with Lester and Angela that is of most interest to us here. He is, despite his new-found assurance, still absolutely enamored of her, and she badly needs someone to comfort her. They have the living room to themselves, and they share his beer. They kiss. Carolyn approaches home in her car, rehearsing her speech to Lester and nursing her gun. Lester tenderly removes Angela's clothes; this is his dream about to come true.

Then the bombshell hits. Angela says: "This is my first time."

Suddenly Lester sees the reality for what it is: she is nothing more than a nervous child. The sexual spell is broken, he covers her nakedness, and comforts her because she is now doubly distressed: firstly at the promise of the encounter, and secondly at what might be taken as a rejection. But before long Lester has regained his natural role, as a fatherly presence; he makes her a sandwich and talks with her in a way that he has long been unable to do with his own daughter.

The First Amendment in the American Constitution guarantees freedom of expression, and every time the "moral majority" or the religious conservatives in America have tried to ban a film the legal battle becomes intense. Landmark novels and films have continued to push the boundaries of what is acceptable in terms of sex and violence, through landmark court cases. The film *The People vs. Larry Flynt*, for example, shows how the right to publish a pornographic magazine, in this case *Hustler*, went all the way to the American Supreme Court. Against the powerful lobby of the religious conservatives stood an even more powerful lobby representing the right to free speech, and the latter won the day. This has been a slow, incremental process, but the end result is that young teenagers, like those in *American Beauty*, grow up with a precocious sexual awareness unimaginable to previous generations. It is an undeniable fact that democracy, with its core belief in freedom of expression, goes hand-in-hand with the spread of pornography, as the collapse of former communist regimes has shown.

The message in Angela's story, though, is that her sexual sophistication was all bluff, but it shows the pressure on youngsters to conform to a norm of sexual activity portrayed in film and other media. While the Right wrings its hands over the supposed attack on tradition and family values in films like *American Beauty*, more left-leaning critics are not much more enthusiastic. For example Leonard Quart says of it: "*American Beauty* provides the blackest of comic portraits of American suburban life. There is nothing nuanced about this film—over-the-top caricatures being the rule and the social reality of the suburbs reduced to a few motifs—cheerleaders, selling real estate, jogging, and growing roses. There is no reason to believe that the film's characters were ever happy and empathetic, and that the distorted and disconnected lives they now lead are a consequence of America's destructive values."[3] Perhaps the defensiveness of this analysis is because Sam Mendes is a British director, but in any case why not believe that the "distorted and disconnected lives" are a consequence of "America's destructive values?" And why dismiss the film's obvious subtleties?

True, the transgressive elements of the film are not subtle, but the scenario is plausible precisely because of the many caricatures. Its emotional intensity has two main sources: the "reversal," as Aristotle required, of Lester's lechery in the face of suddenly glimpsed childhood, and the fact that he dies at the end, shot in the head by Fitts. And here lies the subtlety, which is not apparent to either the Left or the Right: at the end of the film Lester's disembodied voice returns reflecting on his death and his life. The indictment of American suburbia is present in the fact that it took his death to realize how precious his wife and daughter—and everything else—were to him. But his deeper realization is this: "I guess I could be pretty pissed off about what happened to me ... but it's hard to stay mad, when there's so much beauty in the world." We see the plastic bag swirling again in the wind. He concludes: "I can't feel anything but gratitude for every single moment of my stupid little life." The camera pulls up over the tree-lined street and greater suburb, suggesting that Lester's spirit is ascending.

The Right is alienated by the transgressive, the Left by beauty. But we have here a possible answer to the question put by Medved on behalf of the cultural conservatives, which is: why can't the artists of today celebrate our culture? Earlier we pointed out that in a democratic, multicultural world that has lived through revolutions against authority, patriarchy, colonialism and so forth, the artist belongs to no specific cultural tradition, and is inclined to see the dominant culture as deeply flawed. Instead, what *American Beauty* does, along with so many other great American films, is to celebrate *life itself*. Lester's tragic end is down to his "frailties and errors" the worst of which is endemic to suburbia, the triumph of pettiness over a grateful sense of privilege. But his "stupid little life" was astonishing, because life itself is astonishing, and he recognizes this in the end.

Quart does acknowledge the "striking and sometimes haunting imagery" of the film, but concludes "At the same time, it doesn't feel that different in its heavy-handed, melodramatic skewering of suburban lives than another black comedy permeated with loathing for a similar milieu, Tod Solondz's *Happiness* (1999)." Sexual obsession, as we see in *American Beauty*, is only partly about sexual gratification, and more to do with the wider competitiveness central to the American mind. *Happiness* shows this competitiveness taken to an even more absurd and disturbing extreme.

Happiness

If Dr. Hannibal Lecter is the most horrific imaginative product of the madness of the American mind that is violence, then the central character of *Happiness* is perhaps the sickest product of the madness of the American mind that is sexual perversion. Just like Lecter, Bill Maplewood is in the psychiatry game, though this time as a therapist. Bill (played by Dylan Baker) is surrounded by the full spectrum of American sexual misfits—some of whom are his clients—but he himself shocks us most as an unrepentant pedophile. The other characters whose sex lives are a walking disaster include the two sisters of Bill's wife (Joy and Helen) and Allen, one of Bill's clients. The film opens with Joy dumping her boyfriend, who appears to take it very well until he finds the perfect moment to turn unexpectedly nasty. We then cut to Bill in his professional capacity thinking about his grocery list and how boring his client Allen is as he drones on about his obscene sexual fantasies. When Allen gets home he encounters Helen, a sexual predator herself, but oblivious of him. They go up in the lift together as Allen struggles with his desire for her and his sense of inadequacy; she doesn't even know he exists. Once in his flat he pursues his hobby of obscene telephone calling and masturbation. We then see Joy visiting her third sister Trish, Bill's wife. Joy breaks down after one of their boys, Timmy, runs up to her, points a toy laser at her and shouts "Die Aunty Joy, Die!" Sobbing, she confides to her sister: "I don't know what it is but I feel there's so much hostility directed at me." Trish has the solution of course: "You've got to eat more red meat." Trish concludes their conversation with what she thinks will truly cheer her sister up: a confession that the whole family had always thought her sister was doomed to be a failure, but now she saw a glimmer of hope for her. Tears well up in Trish's eyes. "I'm so happy for you," she gushes.

By now we know that this is a comedy, in which the interconnected characters are acting out the typical anxieties of the sex-obsessed, self-obsessed middle-class American. We cut to an idyllic park setting with couples and children. Bill looks on in a tranquil frame of mind, and then pulls out a machine gun and mows them down nonchalantly and at random. He surveys the dead and gently weeping survivors. It turns out that he is recounting this dream to *his* analyst who asks him: "And how is this different?" "I don't kill myself at the end," he replies. Clearly Bill has made some kind of breakthrough in his own therapy. When pressed as to the happiness he feels at the new shift in his recurring dream, he hesitantly agrees that he wouldn't kill people in real life. But he confesses:

> My patients are ugly. Their problems are trite. Each one thinks he is unique. On a professional level they bore me. On a personal level I have no sympathy. They deserve what they get.

Also, we learn that Bill does not have sex with his wife, Trish.

> No. But she's not too interested, either. So really there's no problem there, when you think about it, on a certain level.

Bill delivers this with a slow drawl, preparing us for the exact opposite: that there is a real problem there. We get an indication of this in the next scene when he furtively buys a teen magazine, *Boy's Life*, in the newsagent's and jerks off to it in the back seat of his car in the parking lot. In the next scene Bill's older son is depressed, and eventually comes to his dad for advice. "Dad? ... What does 'come' mean?" Actually Billy knows what it means but is anxious because he hasn't yet achieved this, whereas his classmates have. The previous generation of films would have had a much older boy depressed because he had not had a girl yet, perhaps reluctantly seeking his dad's advice. But the premium on sexual pleasure placed at the forefront of American values, along with the precociousness of educated middle-class youngsters, now shifts that confrontation down the age range to an eleven-year-old. It shifts the highest values from the universals of truth, beauty and justice that preoccupied the classical world, to the sexual orgasm, preferably obtained in sublime indifference to the procreative function (or to the happiness of the sexual partner, if any). So far then, Bill, his son Billy, his client Allen, his wife's sister Joy and her ex-boyfriend have this much in common:

they aren't happy, *sexually* happy that is. In the next scene we find that the parents of the three sisters aren't happy either, as they are in the process of separating. Trish of course is happy, as the contented wife of the successful and loving Bill, the very same Bill who "hasn't got a problem." But what about the third sister Helen, who so far has not revealed to us whether ignoring Allen in the lift is part of a general happiness or unhappiness?

Allen is working through the telephone directory and has reached Joy's number. On answering the phone, Joy takes him to be a friend that Trish has recommended to her as a potential date. Allen takes the cue, and strings her along for a bit until he gets round to his favorite question, to do with women's underwear. He is on the verge of coming, but Trish now realizes sadly that this isn't the date her sister fixed up for her. This brings little further happiness to either party. Allen then has to answer a ring at his door, only to learn from a woman down the corridor (who has a crush on him, incidentally) that their doorman has been murdered; and probably, what is more, that his penis was cut off. Joy in the meantime learns that her ex-boyfriend has committed suicide, but his fellow workers at the call center find it hard to recall who he was. His mother doesn't however, taking the trouble to call Joy at work and express the desire that she rots in hell.

Cut to the other two sisters having dinner. We now learn that Helen is a successful novelist, so she must be happy mustn't she? Anyhow it explains why she would ignore a loser like Allen. But we have to leave her story again as Bill meets Johnny, son of his friend the coach. Bill can't take his eyes off the young boy. The coach is worried that Johnny is gay, and Bill's assurances as a professional psychotherapist don't hold any water for him:

COACH: What do you think would happen if I got him a professional ... you
    know ...
BILL: A professional?
COACH: Hooker. You know, the kind that can teach things ... first-timers, you
    know ... break him in.
BILL: But Joe, he's eleven.
COACH: You're right, you're right. It's too late.

Happiness is intended as a comedy that makes us think, and is, perhaps, successful in those aims. It shows us, through the means natural to comedy— that is, exaggeration—how our obsessions get out of hand. In particular this film shows us a component of the typical madness of America, where competitiveness, secularism and huge wealth combine to make the sexual arena so fraught. At the age of eleven it is too late for a boy to be a first-timer when it comes to sexual experience.

Bill has barely time to absorb the coach's point of view when Billy asks if Johnny could sleep over that night (in a direct parallel to Lester hearing that Angela will stop over). No problem. We cut to Bill doctoring Johnny's desert, and share with him his despondency over the discovery of Johnny's dislike for chocolate fudge: he doesn't want it. What can Bill do to drug the young boy? The conversation goes this way and that as Bill desperately tries to find something the boy will eat or drink, until they settle on a tuna-fish sandwich. We're in business again! Bill gets to "doctor" the sandwich (ironic as Johnny insists on calling him, formally, Doctor Maplewood) just before his wife comes in, and Billy conveniently falls asleep and is put to bed. But we are forced to imagine what happens next, as we cut to the morning. Skipping a few scenes, we find Helen tormenting herself that she is no good, a nothing. So it seems her happiness as a successful writer is not assured. But her self-doubts are interrupted by the phone. You guessed it! Allen has worked through the phone book to her entry, or he has finally decided to call her, knowing she is his neighbor. We can't be sure of that, but we can be sure that he more or less repeats her own words of doubt to her:

> I know who you are and you are nothing. You think you are fucking something, you are fucking nothing. You are empty. You are zero. You are a black hole, and I am going to fuck you so bad you're gonna be coming out of your ears.

Allen is ringing from the office where he works—in IT naturally. He is a geek, a nerd, a loser. She decides to call him back. Still panting he calms himself and picks up the phone. "Data Resources?" She says: "Who are you?" in a husky voice. Terrified, he puts the phone down. She calls back again. Panting, he hesitates and then picks it up. "What do you want?" he demands. "I want you to fuck me," says Helen. He is not sure that he can do that, but she simply says that she will call him back. His world turned upside down, he goes home and gets drunk. Kristina, from down the hall, rings his doorbell and he staggers to open the door. Ostensibly she wants to give him more information about the murdered doorman, but as he begins to collapse she helps him to his bed where he starts to snore. Crouched over him, she tenderly removes his glasses and moves to his side, resting her head on his chest: love it seems is possible even for Allen. But her bliss is short-lived as he suddenly wakes and pukes violently off-screen. "What the fuck are you doing here?" he asks bewildered. "Get out! Get out!" Kristina runs for it.

Little Johnny is in the hospital unaware that the blood in his stool spells big trouble for Bill. His dad the coach gets it though, and we know that things are going to get ugly. But Billy inadvertently offers up another victim for his dad by letting him know that classmate Ronald Farber will be alone that weekend. Bill drives off that evening in the dark, and on his return he looks spent, saying that he needs to lie down. Trish, ever chirpy, says that she hopes he isn't getting whatever brought Johnny down. How can one not laugh at these little ironies that the scriptwriters strew throughout the screenplay? Yet we feel a deep revulsion at Bill's pedophilia, perhaps only slightly assuaged by the inkling that he is a troubled man, and that Coach is probably planning to kill him.

Bill doesn't lie down immediately, but has a chat with Billy first, who tells him that he almost came. Later that night he can't sleep, and turns to his wife, asking her if she loves him. I always will, she replies half-asleep. No matter what? No matter what. "I'm sick," says Bill. "Aww.... Take some Tylenol. You'll feel better tomorrow." But Bill's doom is postponed as the story rotates around the incidents of the other characters' lives, including Kristina and Allen's evening out and the grandparents' separation. Kristina now confesses to a shocked Allen that *she* killed the doorman. He had taken advantage of her, a woman who found sex repulsive, and she had wrung his neck like a chicken's. Allen seems to take this on the chin, but something prompts him then to knock on Helen's door and tell her that he is the sex caller. She pauses for a long while and then lets him in. In another memorably painful comic scene they sit well apart on her sofa, his hand slowly moving across the cushion towards her. Abruptly the choral music stops: "This is not working," she says, unsmiling. "You're not my type." "No," he agrees weakly, and leaves for his room. Changing his mind he rings at Kristina's door.

Joy lurches from one disaster to another in the meanwhile, but in the back of our minds not even Kristina's crime of passion against the doorman can outweigh the enormity of Bill's transgressions. But we get there in the end: Bill and Trish are with the kids at the dinner table, when Johnny's father rings. "Oh great!" says Bill when Trish tells him who it is. "You're a dead man," hisses Coach over the phone. Bill doesn't look too good. Then the doorbell rings: it is the police. They want to question him about Johnny Grasso; he lets them into the living room, goes to the kitchen to tell Trish to take care of the kids, and returns to sit down and face the officers. "Now ... um ... you said something about Ronald Farber?" Pause. "I'm sorry ... er ... I mean ... I mean, Johnny Grasso?" We cut to the following morning as Trish is struggling to get the kids off to school and just misses the yellow bus. She turns and we see with her the graffiti scrawled in big black letters on the house: "Serial Rapist—Pervert."

That evening there is a tense silent supper. Presumably Trish is in shock, living in some awful limbo world between the apparent happiness of married life to the man she loves, and the world to come: the reality of who Bill is and the mockery it makes of their years together. Bill goes up and talks with Billy at bedtime, in what must be the most shocking and moving part of the film. Billy tells him that at school they are taking about Bill as a serial rapist and pervert. Slowly and haltingly Billy extracts from his father a full confession. America's shrink culture is so deeply ingrained in its public life that in *Happiness* this scene was made inevitable. Freud's fundamental innovation of the "talking cure" has taken deep root in the secular part of the American mind, and in this scene it is the simple questioning of the child, in role reversal with his analyst father, that allows Bill to tell us something of the awful stark truth of his condition. He was compelled through his sexual obsession to sodomize the two young boys, the culmination of fantasies that must have built up over years. He tells Bill soberly that he enjoyed it and would do it again if he could.

The essence of the "talking cure" is that one can speak of the unspeakable, and in Bill's face we see perhaps the recognition of the enormity of his transgression. But this is a black comedy, and we won't follow Bill through any further process of remorse or moral development. It is enough that the torment shows in his face. But the logic of comedy now propels us into uncharted territory: Billy' tears and unhappiness reveal an appalling new twist. He is crying because his Dad had preferred to expend his sexual impulses on the other two boys, rather than him. In a world of universal sexual competitiveness Bill's son is a "loser" in the fight for adult attention. In the morning Trish has made up her mind, and leaves with the children and dog.

The ending takes place six months later with the grandparents, the three daughters and the children gathered in a bright sunlit apartment. Helen is recounting how the doorman's body was found cut up in "baggies" in Kristina's freezer, and saying that everyone uses baggies, "that's why we can all relate to the crime." It falls to Trish to say with blank incomprehension: "I can't relate to it."

So, can we relate to *Happiness*, the film? Even writer James Schamus, involved with the production of *Happiness*, calls it "morally dubious."[4] It is a supreme example of what Medved would attack as promoting the "first lie" of Hollywood: that art reflects reality. Such conservatives genuinely believe that violence and sexual perversion on screen (amongst other forms of negative behavior) generate this behavior in society, and quote studies to that effect. Other studies contradict these findings, suggesting instead that Hollywood is right, and that its films are based on observation of real life, but then, statistics are problematic sources of opinion. So we have to ask, would *Happiness* encourage the crime of pedophilia? One has to answer: only if you believe that someone could envy Bill's predicament. From the film it is clear that this man knows he is sick, and it ends with him cut out of everything he holds dear and destined for jail. And it is well known that the experience of a pedophile in jail is worse than for any other crime. How could one envy him?

But this argument is not settled so easily, and is not why this film has been examined. Rather it is the assumption underlying the behavior of almost all the characters, that it is natural to be sexually obsessed, regardless of the exact target of that obsession. Human happiness is defined as sexual happiness: nothing else, it seems, can usurp its total role in human fulfillment. It is only in Trish that her sexuality seems to be in balance with her life as a lover, wife and mother, and so Trish throughout the film is the touchstone of "normalcy." But Trish just appears naïve and unrepresentative, merely the white against which the black is drawn in sharp relief.

American Psycho, Blue Velvet, and Basic Instinct

Neither *American Beauty* nor *Happiness* associate sex with violence, so we return to *American Psycho* to examine that relationship, and then examine the films *Blue Velvet* and *Basic Instinct*. In a society where competitiveness is taken to an extreme, we suggest that sexual relations become another arena for an intense struggle to succeed, to beat the opposition. The horror of failure in general becomes the horror of sexual failure; where the ego fears its weakness, sexual conquest can become the trophy sport that assuages that terror. Bateman's psychological implosion, the necessity to cover over the terrible void that he feels at the core of his being, requires the fantasy of sexual conquest as well as the fantasy of ultimate violence. His environment of high-flying males in the financial markets of the 1980s ensures that he is no exception in his misogyny. In this scene, midway through the film, he is in a bar with his colleagues, talking about women.

ALL IN UNISON: There are no girls with good personalities! (laughter)
VAN PATTEN: A good personality consists of a chick with a little hardbody who will satisfy all sexual demands without being too slutty about things and who will essentially keep her dumb fucking mouth shut.
McDERMOTT: Listen, the only girls with good personalities who are smart or maybe funny or half way intelligent or even talented—though God knows what the fuck that means—are ugly chicks.
VAN PATTEN: Absolutely.
McDERMOTT: And this is because they have to make up for how fucking unattractive they are.
BATEMAN: Do you know what Ed Gein said about women?
VAN PATTEN: Ed Gein? Maitre d' at Canal Bar?
BATEMAN: No, serial killer, Wisconsin in the fifties. He was an interesting guy.
McDERMOTT: So what did Ed say?
BATEMAN: He said, "When I see a pretty girl walking down the street I think two things. One part of me wants to take her out and talk to her and be real nice and sweet and treat her right."
McDERMOTT: What does the other part of him think?
BATEMAN: What her head would look like on a stick.

Unsurprisingly the others don't join in Bateman's laughter. Yet by this time in the film Bateman's depravity has sunk so low as to make it impossible for him to think of women without wanting to slaughter them. Sex and murder become inextricably bound together in the quest to find a meaning outside of the boredom of competitive corporatism: a quest for meaning that we found in *American Beauty* and will look at again in *Fight Club*. In the earlier discussion of *American Psycho* it was remarked that, because Bateman's rage fulfilled itself only in impotent fantasy, he was unlikely to receive analysis or any kind of therapeutic intervention. *Happiness* is even bleaker however: the protagonist not only carried out his sexual fantasies, but, as an analyst himself and receiving ongoing analysis, the very efficacy of any such interventions is thrown into doubt (only the talk with his son perhaps opened the door to his self-awareness). However, in the next two films the psychoanalytical returns as the unchallenged backdrop to sex and violence.

In *Blue Velvet* we find a new symbol of the equation between sex and violence: the use of oxygen to fuel villain Frank's aggression when making love or killing people. *Blue Velvet* was written and directed by David Lynch, and came out in 1986. Medved found it incoherent and absurdly overpraised,[5] while Pratt found it "arguably the most significant, most influential, most crucially important American film of the 1980s."[6] Lynch's films, from *Eraserhead* to *Mullholland Dr.*, are works of art of the highest order, generally juxtaposing "Mom-and-apple-pie" suburban America with a surreal underworld of sexual deviancy and violence. It is precisely because Lynch's films are such well-crafted works of art that they don't necessarily serve our purpose here in exposing the madness of the American mind. As thrillers, *film noir*, or crime mysteries, or in the genre known as "rubber reality," all with exceptional cinematography, they constitute a finessed oeuvre ultimately suggesting a sanity so grounded as to be able to contemplate the darkness without succumbing to it. Nevertheless, there are scenes in *Blue Velvet* that could suggest, to an audience not versed in the tradition of surreal *film noir*, an equation between sex and violence that is far from sane.

The protagonist of the film, young Jeffrey Beaumont, finds a severed ear in a field and takes it upon himself to play amateur detective in an unfolding criminal inquiry. He teams up with Sandy Williams, the daughter of the police officer officially responsible for the investigation, and breaks into the flat of singer Dorothy Vallens, who is somehow involved in the case. Dorothy discovers Jeffrey hiding in her closet and, threatening him with a knife, forces him to undress. This becomes the first association made in the film between aggression and sex, as she prepares to make love with him on the sofa. There is no doubt that he is a good-looking young man, but the transition from a woman scared and enraged to find a male voyeur in her flat, to a woman hot to participate in sexual congress, is rapid in the extreme: there is no emotional bracketing. Are we supposed to buy into this because she is a nightclub singer, and therefore "obviously" sexually promiscuous?

What happens next is far more extreme however: her lover Frank Booth suddenly knocks on the door, and young Jeffrey is bundled back into the closet with his clothes. Frank is into perverted sex; in the near-dark, verbally abusing Dorothy, he forces her to sit with legs apart while he breathes from an oxygen mask. Where Bateman pumps up his sexual aggression through working out, Frank does so chemically. "Mummy, mummy," he moans, muffled by the plastic mask, and crouches down between her legs. "Mummy loves you," comes Dorothy's tutored response, to which Frank utters the immortal Oedipal line: "Baby wants to fuck...." He moans again, screams, and utters a string of obscenities. "Don't you fucking look at me!" he screams. Dorothy turns her head away obediently. He keeps repeating this as he prepares to mount her. He takes her brutally and short, and slaps her afterwards, still repeating "Don't fucking look at me!" He leaves her panting on the floor, his parting shot an allusion to Van Gogh—a cryptic reference to the severed ear that Jeffrey had earlier discovered.

Jeffrey then emerges from his hiding place and attempts to comfort Dorothy. She takes him into his arms and encourages him to feel her body. His tenderness is abruptly ended when she says, "Hit me!" She repeats this demand, and he recoils. Jeffrey cannot deal with this perversity any more, this inversion of all his values, and leaves, despite her plea for him to stay. He is shaken by what he has seen and discovered about Frank's hold over Dorothy (he has kidnapped her husband and son) and haltingly reveals it to Sandy, his girlfriend. "Why are there people like Frank?" he demands, overwrought, "why is there so much trouble in the world?" Sandy responds with a vision of redemption—a deluge of robins bringing light—that stands as Lynch's trademark: the contrasting of a dark amoral underworld with the bright normalcy of mainstream America. But Jeffrey is drawn to the tormented Dorothy instead, and becomes her lover. "I am seeing something that was always hidden," he confides in Sandy, who he nevertheless continues to court.

"I want you to hurt me," Dorothy says to him later on in bed, but he again refuses. They fight and he ends up hitting her, to her apparent delight. The dark world he has become fascinated with opens its doors to him. Next, of course, Frank discovers them and is enraged. Jeffrey is literally dragged into Frank's violent world in which we find that his violence lives alongside a passion for music. As in *Silence of the Lambs* and *Seven*, extreme violence and aesthetic appreciation go together. The exhilaration of this abandonment is summed up in Frank's outburst: "I'll fuck anything that moves! Let's hit the road!" At one point in the tormenting of Jeffrey, Frank, on oxygen again, looks into his eyes and says: "You're like me." This is perhaps what Jeffrey is afraid of, what Lynch's audience is secretly, and delightedly, interested in: the Frank in all of us. And when Jeffrey finally snaps and punches Frank in the face, all hell breaks loose: not the "love letter" that Frank threatens him with (a bullet), but a strange set of kisses, kisses of recognition at knifepoint. The wild man in Frank acknowledges the wild man as yet undeveloped in Jeffrey, and so by extension in all of us. Then, to the sound of Roy Orbison's "In Dreams," Frank beats the crap out of Jeffrey: an association between music and violence that was pursued relentlessly in Kubrick's *A Clockwork Orange*.

The image of Bateman working out and then admiring his physique as he screws two prostitutes, or the image of Frank sucking on his oxygen mask as a prelude to either sex or violence, sums up for us a unique madness of American sexuality: male competitiveness so pumped up as to become murder. The context for it is an obsession with sex as achievement, as lifestyle accessory, as trophy sport; not even an eleven-year-old can escape it.

Lecter is the grotesque figure as foil to the earnest Starling; Frank is the grotesque figure as foil to the innocent Jeffrey. But Lynch's vision is the darker one: Jeffrey's rite-of-passage encounter is tinged with the possibility that somewhere he too incorporates Frank's madness. In the next film the grotesque figure is a woman as foil to a man clearly on a knife-edge between moral outrage and uncontrollable passion.

Basic Instinct pits Sharon Stone as heiress novelist Catherine Tramell against Michael Douglas as police detective Nick Curran. Tramell fits Aristotle's definition of the monstrous or grotesque, in that her motives appear inscrutable, whether she is or is not a serial killer as Curran suspects (either of which possibilities the film leaves open). But the complete implausibility of her character provides an extremity of situation against which the portrait of Curran develops in its complexity and plausibility. Medved makes the usual mistake of the Right in assuming that transgressional content invalidates a film. He says: "I know many people who would never dream of spending $7.50 to go see *Basic Instinct*, but they can nonetheless describe much of its content with reasonable accuracy."[7]

Medved is presumably talking about the famous scene where Sharon Stone crosses and uncrosses her legs in her first interrogation, an "overrated scene" as Pratt rather oddly describes it. But Medved is wrong to think that because of this, or any listing of its transgressional content—its "message" as he likes to describe the content of such works—a person might know the film with reasonable accuracy. Even Pratt, whose analysis is at length compared to Medved's, seems to believe, quite wrongly, that Tramell "has literally gotten away with murder several times over."[8] In the film, it is Curran's former lover and police psychologist colleague who carries out the murders.

But what is of interest here is firstly the association of sex and violence throughout the film, and secondly Michael Douglas's performance as Curran. We insisted in the Introduction that this examination of the American mind driven to excess was not just to paint a portrait of the unique American madness, but also to show clearly the unique strengths of the American mind when rolled back from the brink. In both *Basic Instinct* and *Falling Down*, Douglas plays an ordinary American man on the edge, with an intensity and conviction that is perhaps the best icon for both aims of this book. In the former film Douglas pulls back from the brink, and in the latter he goes over the edge, but in both cases his struggle is deeply illuminating about what it is to be American.

What Douglas conveys above all in *Basic Instinct* is a *moral* energy that erupts from time to time into a fury that is both sexual and violent. But the source of that energy is always clear: it is outrage at murder and lies, and the human coldness that can kill and lie, especially if the human face of killing and lies happens to be that of a beautiful woman. By Riesman's analysis Curran is an inner-directed man whose torment is naturally guilt; by Lasch's analysis Curran suffers from a superego constructed in the absence of traditional authority, and prone to erupt into rage. In reality Curran embodies many of America's best qualities, and to this extent is a noble character, but, as Aristotle would have it, he is brought low through his "frailties and errors." Hence we identify with him in facing the terrible, grotesque figure of Catherine, and eventually the horrible reality of a policewoman as serial killer. We feel pity and fear for him. His is a truly American situation of a pumped-up aggression that has a proper moral focus, yet threatens to unravel at every turn, because his moral energy is so intertwined with his sexual energies.

7

The Apocalypse and Armageddon

KEY FILMS: *The Rapture, The Passion of the Christ*
ADDITIONAL FILMS: *Left Behind* trilogy, *Apocalypse Now,*
The Birds, The Terminator, End of Days

In the U.S. election year of 2004, liberal U.S. commentators grumbled that George W. Bush (the Republican contender) was running a theocracy, and that it was easier for candidates to profess "freethinking" tendencies at the founding of America in the eighteenth century than it was at the beginning of the twenty-first. A recent American poll showed that while a majority might accept a Jewish candidate for President, an avowedly atheist candidate stood no chance. British journalist Alexander Chancellor, writing in *The Guardian* on the subject of the 2004 election, suggested that "In Britain, flaunting religious faith is a political liability; in America, it is a political necessity."[1] Religion in France appears to hold even less credibility in the political sphere, or to put it another way, France can be thought of as the epicenter of Western secularism, Britain being not far behind.

It is sometimes hard for a British person to understand that American society is so deeply religious compared to the more secular cultures of Britain and France. But the considerable number of films with a Christian basis produced in America testifies to this. While many are positive, humorous or thoughtful, e.g. *Witness* and *Oh God!*, some highlight particularly Christian pathologies of thought, of which the Apocalypse is the most visible. Many Americans believe that religion is a force for good in society, and that, for the individual, it is an essential part of what it is to be fully human. Thoughtful commentators throughout the 20th century have suggested that its absence leads to a deep alienation and sense of meaninglessness. On the other hand secular objections to religion are intrinsic to much humanist thought (particularly if it has a Marxist basis) mainly regarding religion's potential for fundamentalist dogmatism, and that its history is dogged with authoritarian power structures and the use of imprisonment, torture, and murder for religious reasons. This history can be contrasted with the genuine advances of secularism, which include democracy and freedom of expression as overarching principles behind more specific advances, including universal welfare and education, the abolition of slavery, the emancipation of women, and gay rights. Religion in America, as elsewhere, has a history of resisting these genuine advances in society.[2]

The two films mentioned above both show that American cinema is able to convey a genuine religiousness that is free of dogmatic assumptions. In *Witness*, directed by Peter Weir and starring Harrison Ford, a hard-boiled Philadelphia cop is given sanctuary in an Amish religious community (such a community is virtually unknown in Europe). It is a community that expresses its religiosity through a rejection of modern lifestyles and values, turning instead to a life of rural simplicity and pacifism. What *Witness* does so well is to juxtapose the secular values of a very modern police officer with the religious values of such a community, and show that there is merit in *both*. In Carl Rayner's *Oh God!* religiousness is presented more as an optimistic and deeply caring relationship with others, while "God" is personified as an old man, looking for all the world like a golfing enthusiast. The film is a comedy, imagining what it would be like for an ordinary man—a supermarket manager—to be chosen by "God" to spread His message, only to find that "God" was, to appearances at least, just as ordinary. This film is entirely free of dogmatic Christianity, and while it doesn't push any of the issues that it raises particularly deeply, it conveys what many find to be the essential *warmth* of true religion. (Films made in the U.K. and continental Europe, where they do deal with religious issues, rarely convey this: Bergman's films for example all express the bleakness of what could be called an exhausted Christianity.)

However in this chapter, we are looking at the darker sides of religion; at a peculiarly American pathology of Christianity summed up in the idea of the *apocalypse*. The term originally meant "revelation," but has acquired a secular meaning as Mick Broderick points out: "It is a term used indiscriminately to connote and conflate, amongst others, notions of 'anarchy,' 'chaos,' 'entropy,' 'nihilism,' 'catastrophe,' and 'doomsday,' yet by removal from its original mytho-religious association it assumes a randomly clichéd definition."[3] Broderick is writing in a collection of essays called *Crisis Cinema— The Apocalyptic Idea in Postmodern Narrative Film*, which largely uses just such secular meanings in its discussions. Here we are interested in the specifically religious meaning of the term "apocalypse"—and a set of related concepts—as it has come to circulate amongst American Christians at the end of the twentieth and start of the twenty-first century, and as it appears in film. Heather Hendershot discusses selected films in this genre and evangelical

Christians as a large market for such films, citing *The Omega Code* as an apoc-alyptical film, almost unknown outside such circles, that surpassed *Fight Club*'s per-screen box office average.[4]

Michael Northcott's work on apocalyptic religion in America was intro-duced in Part One, where it was suggested that increasing American paranoia is partly the result of a shift from postmillennialism to premillennialism. Hal Lindsey's *The Late Great Planet Earth* is regarded by Northcott as a key apocalyptic text, and was an influence on Ronald Reagan.[5] Hendershot tells us that it sold over fifteen million copies just in America, and that *The New York Times* declared Lindsey as the best-selling author of the seventies.[6] Lindsey himself is adamant that the postmillennialist position was successively demolished by the two world wars, adding: "No self-respecting scholar who looks at the world conditions and accelerating decline of Christian influence today is a 'postmillennialist.'"[7] (However, the Microsoft Word 2003 spell checker accepts "postmillennialist" while failing to recognize "premillennialist:" does this mean that Bill Gates has failed to move with the times? Or that he is an optimist rather than a pessimist?)

We saw earlier that conspiracy theorists are self-reflexive about the recap-tion of their ideas in the broader community; so are the millennialists. Tim LaHaye, mentioned in Part One, is perhaps the most significant popular writer on the topic since Lindsey. He devotes the opening chapter of *Mind Siege* to an imaginary story set in the future in which the forces of humanism over-whelm Christianity and where fundamentalist Christians could be considered legally insane.[8] This is meant to outrage his audience while offering them the continued perception of humanism as an evil "religion." The irony is that since the time of Locke and Mille, secular humanist legislature has insisted that private belief of any kind is beyond the domain of the law. Belief in the apocalypse is not a matter of the law, but all the more reason to argue that in its extreme forms it *is* a form of insanity, the *acting out* of which is increasingly a threat to world peace. We can identify it here as a part of the American madness, and in the work of LaHaye we also find a relationship between apocalypticism and a particular form of paranoia, an unjustifiable fear of *humanism*.

Pratt ignores the whole issue of apocalypticism in relation to paranoia, perhaps representing a secular dismissal of anything outside the Marxist analysis of history. Others relate to it in secular terms, for example Christopher Sharret, writing on apocalypticism and masculinity says, also in a some-what Marxist vein: "As a perpetual wish-dream within dominant culture, the apocalyptic prefers conflagration and self-immolation to radical transforma-tion."[9] Elsewhere he cites *Taxi Driver* as a preeminent example of apocalyptic art of the 1970s.[10] (This film is analyzed later in the chapter on secular nihilism, alienation and self-destruction, rather than in a religious apocalyptical sense.) Wheeler Winston Dixon offers this secular train of thought: "Time is running out. I can feel it. The romance of Armageddon is being replaced by the specter of inevitable destruction, albeit on a smaller scale. ... The twenty-first century will be defined not by wars, but by terrorist incursion." [11] Not if Lindsey and LaHaye—abetted by a slew of American apocalyptical films—can help it. *The Late Great Planet Earth* has a film version, "cobbled together from stock footage and some hastily recreated sequences and narrated by a transparently desperate Orson Welles," [12] while LaHaye's bestselling *Left Behind* novels have been made into a film series (discussed below).

The term "Rapture" is a relatively new one, with currency mainly amongst Christian fundamentalists (or evangelicals as they prefer to be known) in America. It signifies the elevated mood, or the anticipation of that moment, when the Day of Judgment will come and Jesus will re-appear to usher in a world free of sin and suffering. Only the "saved" will enter this new world, the rest being condemned to eternal damnation, while the transition to the new world will, of course, be cataclysmic. Any and all disasters around the planet are assumed to be portents of the coming Apocalypse, as we are living, so the fundamentalists hold, at this time in the "End of Days." Websites abound that give free rein to these deranged imaginings: for example "Rapture Index—The prophetic speedometer of end-time activity" lists dozens of categories under which "end-time" events are considered, such as hurricanes, earthquakes and mass murder. [13] However, since the exact date of the "Rapture" or its equivalent has been predicted as coming "real soon now" for the last two thousand years at least, the website carries this warning:

> Because date-setting can cause emotional harm to some people, we do not allow date-setting on the message board. A couple of years back, one participant threatened to kill himself after he thought he'd missed the rapture. [14]

Liberal commentators are concerned at rapture as the underlying motivation for Christian fundamentalist support for the U.S. invasion of "Babylon"— i.e. modern-day Iraq. It is not at all clear whether George W. Bush can be regarded as rapture-motivated, but it appears to be a quintessential part of the American madness in a way that it is generally not for the British or European mind.

The Rapture, written and directed by Michael Tolkin, and *The Passion of the Christ*, co-written and directed by Mel Gibson, have been chosen to illustrate this. Neither of these films is particularly well-made or worth watching as *a film*, though it has to be said that Mel Gibson's film has a far higher budget and better production values. That doesn't make it easier on the eye however, because it is a film of relentless graphic violence, dwelling on the alleged capture, torture, and crucifixion of Jesus. In a sense this is apocalyptic because of the narrow focus that Gibson has taken on the Jesus story, and also because of the accompanying imagery. Its madness lies perhaps with a typically American obsession with violence, this time in a religious context: why did Gibson not choose what is universally considered to be a far more significant element of the Jesus story, that is, love (*caritas*, *agape*)? It is the film *The Rapture* however which truly shows how the Apocalypse can take a hold on a person's mind and become the archetype for a very specific act of madness.

The *Left Behind* trilogy will be discussed to show that ideas of the Apocalypse—or to use a term with more secular currency, Armageddon—are found far and wide in American film culture, and a number of other films will also be introduced: *Apocalypse Now*, *The Birds*, *The Terminator*, and *End of Days*.

The Rapture

The low-budget character of *The Rapture* announces itself in the opening shot, which is set in a call center, as unconvincing a set as the cheap special effects used to convey the Apocalypse at the end of the film. But a low budget may simply mean that the film has set out to deal with difficult issues that the mainstream has little patience for, and there is no more difficult an issue than religion. For our purposes it doesn't matter if the film is ultimately a low-budget masterpiece or a low-budget flop: what counts is that it tellingly reveals some key elements of the American madness. In fact *two* such elements are juxtaposed in the film: sexual obsession and apocalyptic religion. The opening shot introduces us to the central character of the film in her work-day setting, known to us just as "Sharon," played by Mimi Rogers. In the next scene she is perched seductively next to Vic, her boyfriend, in an expensive car. They are cruising the hotels in search of another swinging couple for a partner-swapping session, and before long we are watching two couples undress in Vic's apartment. Leading up to the sex session with strangers Randy and Diana is a conversation which prepares us for an anything-goes experience:

> DIANA: What are you looking for now?
> SHARON: Now we're looking for something a little less obvious.
> VIC: But fun. Definitely fun. We're very social people.
> RANDY: You might be asking for something you couldn't handle.
> SHARON: I can handle it.
> RANDY: What if things go out of control?

SHARON: What's control got to do with it?
VIC: I think he wants to find out if you have any limits.
SHARON: Tell him that I haven't found them yet.
VIC: Sharon hasn't found her limits yet.

The film by this point is preparing us for the stark contrast it wants to pose between Sharon's boring work, over-compensated for by swinging sex, and the meaning that religion could give to her life. The next day at the office during her coffee-break she sits down, perhaps to contemplate the delights of the previous night, but overhears a conversation between fellow workers. They are clearly religious and seem to be discussing some imminent and important event, with references to prayer and to "the Boy," a character who will play an important role in Sharon's life later in the film. At this point she is skeptical and listens with a superior smile on her face.

The film cuts to Sharon's bedroom, where Randy from the previous encounter is in bed with her (he is impressed, it seems, that she remembers his name). Randy is played by David Duchovny, star of *The X-Files*, and famous for his earlier soft-porn career. While it is a genuinely open question as to the moral implications of casual sex and swinging, Randy is encouraged by Sharon to confess something much more extreme: that he once killed a man for money. Both women and men who defend their right to engage in casual sex tend to do so on the basis, firstly, that it does no harm, and secondly, that the pleasures of such behavior are a positive good. Western psychologists from Sigmund Freud to Wilhelm Reich are there to back up such theories, and it appears that this viewpoint is central to the lives of millions of non-religious Americans, though when pushed to the extreme it forms a core part of the American madness. But there is no conceivable psychological, ethical or cultural support in America for the idea that murder can *ever* be justified, particularly when undertaken in cold blood and for money (judicial execution is a quite a different issue).

We are watching Sharon and Randy in bed after his revelation that he had killed a man for cash. "For how much?" is the first question that comes to her mind. "For a thousand dollars," he replies. "That's not very much money," comes her response. Although he subsequently expresses regret at his action, we are now left in a morally ambiguous space: is Sharon really so depraved as to be unable to dredge up the slightest repugnance over this act of murder? Does not the intimate touch of this man now carry a different meaning? This is the first question mark that must hang over this film: it may be a device to show us just how lost Sharon is, but as such it is clumsy and psychologically implausible—in Prince's terms it is poor emotional bracketing. The equivalence that we are asked to make, between the moral bankruptcy of sexual swinging and the moral bankruptcy of murder, is one that the secular, humanistic tradition balks at. Only a religious fundamentalist would suggest it, and even then probably very few. But the scene merely continues with Sharon expressing the emptiness of her life, and Randy suggesting that she is depressed and should see a therapist.

Sharon doesn't see a therapist, but is increasingly aware of evangelical religion around her. Sharon is being forced in that direction, firstly by doorstep evangelicals, and then through the next swinging session where Vic is making love to their latest sexual acquaintance, Angie. Sharon is curious about an extensive tattoo on Angie's back which depicts apocalyptic scenes, but at first Angie is reluctant to talk about it. Sharon presses her however, and in the end Angie's partner, who has been making love with Sharon, says simply: "Tell them." We are not party to Angie's account, but next day at coffee break Sharon confronts her religious co-workers by claiming that she has seen the "Pearl," an image of which was depicted on Angie's back. They are suspicious of Sharon at first, and reluctant to share with her, but before long they too are repeating the apocalyptic message: Christ is about to return. Sharon responds as any educated humanist might:

> There are five billion people on the planet. There's I-don't-know-how-many religions. Why does the God of some little country on the Mediterranean have to be the God for everyone? Isn't that a little arrogant? I mean, really? The Buddhists get along okay without Jesus Christ. The Hindus get along okay without Jesus Christ. The Moslems seem to be getting along okay without Jesus Christ.

To which her co-worker responds that none of them are saved. For the secular humanist, this response represents the core madness of Christianity, and so is not especially American in its nature. But one could argue that the American version of Christianity has revived an early Christian millenarianism in a unique manner, vividly portrayed in this film. But, again, the film lurches towards this exposition in a clumsy and unconvincing manner. Sharon's life-long objection to taking Jesus into her heart, so well expressed when she points out his absence in other major faiths, appears not just to waver, but disappear entirely within a few moments of reflection. At night with Randy a little later she suddenly makes up her mind, kicks him out of bed, and insists on changing the sheets. "This bed is unclean," she says. He objects that she had only changed the sheets the day before, but she is adamant: "I need a new direction in my life. There is a God, I know it, there is a God, and I'm going to meet Him."

In the next bizarre scene Sharon picks up a hitchhiker who thinks he looks so dangerous that even he wouldn't give himself a lift. She takes him to a motel where her reasons are revealed: she steals his gun and forces him to leave. After a good draft of brandy for courage she points the gun under her chin, but does not in the end have the resolve to pull the trigger. Clearing the gun and bottle into the drawer by her bed she closes it, but then reopens it and reaches for the Bible we have seen there, which she takes out for study. She drifts off to sleep and the image of a revolving pearl suggests to us that she is now really dreaming of it. Sharon is converted, and Vic can tell that something has changed by her "goofy" smile. In a kindly fashion he draws the obvious secular conclusion, that she has fallen in love. Which, in a sense, she has. At her call-center job she is now much livelier, and attempts to talk with each customer about "God." Naturally her boss is concerned that she is getting through fewer calls in a day and summons her to his office, only to reveal that he too is converted.

The idea of Judgment Day is central to all three monotheisms (Judaism, Christianity and Islam)—but totally absent in far Eastern religions. Hence it is part of what is unique to the Western mind, and in this film it plays out in a very American way. The problem with any idea of a new Millennium, or a day of salvation or Judgment Day, is that it never seems to come. Hence the website cited above makes it clear that "date-setting" is not allowed. For the secular world the great puzzle is how the believers cope with this seemingly infinite postponement; after all the idea that Judgment Day was only a few years away is prevalent in the Old Testament, is recounted in lurid detail in Revelation, and was the firm belief of early Christians. Naturally for most Christians, some two thousand years later, this element of their religion has been somewhat downplayed, particularly after the uneventful passing of the year 2000. But for the minority of the religious right in America the Apocalypse is a firm belief. (There is also a non–Christian New Age version of it pursued by equally well-meaning people more to the left of the political spectrum.)

In the next scene we meet the "Boy," a child with the apparent gift of prophecy. Sharon has joined a religious group centered on his prophecies, and the boy, whispering to his father (who repeats his words to the devotees), is answering questions. He tells them that they have to wait for "God's" return. "How long?" comes the natural question from an older woman in the circle. "Probably a few years. Five years, six years," comes the reply.

Apocalyptic groups, such as the Jehovah's Witnesses, are fascinating because of their ability to survive despite actually naming dates, which come and go without the predicted apocalypse ever materializing. These dates are most likely to be set about five or six years away, possibly because this is a psychological timeframe that somehow works for most believers. It is a timeframe in which people can make major changes in their lives, such as moving to a remote region of America, joining a religious group, and recommitting their life's work and savings to the cause. But within five years all kinds of new prophecies come and go, and it is easy to forget the initial fervor that the proposed date brought about. At the same time a thousand easy answers are to hand as to why the *exact* date was inaccurate, the principal one being: "God moves in mysterious ways." The very failure of the prophecy is proof that "God" is testing the believer, or that the believer's faith is not yet strong enough. A redoubling of effort is needed. Perhaps a small percentage of believers are actually disillusioned by the receding horizon of the Apocalypse and eventually quit the movement (whatever it is), but they are probably more than made up for by newcomers.

But none of this impinges on Sharon's consciousness at this moment: members of the group get up and hug one another. This scene places in stark contrast the secular world, where love and intimacy are only possible when channeled through sexual encounters (it seems), with the religious life, where love and intimacy are the hallmarks of the whole daily life. The price for this greater love, if we can accept for the moment that it is real, *appears* to be the abandonment of one's critical faculties. But we have no idea at this point in the film how Sharon will eventually abandon reason on a catastrophic scale.

Sharon returns from her church meeting to confront Randy, who appears at least to put up a good fight in the teeth of her religious convictions, but, mysteriously, he too succumbs with no graduated stages. We then jump six years into the future to see Sharon and Randy together in a church with a little girl sitting between them. In the meeting the Boy is now old enough to speak directly to the flock:

> So far, we're still in the realm of signs and wonders. But the Rapture is coming. It says so in the Bible. Our bodies will be transformed into spirit. And then we will be caught up in a cloud to meet God. The end is coming soon ... This year ...

This is the first time in the film that the term "Rapture" is mentioned. Randy and Sharon are now happily married with a small daughter, Mary, apparently living the perfect Christian life and proselytizing wherever possible. Sharon's happiness is not to last however, because Randy is killed by a disgruntled employee in an act of typically American violence. The sacked worker turned lone gunman goes on the rampage and Randy, while trying to stop him, is shot. At the funeral Sharon appears serene and tells her distraught friend: "Paula, the universe you live in is a cold and empty space. The universe I live in is filled with God." But little Mary, continually exposed to a Christian doctrine that her young mind interprets even more literally than her mother, keeps asking when she will see Daddy again. She cannot separate the idea of the "Rapture," as a future event manifesting through divine intervention, and her own death, because the end result is the same deeply appealing vision: of going to heaven and being reunited with Daddy.

From the secular standpoint heaven is a fiction, whether reached through an apocalyptic "Rapture" or through the death of the individual. Sharon's state of mind is now doubly suspect: "brainwashed" by her cultish beliefs, she is now tragically bereaved, making her apparent serenity implausible. In the next scene she watches as a series of pictures appear from processing by a photo-booth in a shopping mall. These are ordinary scenes, quite unrelated to her life, but Randy, wearing the clothes from the time of his death, is superimposed in each one. She is seeing things. On the last shot Randy is in the desert and a voice-over from the Boy recites from Revelation. But when consulted during their next church meeting the Boy is unsure whether Sharon's vision is from "God" or Satan, and when Sharon asks the church group to go with her to the desert, the Boy simply says that they haven't been invited.

Sharon and her daughter Mary are convinced that "God" has called them to the desert to be taken up in the Rapture, and so they set off and camp out, with provisions sufficient only for a short period. As the days begin to drag out it is Mary who becomes impatient. Amidst the harsh indifference of the semi-desert landscape, their only friend is a local policeman who brings them a few candy bars. Sharon begins to waver, but it is the simple equation in Mary's head that drives her inexorably to the desperate act to follow. For Mary, this hopeless life, lived with neither the comforts and security of home nor the promised Rapture is hell. Heaven, the outcome of the Rapture, is within such easy grasp if they were only but to commit suicide: why wait wearily and hopelessly in such dreadful circumstances? Sharon finally buckles under the horrible logic of her predicament and shoots her little daughter Mary. Thankfully—as Mel Gibson was not the director—we are spared the graphic details of the child's blood spattered on the rocks. But Sharon, again, cannot use the gun on herself and she is picked up wandering along the road by the friendly policeman. He quickly ascertains the truth of the situation and locks Sharon up in his local jail on suspicion of child murder.

There is a chance here for the film to return to reality, for us to confront with Sharon the whole course of her derangement, and some possible redemption through counseling, analysis, or atonement. But after a few days in jail the Rapture *does* actually arrive, in a memorable scene where the bars of her prison disintegrate and fall away. (In all fairness to the director this scene was well-realized, despite the low budget.) The Apocalypse comes, but it is the policeman who is taken up to heaven, leaving Sharon behind. Her faith, in the end, is not strong enough.

Tolkin is using the film to attack Christianity, and so it is a caricature, especially in the idea that a new convert is inevitably focused on the Second Coming. That simply isn't how most Christian converts experience their newfound religiousness. Medved complains of the film that "Naturally, those who belittle religious thinking deliver all the best lines."[15] Since the time of the

European Enlightenment, it has been a Western right to insult religion, in stark contrast to the Islamic world which has not yet experienced such a liberation. It is America's strength to defend that right, though the right to insult religion does not necessarily guarantee works of artistic merit. Nor does blind faith either, as Mel Gibson's attempt to portray the passion of Christ shows us: it probably only further diminishes the image of religion in the secular mind.

The Passion of the Christ

The Passion of the Christ starts with a tearful Jesus approaching his disciples at night and reproaching them for not staying up with him. John asks what has happened to him and if they should call the others, but Jesus says: "No, John. I don't want them to see me like this." With this line we already know that Gibson, unlike Pasolini in his film version of the Gospel of Matthew, is inventing lines not in the Gospels. Hence we are immediately interested as to what interpolations Gibson is making and why. While it is true that three of the four Gospels record Jesus as distraught and overcome at this point, not one of them suggests that Jesus is in any way embarrassed about his state of mind. What Gibson has done at a stroke is to turn Jesus into the man that we might all fear ourselves to be on hearing about our impending horrible execution: a coward. Gibson then adds another line not to be found in any of the Gospels. "He seems afraid," says one of the disciples as Jesus wanders off, clearly overcome. The next scene is pure Gibson invention: Satan now appears and offers Jesus solace. A snake crawls out from under Satan and reaches Jesus. Gibson now places his characteristic stamp on the film—literally—as Jesus, drawing himself up to his full height, crushes the snake underfoot.

Whatever happened to the central message of Jesus of love for one's neighbors, and to turn the other cheek? Poor snake. But Gibson has introduced the first image of violence into the film, and it will not be long before it fully descends into a bloodbath. True, the Jesus story is rich and complex, and one could focus on any of a number of themes in it. But to focus on *violence* must surely be to thoroughly betray all the dominant themes in the story. Yes, we know that Jesus died a horrible death (at least if we accept the story, for which there is no proper historical evidence). But in this moment of anguish for Jesus, why not select other passages from that scene in the Gospels, for example John 14:27 where Jesus says: "Peace is my parting gift to you, my own peace, such as the world cannot give." (Many accounts of great modern religious figures, such as the Dalai Lama or Jiddu Krishnamurti, suggest that this very special kind of peace is precisely the gift to us bestowed by the presence of these individuals.) But peace is certainly not the gift that Gibson wants to bestow upon us as we leave the cinema or any screening of this film. Relentless, bloody violence is his gift, and as such it is highly indicative of the madness in the dark heart of the American mind.

In the film the capture of Jesus is told in a fairly conventional way, and he is led off in chains. But in a bizarre flashback to his life as a carpenter in the house of his mother, Gibson comes up with an irrelevant but almost comic invention. Jesus had made a "tall" table, which his mother inspects with suspicion, having to imagine the necessary Western-style chair to sit at it on. "This will never catch on!" she says, in a humorous moment of light-hearted relief, presumably designed to contrast with the horrors that Jesus is about to undergo. But what on earth Gibson was thinking of? (There is of course no such account in the Gospels.) Could it be part of his cultural arrogance, a way of dismissing or even denigrating the cultures of the East and of Africa which, if they use tables at all, use low ones? And which certainly do not use the typically Western tall chair? Does squatting on the ground or sitting on cushions somehow signify for Gibson the irredeemable "otherness" of these cultures? Is he mocking them from the vantage point of his imagined American superiority?

The next section deals with the trial of Jesus and effectively amounts to Gibson's attack on Vatican II (which sought rapprochement with Jewish communities by downplaying the role of Jews in Jesus' indictment) though this is not that relevant to our exploration. It does remind us however of what is great about American culture: that its artistic productions have the constitutional freedom to present provocative views on any subject on earth. To be fair to Gibson, he goes into some detail regarding the role of Pilate and his unwillingness to condemn Jesus, but this leaves the Jews at fault and is exactly what Jewish groups have most objected to. The Pope however apparently approved of Gibson's film.

Once found guilty Jesus is whipped to the gasps of the onlookers, but their reaction is a trifle implausible, considering how commonplace this punishment was at that period. But the point of the scene is to ram home the sufferings of the Lamb of "God," and Gibson gives us a seemingly endless visualization of it. The crucifixion likewise spares us no details: for example a veritable Niagara Falls of blood spurts from Jesus's side when pierced by the spear. The process of his dying is accompanied by thunder and lightning, earth tremors, gales, and the crashing down of temple buildings; finally Satan screams out in rage at having been cheated of his victory. Gibson's *Passion* may yet be the worst Jesus film ever made, while many critics hold that Pasolini's the *Gospel According to Matthew* is the best. Yet Gibson is an avowed Catholic and Pasolini was an atheist communist homosexual; an outsider to conventional religion on three counts. A plot synopsis of Gibson's film could go like this: "Jesus starts as a sniveling coward, having learned his fate, but ends up taking his punishment like a man. The end." But any desire to see worthwhile films on this topic aside, Gibson's *Passion* usefully shows us how the American mainstream give credulity towards two madnesses at once: violence and apocalypticism. Where Tolkin set out to insult religion in his portrayal of the Apocalypse, Gibson's adherence to outof-date Catholic dogma creates an even less appealing and insightful portrayal of religion.

Gibson's film is an offering from a believer, while Tolkin's *The Rapture* is intended to show that becoming a Christian inevitably leads to delusional apocalyptic behavior. Medved is right to criticize this, because extreme apocalypticism is not part of mainstream Christian thought, especially not in Catholicism. But our job here is to examine the extremes of the American mind, and so we move to apocalyptical films offered by believers whose purposein making them is to *convert*, not parody.

The *Left Behind Trilogy*

The *Left Behind* trilogy is so uniquely an American production that it is not much known outside the USA. It is acclaimed on the first film's DVD cover as "the best movie in the Apocalyptic genre!" Unlike *The Rapture* it takes the logic of Revelation and the Apocalypse several steps further, to consider the obvious weakness in the original idea: that only 144,000 people were to be saved on the Day of Judgment (twelve thousand each from the twelve tribes of Israel, according to Revelation 7:4). As the world now contains in excess of 6 billion people, and perhaps 2 billion of them Christian, then what happens to every one else? Those that get "left behind?"

To Catholics the last book of the New Testament, the Revelation of John, is something of an embarrassment and is mostly ignored. It is only within Protestant traditions that it became important, and this may be because Protestantism can be partly understood as a turning back to Old Testament values, a denial of the uniquely devotional flowering of Christianity in Catholicism. In his analysis of millenarianism Michael Grosso makes it clear that Revelation hardly embodies the values of Christ. He says, "It needs to be pointed out that this all-important document of western history that it exudes the language of the will to power. There is scarcely a trace of love, forgiveness, or humility, such as one associates with the Jesus of the Gospels."[16] By saying that Revelation is an "all-important document of western history" Grosso betrays his own feelings towards it: he is clearly enamored of it. But it never occurs to the enthusiasts for Revelation, such as Lindsey and

LaHaye, that the text does not embody core Christian teachings; their love-affair with its lurid spectacle is unhindered. The history of apocalyptic thinking in the Old Testament, through Revelation and the millenarianism of the Middle Ages is well-documented by Grosso, who also suggests that Marxism should be thought of as an expression of this utopianist tradition[17] (a thesis also explored in John Gray's *Black Mass*[18]). The common factor in both cases is that the promised utopia will be ushered in after a "final battle"—Armageddon in one case, and revolution in the other.

The tragic consequence of this doctrine is that signs of impending chaos are interpreted as *positive* indicators, as we saw with the "Rapture Index." Marx was also very much prey to this, as is the Marxist tradition, especially vis-à-vis the hoped for end of capitalism.[19] Even worse is the temptation to help things along a little, as a religious justification for acts of nihilistic destruction. The move in the American mind from postmillenarianism to premillenarianism, from optimism about America to a pessimism and a turning to Israel instead, gives us the extreme cinema of the *Left Behind* trilogy. The films are based on a book series by Timothy F. LaHaye and Jerry B. Jenkins, who rank ninth amongst best-selling authors at Amazon.com in the ten years since the series started. This is a staggering statistic, and tells us that the ideas in the *Left Behind* series are far more popular than any critical assessment would suggest. As well as being a fundamentalist Christian minister, author, and speaker, Tim LaHaye has been involved with far-right U.S. organizations promoting the end of separation of church and state: the undermining of the very basis of American public life.

The three *Left Behind* movies have three different directors, but all of them star Kirk Cameron, also a Christian, as Buck Williams. The film opens with Williams, an American news journalist, reporting on an all-out attack on Jerusalem involving seemingly thousands of enemy planes, which are mysteriously destroyed without a single Israeli shot being fired. A figure resembling an Old Testament prophet enters Buck's field of view as he films the "miracle" and tells him that they are entering a covenant for seven years. The utter absurdity of this opening is not redeemed at any point in the trilogy: it's all equally implausible. But this isn't the point: it is a question of whether the absurdities heaped up in this trilogy are merely random imaginings of fantasy / science fiction, or whether they represent a culturally significant set of ideas.

Unfortunately it is the latter. It is no accident that the opening scene of the series is set in Israel; this nation and its re-emergence are central to American apocalyptical thinking. (Christian operations such as "Operation Exodus," funded by the Ebenezer Emergency Fund International, help Jews from all over the world—including the former Soviet Union—to settle in Israel, because this will hasten the Biblical prophecy of salvation.[20]) Also visibly present in the films are all the essentially American paranoias regarding global currency, banking, and the U.N. These fears are focused in the films on the character of Nicolae Carpathia, who is—guess what—Secretary General designate of the United Nations. His mission to start with is the ending of world hunger through a "secret formula" for growing wheat in deserts. Meantime the "Rapture" takes place in a much less dramatic way than imagined in the film of that name: people simply disappear, leaving their clothes behind. It is down to Nicolae to announce to American audiences that the disappearances are a world-wide phenomenon (he speaks with a Russian or East European accent, and his name is an obvious reference to "Old Nick"). Naturally, the U.N. has "taken a leadership role in stabilizing the world." This idea is clearly scripted to bring terror to the American mind (with its deep paranoia about the United Nations), even if we did not anticipate at this point that Nicolae will turn out to be the Antichrist.

Actually "disappearances" are a wider part of American paranoia, surfacing in the recent U.S. TV series *The 4400* and Spielberg's mini-series *Taken*. In these stories the missing people are abducted by aliens over a fifty-year period, the twist in *The 4400* being that a spaceship returns them as humans with supernatural powers. Such dramatizations can be thought of as mainstream science-fiction fantasies, so why treat the highly obscure *Left Behind* films as actually more indicative of a uniquely American madness? Because, again, of the Old Testament connection. Science fiction is a new, though admittedly largely American, cultural invention, but the Old Testament has supplied myths and images made immensely powerful through their repetition and restatement over the centuries. A secular English or French audience may not immediately grasp that America is so deeply shaped in its imagination by the Old Testament, but any examination of the extraordinary rise of the religious right since 9/11 should convince them of that. 9/11 itself was the biggest single apocalyptical image to reinforce and re-stimulate the imagination of Revelation.

At the United Nations Nicholae is closer to his dream of the "secret formula"as he attempts to bribe its inventor, Professor Rosenzweig, with detailed drawings of the Temple of the Rock, itself deeply significant in the unfolding mystery. He is ever closer to his dream of world peace (yes, have patience, the Antichrist knows what he is doing), and announces to a startled world that the disappearances are due to radiation from nuclear bomb testing. His dastardly next step is to attempt total nuclear disarmament, along with a program to feed the hungry of the world. Buck Williams is attempting to piece together the puzzle, aided by his friends who show him that all this is foretold in the Bible. This includes the prophecy that the Antichrist will take up his place in the Temple of "God" in Jerusalem. The Arab world won't object because peace will be made ... by the Antichrist. Buck finds the evidence in the Bible "compelling." This is how it will unfold: bankers calling in billion-dollar loans to the U.N. will own the "formula" and control the land involved in the deal, and Nicholae, now officially Secretary General (or is that President?) of the U.N. will be able to control the whole world. Nicholae explains that building the new Temple in Jerusalem is not just for Jews, but for every man and woman in the world: an incentive for all world leaders to sign "the peace treaty" for the seven years of peace to come.

In one of the most bizarre scenes in the film Nicholae now plays host to international statesmen in a U.N. debating chamber look-alike and offers them part of the new global power; their states happen to include desert tracts of land from which the new food production will flow. But the bankers who originally put Nicholae into office protest and are shot by him. He then semi-hypnotizes the delegates to believe that one of the bankers killed the other and then turned the gun on himself. Only Buck seems to doubt the story; he is immune to Nicholae's powers because he has accepted Christ into his heart. He returns to the church where his friends welcome him, and, inexplicably, the first film ends here with no hint as to what a sequel might unfold. In the second film, *Left Behind: Tribulation Force*, Buck appears on TV to remind us of the events so far, and to confirm what was merely hinted at in the first film: that amongst the disappeared are *all* the world's children. (Unlike films such as the *Handmaid's Tale* or *Children of Men*, there seems to be no anxiety about this, no effort to quickly beget the next generation: the *physical* world as we know it is of little interest to the premillennialist). Next we hear that Rabbi Ben Judah, the "world's leading religious scholar" will announce "the single biggest piece of news in history." Before this we watch as Nicholae is begged to create a single world currency to rescue the markets from collapse. He graciously concedes, adding that since now there is a single currency, world peace is the only choice. He calls on all nations to disarm and put aside their religious differences. In fact he casts aside religion altogether, as the world applauds. As Buck now points out, Nicholae is not so much Secretary General of the U.N. as "President of the whole planet." Buck and his church friends know that you cannot defeat the Antichrist, as he is predicted by the Bible, but you can *fight* him: they set up the "Tribulation Force" to do that, and to defend all the Christians that Nicholae will now be hunting down. In the beleaguered church a preacher runs through the staple images of Revelation: the Four Horsemen of the Apocalypse, the Antichrist, the Rapture, and the "Tribulation": the coming period of famine, war, pestilence and so on. A false peace is coming that will reign, promising world unity.

Is this all part of a deeply American madness? To conceive of the Secretary General of the United Nations as the Antichrist? To be so paranoid about the other nations of the earth that the idea of global currency, global disarmament, and global peace must automatically hide an evil so monstrous that only Satan could be its author? Could any of this rub off in even the smallest way on American policy makers, Neocons, and White House advisors? If *Left Behind*—and its remarkably similar cousin of a film series, *The Omega Code*—were the amateur ravings of just any science fantasy writer then one would dismiss these paranoias, though that could well be a mistake. Northcott says:

> American premillennialists hope to bring forward the end of history by supporting a war in the Middle East which, as well as shoring up America's access to oil, is intended to secure the Jewish resettling of the Holy Land and the rebuilding of the Temple in Jerusalem.[21]

Northcott is convinced of the connection between White House Neocons and American premillennialists, but this may be partly a result of the Marxist-inflected brand of his Christian thinking.

But back to Buck. Nicholae takes him to the roof of a skyscraper looking out over a big city, and in a scene reminiscent of the one in which John Milton offers Kevin Lomax a partnership in his law firm, Nicholae offers Buck a key media job. Buck negotiates on the terms and Nicholae says "Do we have a deal?" He gestures over the expanse of city behind him: it is the Devil offering Christ the world from the tower. Buck wants his first assignment to be the signing of the peace treaty with Israel, but is told instead that he is covering the momentous announcement from Ben Judah. Nicholae meanwhile is backtracking on the no religion thing, deciding instead to create a single religion for the whole world. The word "Global" now appears more and more in the film: it is the word, it seems, that most easily triggers American paranoia. But all the threads are taking us to Jerusalem, and it seems that Rabbi Tsion Ben Judah has written a speech claiming that Nicholae is the Messiah. Ben Judah was originally going to announce that Jesus Christ was the Messiah, but his speech had been rewritten for him by Nicholae. Buck finds Rabbi Judah and persuades him to visit the Wailing Wall with him, where he believes that two prophets breathing fire will persuade him out of his allegiance to Nicholae. Miraculously circumventing armed guards with orders to shoot, they approach the prophets.

In another astonishing scene, this time of the most extraordinary cultural arrogance, the prophets lecture the learned rabbi on Jesus as the onlybegotten Son of "God." "For God so loved the world that he gave his one and only Son, that whoever believes in Him will not perish, but have everlasting life. For God did send his Son into the world not to condemn the world, but to save the world through Him." The rabbi asks hesitantly: "And the name of the Son?" The prophets respond: "Christ Jesus," at which Buck smiles smugly in heartfelt religiosity. The guards suddenly wake from their trance and pour machine gun fire into the prophets, but the bullets go straight through them, and they respond with roaring fires that consume the soldiers. Nicolae has cut the live transmission, so the world remains ignorant of this astounding moment, and all hinges on whether the rabbi will deliver his speech as scripted by Nicholae or will instead announce that Jesus is the Messiah. The world's greatest religious scholar (odd that he wasn't a Muslim or a Buddhist, but there you go) now announces to the world that "The Bible has given clear prophecies that could be fulfilled by only one person in the entire human race. Based on 456 messianic passages and 558 references from the most ancient biblical writings, there are 109 distinct prophecies of the Messiah.... There is much speculation that the Messiah indeed walks amongst us today." The suspense is killing. The rabbi goes on to list the qualities of the Messiah, as we see Nicholae nodding in agreement in his executive plane. Yes, he was born to a rare bloodline. Yes, he was pierced but had no bones broken. Yes, he was in Egypt as a child. But his face darkens as Ben Judah suddenly lists those requirements that Nicholae plainly cannot fulfill: to be born in Bethlehem and to have been resurrected. Nicholae orders the transmission cut, but it is too late: the whole world hears the astounding news. Yes, the Messiah was Jesus Christ! Buck congratulates the rabbi, who is still wearing his Jewish skullcap, the sign of his Judaic faith.

The second film ends with Nicholae throwing a tantrum in his jet, while Buck returns to his church and rejoices. In the third film a new American President, Gerald Fitzhugh, answers to Nicholae in what can only be an image representing the deepest paranoid fears of Christian fundamentalists: American power subordinated to the U.N. Secretary General. In fact all power now resides with the "Global Community" or GC, led by Nicholae, and the Christians have become a persecuted underground, reminiscent of the martyr church under Roman law, hidden in the Catacombs. The new U.S. president is curiously hands-on, personally interrogating the arrested Buck over his possession of forbidden "hate literature"—the Bible (an inadvertent double irony for the more tough-minded humanist). Nicholae as the "Beast of Revelation" is aiming to wipe out the Christians with a deadly virus (a plot element in common with *The X-Files*), and Fitzhugh is gradually convinced by Buck that he must stop him. In the very moment that Fitzhugh shoots Nicholae with a porcelain gun smuggled through metal detectors, World War Three breaks out. Nicholae forces the President through mind control to strangle himself, and then hurls him out of a tower building. But he survives the fall, and Nicholae asks himself "That's not humanly possible, is it?" Of course not: it's the power of Jesus.

A little later the President, alone in the ruins of the White House, is then properly converted by Buck. By taking Jesus into his heart he is able to return to Nicholae's headquarters and, made invisible by his faith, he gets past the guards and confronts the Antichrist. A bolt of lightning descends from the heavens and destroys them both: the Antichrist and the craven President of the United States of America who had obeyed his orders. The joy of the Christians, and their total triumph, is sealed when they discover that their communion wine is the antidote to the virus.

So, millions disappear in the Rapture; the Secretary General of the United Nations is the Antichrist; the world's leading Jewish scholar confirms that Jesus is the Messiah; and communion wine is the antidote to a deadly virus. The films show what Americans fear most: the United Nations, disarmament, a global currency and world peace. How can any educated person, on either side of the Atlantic, entertain such nonsense? Yet we need to take this fantasy seriously. Firstly, as already pointed out, the books behind the films are best-sellers. Secondly, a study by an American national survey research company called McLaughlin & Associates shows that 42 percent of all Americans agree with the statement: "Events such as the rebirth of the State of Israel, wars and instability in the Middle East, recent earthquakes, and the tsunami in Asia are evidence that we are living in what the Bible calls the Last Days."[22] It also shows that 52 percent of all Americans agree with the statement: "The rebirth of the State of Israel in 1948 and the return of millions of Jews to the Holy Land after centuries in exile represent the fulfillment of Biblical prophecies." Interestingly the proportion holding these beliefs is highest amongst female Republican black Americans on low incomes living in the South of the U.S., rising to some 75 percent; while the proportion holding these beliefs is lowest amongst male Democrat white Americans on high incomes living in the Northern states, dipping to 16 percent. Only 8 percent of American Asians hold these views, not surprising as their cultures (in the *far* East at least) have no apocalyptic traditions.

From a European perspective all this is incomprehensible. The secular mind assumes that these beliefs were all abandoned in the 18th century, and can find no purchase on the questions that they raise today. But it might provide some insight into the American mind to consider the actor Kirk Cameron, who plays Buck Williams. Cameron is a believer. He was born in 1970, placing him in his late twenties and early thirties throughout the making of the films, and has clearly undergone a conversion experience at some point. His promotional video (included in the DVD of the last film in the trilogy) promotes *The Way of the Master* Christian website. The video starts with an account of a fireman found guilty of grave neglect of duty as a house burned down, killing its occupants. The analogy is with those who are "saved" but stand by idly as those who aren't unwittingly enter the flames of hell. "Who do you know who isn't saved?" says the graphic titles, and Cameron, looking straight into the camera, presses home the point that there is little time left.

Now, one may have sympathy with those who have found religion in one way or another: so far, so good. But it seems clear that since the Western Enlightenment of the eighteenth century, religion and intelligence have rather parted company, and the *Left Behind* films demonstrate this well. It is not suggested that Cameron is stupid: he is clearly a gifted young actor, and is pursuing his goals with clarity and determination. But there is no Western tradition of applying the usual faculties of critical thinking to religion, and so inspired people like Cameron are free to promote the most ridiculous of ideas. One can imagine him as a young Christian actor, fired by a conversion that may have taken place quite recently, thoroughly enjoying his role in *Left Behind*. He plays a major part in the destruction of the Antichrist. He helps the world's greatest Jewish scholar to understand, after two millennia of denial, that Jesus is the Messiah. And, most touchingly, he sits down quietly with the President of the United States of America in the ruins of the White House and helps the man take Jesus into his heart. Unlike the fireman who stood by and did nothing, Cameron, in his role as Buck Williams, helps to save the soul of the U.S. President and ensure the triumph of Christendom. What could be more appealing?

Bizarre religious beliefs are not of course unique to America. But the American version of apocalyptic and millenarian doctrines brings something unique to these ancient Western prophecies. Europe on the whole does not provide a hospitable ground for the public promotion of such ideas, religion having been relegated to the private sphere and its ideas fiercely deconstructed by the secular mainstream. We saw that when Sharon in *The Rapture* was still skeptical she said of Christianity: "Why does the God of some little country on the Mediterranean have to be the God for everyone? Isn't that a little arrogant?" This bigger perspective acts as a corrective on the wilder claims of religion, or at least it ought to. But America is very different from Europe, as the case of Darwinism shows: it is against the law in many American states to teach this "doctrine" in schools, especially in the South. Even the popular *Harry Potter* books have been the subject of over 3,000 attempts by Christians to have them banned from public libraries.[23] This is not because they show secular skepticism, or promote scientific views, but because they are about wizardry, a topic unacceptable to Christians.

The secular version of the Apocalypse is any vision of the future in which civilization is wiped out: we could call this "Armageddon" to distinguish it. For mainstream America, where it is not inclined to the Christian version of the Apocalypse, a nuclear-, disease-, or war-induced Armageddon is a widespread fear which many films address. The *Terminator* films and *Twelve Monkeys* are good examples where a devastated future sends a character (robot in the first case, man in the other) back in time to try to change the course of history. Another series that deals, like the *Terminator* films, with an Armageddon created by robots or computers gone bad, is the *Matrix*. This trilogy will be discussed later, in the context of Virtual Reality, but first some more American films in which Armageddon appears in various guises.

Apocalypse Now

Rambo: First Blood represents an American aggression that is ultimately comicbook: Rambo defeats a small army and blows up a town single-handed, or rather with ridiculous phallic weapons. His madness is the tragedy of a soldier who has been through hell, only to find that his country meanwhile decides the war he fought was pointless. In *Apocalypse Now* we find a different portrait of the madness that was Vietnam, painted through the key protagonists, Colonel Kurtz (Marlon Brando) and Captain Willard (Martin Sheen). Willard is sent upriver to Cambodia to terminate the mission of Kurtz, a green beret gone mad, who is worshipped by the locals as a savage god. It is the American version of *Lord of the Flies* (though its actual literary source is Conrad's *Heart of Darkness*), and owes much to European nihilism, including that of T. S. Eliot.

On the riverboat journey we are presented with a cameo of the American madness at war: the crew inspects a sampan apparently occupied only by farmers, their livestock, and their produce. Unwilling at first, a soldier is shouted at repeatedly by the boat's captain to investigate every basket, under the insane eye of the crew's machine-gunner. Twitchy-fingered, the tension escalates as the farmers are roughly pushed aside; the Americans scream orders at each other. As the soldier is made to investigate an overlooked container a woman on the boat lurches back to protect its contents, and the sampan is suddenly raked by machine-gun fire. The woman had merely turned to protect a puppy sleeping in the container, but becomes the only survivor of the maelstrom, lying injured amidst her massacred family. The soldier demands they take her to a hospital, but Willard points his gun at her head and then coolly shoots her dead. "I told you not to stop for inspections," he tells the boat's captain: his mission takes priority. The Americans, as part of their campaign against the Taliban in Afghanistan, dropped bombs on wedding ceremonies because of the same nervous irritability. Men, women and children were blown to bits for no reason at all. Whoops! Sorry! This is an American refrain heard in too many countries, alas.

It is Marlon Brando's Kurtz who is the most memorable creation of *Apocalypse Now*, the American insanity writ large in a jungle setting of savagery and idol-worship. Like Hannibal Lecter in *Silence of the Lambs* or John Doe in *Seven*, Kurtz is *aesthetically* insane: he reads from T. S. Eliot's poem "The Hollow Men." His Armageddon is removed from its Western monotheistic roots, and will end "with a whimper, not a bang." He reads not just Eliot, but from *The Golden Bough*, a classic piece of white man's nonsense with respect to "idol-worship" and the older Nature religions.[24] "He took his orders from the jungle anyway," reflects Willard.

Kurtz is Nietzschean in his respect of the perfect will to power, the "diamond" genius that kills inoculated infants as enemies. Kurtz has gone mad through the contradictions of war: "We train young men to drop fire on people, but their commanders won't allow them to write *fuck* on their airplanes, because it's obscene." This simple line sums up Kurtz's anger, but really (one might suggest) it is the anger of Francis Ford Coppola, the co-writer and director of the film, an anger on behalf of a generation of anti–Vietnam war protesters. Willard is by now as insane as his quarry, and ritually kills Kurtz. Afterwards he turns over the pages of a think-tank paper written by Kurtz entitled: "The Role of Democratic Force in the Underdeveloped World." Scrawled in red ink across one of its pages Kurtz has written the epitaph for all American military insanity: "Drop the Bomb—Exterminate them All!"

Coppola vividly presents a secularized version of the Apocalypse in his film, and as such visualizes an aspect of the American madness, but it is fair to question its attack on militarism generally. One can agree with Medved that Hollywood's representation of war is often unrealistic and slanted against the service personnel and their officers who risk so much for their country. Nevertheless, the points he makes under the heading "Antipathy to the Military"[25] are not as telling as arguments from more Left-leaning sources, such as Willem M. Hagen and Leonard Quart, both of whom consider the film from historical and political perspectives. Hagen points out that the film fails to convey what most people imagined Vietnam to be like because its artistry was too high: "One is left with an aesthetic of intensities."[26] Quart comments on Coppola and similar directors: "... in the seventies these were directors who substituted inventive metaphors and symbols and startling images for an ability to penetrate the heart of darkness which was Vietnam."[27] Perhaps the reason that the film failed to impress either the Right or the Left is again the distinction between the terrible, and its ability to invoke pity and fear, and the merely grotesque. Kurtz is obviously grotesque, but cannot be understood as the foil for Willard, as Willard himself is from the start a character beyond mere "frailty and error": he is a grotesque in the making.

The Birds

In the dark side of the American imagination the Apocalypse, or Armageddon, or any number of disasters is always around the corner. In Alfred Hitchcock's *The Birds* it is Nature that turns and menaces humanity, and it is not long before mention of the Old Testament is brought into the drama. In the scene where Melanie is trying to alert the outside world to the attacks of the birds on the school, a drunk soon spots what's going on:

> DRUNK: It's the end of the world!
> HELEN: What's this about the school?
> DEKE: Bunch of crows attacked the school, Helen.
> DRUNK: It's the end of the world. "Thus saith the Lord God to the mountains, and to the hills, to the rivers and to the valleys; Behold, I, even I, will bring a sword upon you, and I will destroy your high places."
> HELEN: The Lord's not destroying anything, Jason.
> DRUNK: "In all your dwelling places, the cities shall be laid waste, and the high places shall be laid waste!" *Ezekiel*, Chapter Six.
> HELEN: "Woe unto them that rise up early in the morning that they may follow strong drink."
> DRUNK: *Isaiah*, Chapter 5. It's the end of the world.
> MELANIE: Yes, all right, I'll wait for you. Good-by. (she hangs up)
> MRS. BUNDY: (laughing) I hardly think a few birds are going to bring about the end of the world.
> MELANIE: (turning to her) These weren't a few birds.

The Birds was released in 1963, so it is interesting to note that in that period of heightened modernism two characters can still quote the Old Testament so fluently, a continuing feature of American cultural life that is evidenced again in *The Devil's Advocate*, where Lomax and his mother trade quotations. That would have been much less likely in Britain and Continental Europe either in the sixties or now. It shows again that the Apocalyptical is simply part of the language in America, just as much in the mainstream 1960s as it is amongst millennial fundamentalists in the 1990s.

The Terminator and End of Days

Arnold Schwarzenegger found his métier in the *Terminator* films, playing a robot sent from the future to save the world from a machine-made Armageddon, or to prevent human interference with it. The first *Terminator* film shows a future where machines relentlessly hunt down the human

Resistance—a secular version of the Apocalypse where "Judgment," as it were, has been made: humans are irredeemable and need to be exterminated like vermin. They live in underground warrens, emerging to fight the death-ray robot patrols, and must travel back in time to prevent the leader of the Resistance or his mother being murdered by time-traveling robots. The image of this underground resistance is, quite possibly, a retelling of the Masada story as mentioned earlier—a retelling that crops up in many films. These include *Soldier* (1998), *Extreme Measures* (1996), *Demolition Man* (1993), all the *Terminator* films, and all the *Matrix* films. The common factors are a community under siege including men, women and children; a badly clothed and badly fed population (in *Demolition Man* they eat ratburgers); a badly armed but brave collective non-hierarchy; an underground environment of city tunnels or mountain caves; and an enemy that is relentless and like a machine. In the *Terminator* series the enemy *are* machines; in *Demolition Man* and *Extreme Measures* they are the police. Also required is a cute unsmiling kid in shabby brown clothes who watches wide-eyed and learns from the hero conveniently parachuted into the situation (as in *Soldier* or *Demolition Man*). In *Aliens* (1986), the unsmiling urchin is a little girl, the sole survivor of her community: a direct parallel with the surviving children of Masada.

But Arnold Schwarzenegger is not content with merely secular visions of Armageddon; he also features in a film called *End of Days*, which returns to an explicitly Biblical vision of the Apocalypse (perhaps also a return to his roots in Catholic Austria). *End of Days*, like *The Rapture*, is poor film-making, though it is mainstream mind-rot as opposed to a personal and obscure investigation of the issue. The very term "End of Days" is part of the language of Christian millenarianism, as is "Last Days," "Revelation," and "The Rapture." In the film *End of Days*, Schwarzenegger must prevent the devil from siring a new Antichrist who will destroy humanity. He has to protect a young woman (marked out by a sign in the heavens) both from the Catholic hierarchy who want her dead, and from the sexual attentions of the devil. Copulation must take place in the final hour of the 20th century, on the eve of the new millennium, making this film more directly millenarian than other Apocalypse films. Where the *Terminator* films are amongst the best in their genre, *End of Days* combines pointless over-the-top trademark "Arnie" violence with titillatory pseudo-occultist claptrap. Deservedly, the film bombed.

The Apocalypse and Critical Distance

The films in this chapter were not selected on artistic merit, but to demonstrate how apocalypticism and its secular derivatives feature in the imaginative life of America. Nevertheless it is worth looking at the issue of critical distance in these films, given that they contain transgressive material and are certainly supposed to have emotional intensity. *The Rapture* is unusual in that it is intended as a satire, that is as an attack on its central idea, but is taken seriously by many religious commentators; except Medved, who expects his readers to find the synopsis of it enough to condemn it, along with Tolkin's response to the charge that he was unfairly attacking religion: "'It's not antireligion,' he answered, 'It's anti–God.'"[28] One could argue that its protagonist Sharon is brought low by frailty and error, but the implausibility of her transitions—poor emotional bracketing, one could say—suggest that Tolkin was in a hurry to polemicize against religion, rather than leave open the possibility that religion as a whole might be sound despite the excesses of a few. In Medved's words, "Throughout the film Christian believers are portrayed as twitching zombies, with an obvious edge of madness behind their fervent beliefs." Having said this, it compares well with most of the remaining films in this section. Films like the *Left Behind* series, the *Omega Code* series and *The Late Great Planet Earth* make no pretense at critical distance, other than the pseudo-reflexivity remarked on earlier in the context of conspiracy theories. This wouldn't matter if these films circulated in a very small cultural ghetto, but it is in fact a large cultural ghetto ("ghetto" because it is insulated from constructive debate with other cultural strands). As Hendershot notes, mainstream criticism may nod to the conservative Christians, but they are "still dismissed as weird cultural outsiders." She adds: "... it is quite problematic to conceive of Christian apocalyptic belief as marginal to American culture."[29]

8

Native Americans
and Cultural Genocide

KEY FILMS: *Little Big Man, Dead Man*
ADDITIONAL FILMS: *Natural Born Killers,*
U-Turn, Thunderheart, Broken Arrow,
The Outlaw Josey Wales, Dances with Wolves

At the heart of a very specific American paranoia is a collective guilt about the virtual genocide practiced on the Native Americans. This theme appears remarkably often in American cinema. The term "cultural genocide" is used by the Dalai Lama to describe the impact of the Chinese invasion of Tibet. It is clearly not a conventional or total genocide, because only a small proportion of the population were killed by the Chinese, but the destruction of Tibetan culture—which was deeply religious—was carried out wholesale, and intentionally. Similarly Native Americans have survived in some numbers after the various wars with the white man, but their culture was systematically targeted for eradication. Symbolic of this is the image of the needless slaughter of the Plains buffalo, or bison, in their millions, one of many extinct-tions or near-extinctions of animal species inflicted by the white man on North America.[1] (The passenger pigeon was hunted to total extinction, and the American bluebird nearly became extinct because of the introduction of European birds that took its habitat. In Hitchcock's *The Birds* a salesman in the café scene with the drunk insists: "Gulls are scavengers, anyway. Most birds are. Get yourselves guns and wipe them off the face of the earth!") Another Native Americans cultural target was their religion. The destruction of the buffalo had no cultural justification—other than the general plundering of natural resources by the white man—whereas the destruction of Native American religions had an obvious source in Western history: the extreme intolerance of Abrahamic religion towards the older, nature-orientated religions.

The link between the issue of the Native Americans and American paranoia is complex, though their increasingly positive presence in film prompted this complaint from Medved, discussing the film *At Play in the Fields of the Lord*, "although this line [in the film] equates Christianity with the superstitions of the naked and painted jungle dwellers, the rest of the movie treats native religion with far more respect than it accords any Western faith."[2] Medved is committed to the idea that "Western faiths"—by which he means, out of the three monotheisms, just Judaism and Christianity—are superior to Native American faiths, unaware of the concerted move amongst academics and beyond to study them seriously.[3] In Jacquelyn Kilpatrick's *Celluloid Indians—Native Americans and Film*, she says of much recent academic study: "Given the misuses to which Native American images have been put, these studies tend to have an irritated if not genuinely angry tone."[4] What is remarkable in her work—as a woman of Cherokee descent—is that she takes a more positive tone in regards to recent films portraying the Native American.

In fact there is a long tradition of what is known as the "revisionist Western" or anti–Western, where some or all the assumptions of the traditional American Western are overturned. Here we are particularly interested in the reversal of the traditional depiction of the Native American as bad and the white man as good. Early examples of this include *Broken Arrow*, released in 1950, which has a fine performance from James Stewart as Tom Jeffords, a man who strikes up a friendly relationship with the Indians in his quest to deliver the mail. Kilpatrick tells us that the film was made partly as resistance to McCarthyism,[5]—its writer Albert Maltz was blacklisted[6]—though the work more obviously cited in respect to communist paranoia in the 1950s is Henry Miller's *The Crucible*.[7] However, an early work like *Broken Arrow* still conforms to many stereotypes, and it is not until the films of the 1980s and 1990s that Kilpatrick finds a more truly sympathetic portrayal of the Native American, finding for example Cimino's *The Sunchaser* to be a "good film" and Jarmusch's *Dead Man* to be a "great film."[8] Another work that usefully traces this development is *The American Indian in Film* by Michael Hilger, who gives the "kindly eyes" of Old Lodge Skins (discussed below) as an example of the image of the Native American in film that dominates his imagination, though it is still a stereotype.[9] While this may be true, the value here of exploring these images is to investigate the *white* American mind.

A book on the American painter Jackson Pollock records that his Jungian analyst believed that Pollock's interest in Native American art and culture was to be understood and encouraged through Jung's dictum that "a colonizing people 'inherit' the racial memory of the natives they displace."[10] Is it possible that the progression from the early Native American stereotype in film to the revisionist, and sympathetic portraits of more recent times, is a further illustration of this dictum? And what if that "racial memory"—or rather the term that Jung later used, the "collective unconscious"—dwells in the American mind as guilt and paranoia? Pollock's paintings, used by the CIA during the height of cold war paranoia to promote American culture,[11] are an expression of an inspiration drawing on Native American art, coupled with raw American energy and creativity:[12] what if films like *Dead Man* and *Dances with Wolves* are part of that same psychic movement? If so, we reveal a uniquely American obsession.

We can find traces of this in widely disparate sources. For example Johnny Cash's 1964 album *Bitter Tears: Ballads of the American Indian* explored the plight of the Native Americans, including the story of Ira Hayes, a young Marine of Native American descent who participated in the flag raising on Iwo Jima. Hayes became an overnight celebrity, only to die in obscurity on the reservation where he was born. Robert Pirsig, author of *Zen and the Art of Motorcycle Maintenance*, devotes part of his second book to the idea that an important national characteristic of the American mind is shaped by the Native American heritage. The "Plains-talking" style of white Americans such as Woody Guthrie, Gary Cooper, John Wayne and Robert Redford has its source, according to Pirsig, in Native American culture. More than just a way of speaking, Pirsig suggests that "the Indians were the originators of the American style of life. The American personality is a mixture of European and Indian values."[13] Writing in the late 1980s Pirsig considers this mixture, and the Native American legacy as a whole, to be "the central internal conflict in America today."[14]

To show how the Native American issue highlights elements of the American madness, two key films have been chosen here: *Little Big Man*, directed by Arthur Penn, and *Dead Man* directed by Jim Jarmusch. *Little Big Man* (received by some as an indictment of the Vietnam war) is a film adaptation of the novel by Thomas Berger, and uses comedy to soften the blow of its often sharp satire, while *Dead Man* was written by Jarmusch himself as a more extreme indictment of the madness of the white man vis-à-vis the Indians. Other films touching on Native American issues that will be discussed include: *Natural Born Killers*, *U-Turn*, *Thunderheart*, *Broken Arrow*, *The Outlaw Josey Wales*, and *Dances with Wolves*.

Little Big Man

Little Big Man is the telling, to a young "politically correct" university researcher, of the life story of Jack Crabb, a very old man indeed. The story is so long and convoluted that it is not worth re-telling it here in its original sequence, other than to say that Crabb's life is intimately bound up with Native Americans; that he is adopted by Old Lodge Skins (played by actor Chief Dan George); and that he is a witness to Custer's last stand. Instead we focus on Custer, as representing the American madness that had as its target the Native American, and on Old Lodge Skins, as representing the Indians' own analysis of what is wrong with the white man. Michael Hilger agrees that "*Little Big Man* emphasizes the guilt and madness of white culture in its depiction of Merriwether, Hickok and Custer ..." (three principal white men in the film), and also adds that he considers the film to draw parallels with the American role in Vietnam.[15] Kilpatrick considers it the best received film of the Indian experience made in the sixties, seventies and eighties.[16] (Additionally, she considers the original Berger novel to be uniquely even-handed in its treatment of whites and Indians, and that it does a better job of making the Native American belief system comprehensible.)

The portrayal of Custer in a film comedy like *Little Big Man* is quite naturally a caricature, but one that is widely recognized as quintessentially American. Half way through the film Crabb (played by Dustin Hoffman) has realized that Custer is central to the disaster befalling the Native Americans around him. Although the Second Treaty of Fort Laramie in 1868 had, in effect, guaranteed the Indians exclusive possession of the Dakota territory west of the Missouri River, white miners in search of gold were settling in lands sacred to the Dakota Indians. Having decided that the occasional minor breach of the treaty in raids on white settlers by the Indians was sufficient justification to revoke the treaty wholesale, troops were sent in to clear the area of Native Americans. The first attempt ended in the disastrous Battle of the Little Bighorn, also known as Custer's last stand, after which the whole area was flooded with troops, forcing on the Indians a total surrender. Although Crabb doesn't yet know this sad unfolding of history, he decides to sneak up on Custer in his tent and kill him. Unfortunately his nerve fails him, and Custer turns to survey what to him is a worthless specimen. He knows Crabb and tells him that he won't hang him because: "Your miserable life is not worth a reversal of a Custer decision." Earlier he had intervened when his men had wanted to hang Crabb as a renegade, eliciting from Crabb a totally fictitious story justifying his presence amongst the Indians. Custer believed him, or wanted to believe him just to pull rank on his men, and then lectured them on how their "summary judgment" was mistaken, and how hard it is to admit to an error. So Crabb lives to make the attempt on Custer, and is spared again because Custer never makes a mistake, or at least never reverses a decision founded on his supposedly unerring judgment.

Later in the film Custer, again in spite of his men, takes Crabb on as a scout. He does so on the perverse logic that Crabb's advice would be more lies, this time designed to send him in the opposite direction of the Indians he wants to hunt down and kill. In an off-screen aside Crabb tells us that Custer's hate for the Indians and his ambition to be President of the United States had "combined on him" and made him determined to secure one more dramatic victory over the Indians. Custer intends to take the opposite of Crabb's advice, but Crabb knows this, and in a double reversal of logic tells him the truth. The outcome of Custer's arrogance and perversity (in the film at least) was the carnage of Custer's last stand, where every soldier, including Custer, was killed by the Indians. It is hard to convey in words the manner of Custer (played in the film by Richard Mulligan) but it perfectly represents the madness of the white man bent on destroying the Native Americans, and the personal madness of Custer's arrogant buffoonery, the end-product, in the film-maker's imagination at least, of Western civilization. Note that it is not suggested that Custer was like this in real life, merely that the film has constructed a certain type of character that is universally recognizable. Kilpatrick draws comparisons between Custer's portrayal here and the commanding officer of Fort Hayes in *Dances with Wolves*,[17] while Kolker draws the obvious parallel between Custer and Buffalo Bill (Paul Newman) in Robert Altman's *Buffalo Bill and the Indians*.[18]

But the greatest pleasure of *Little Big Man* is to see another performance by the Native American actor Chief Dan George. He also appears in Clint Eastwood's *The Outlaw Josey Wales* (another classically revisionist Western), and both by what he had to say, and by his manner in saying it, is mesmerizing. There is no better or more poignant contrast to the American madness than the Native American sanity, and Chief Dan George is amongst a number of actors who often appear in such films and who convey this so well (two others are Native American actors Graham Greene and Gary Farmer). This is not to say of course that the Native Americans have no madness unique to their own culture; of course they do, as do all cultures. But what is interesting is how often American filmmakers draw on the Native American sanity to highlight aspects of white American madness.

Jack Crabb is "adopted" fairly early on in the film by Old Lodge Skins, whom he addresses as "grandfather." Old Lodge Skins is a warrior of long standing, and is amongst the first of his tribe to recognize that the white man is here to stay. Also that he is insane. Throughout the film Old Lodge Skins reserves the term "human" only for the Native Americans. "Black white men," i.e. peoples of Afro-Caribbean descent, were placed in an ambiguous category, though they definitely weren't as mad as the white men. Jack Crabb has become an honorary Indian in the eyes of Old Lodge Skins, and therefore counted as a "human," and therefore not insane. But this is not a new idea, for example Carl Gustav Jung encountered it in the 1920s when he visited New

Mexico. He reported the following revelation in his autobiography *Memories, Dreams, Reflections*:

> I asked him [a Pueblo Indian] why he thought the whites were all mad.
> "They say that they think with their heads," he replied.
> "Why of course. What do you think with?" I asked him in surprise.
> "We think here," he said, indicating his heart.
> I fell into a long meditation. For the first time in my life, so it seemed to me, someone had drawn for me a picture of the real white man.[19]

This passage is most illuminating, as is the subsequent account that Jung gives of how his own self-image changed, and how his understanding of the colonial history of the West was placed in perspective. Chief Dan George, one could say, allows the white man to see himself through another culture, through eyes that are perceptive but also sympathetic. In his role as Old Lodge Skins one hears not only the intelligent script created for him by a revisionist white script-writer, but also his own true voice as a Native American actor: slow, patient, full of humor. Old Lodge Skins is friendly to the white man, despite his acute understanding of their madness. Even after white soldiers have raided their camp, killed many Indians, and left him blind, Old Lodge Skins retains his balance. Young Jack Crabb only slowly realizes the old man's condition, because Old Lodge Skins explains it in a curious way: that his wound had cut the "tunnel" through which light travels to the heart. His "eyes still see" but his heart no longer receives it. Note that Old Lodge Skins talks about the tunnel through which the light travels, or optic nerve as we would call it, as connected to the *heart*, not the brain. We consider this quaint, and anatomically incorrect, but the Pueblo Indian and Old Lodge Skins can't both be making the same mistake by accident. They are showing us a more ancient way of understanding the world, perhaps a truer one, which sees the centre of gravity of a human being as existing in the heart, not the head.

The conversation continues, with Jack Crabb overwrought at the suffering inflicted on his Indian friends. Old Lodge Skins reaches for an old trophy, a scalp, and explains to him:

> Do you see this fine thing? Do you admire the humanity of it? Because the Human Beings, my son, they believe everything is alive. Not only man and animals, but also water, earth, stone. And also the things from them, like that hair. The man from whom this hair came, he's bald on the other side, because I now own his scalp. That is the way things are. But the white men, they believe everything is dead: stone, earth, animals, and people, even their own people. If things keep trying to live, white men will rub them out.

The white man sees what he considers the essential Native American madness in this soliloquy: firstly the practice of taking scalps, and secondly the superstitious ideas that the dead enemy "lives" in some spirit world (and is portrayed, picturesquely, as bald). But Old Lodge Skins has hit on a key element of the white man's madness: the inability to conceive of all natural things as alive, of all natural things as a living interconnected whole.

After the carnage of Bighorn, Jack Crabb visits Old Lodge Skins for the last time. The old man, while content enough with the day's victory, knows that the game is up for him and his people. He tells Crabb that he wants to die in his own land where Human Beings are buried in the sky (in a similar ritual to, for example, that in Tibet). Crabb is naturally shocked and asks him why he wants to die, to which the old man responds that there is no other way to deal with the white man, you cannot get rid of them. Crabb has to acknowledge this fact, that there is an endless supply of the white man. Old Lodge Skins then invites Crabb up a small hill to the ceremonial burial ground, and stands facing out over the plains, chanting. He then invokes the sacred presence:

> Come out and fight. It is a good day to die. Thank you for making me a Human Being. Thank you for helping me to become a warrior. Thank you for my victories and for my defeats. Thank you for my vision and the blindness in which I saw further. You make all things and direct them in their ways, O Grandfather. And now, you have decided the Human Beings will soon walk a road ... that leads nowhere. I am going to die now, unless death wants to fight. And I ask you for the last time to grant me my old power to make things happen. Take care of my son here. See that he doesn't go crazy.

But in a moment of dignified comedy, the old man does not die, and has to accept his fate; to live on and watch his people hemmed in further—to watch the world lose its "centre," to watch the "Human Beings" walk a road to nowhere. We note also that he makes it clear that in his blindness he saw further, that his understanding deepened, or perhaps that the ancient shamanic skills of seeing into the spirit world sharpened in him. The text of these extracts, the mere written record of the words spoken by Chief Dan George in this film, only hints at the meaning that his voice and personality gives to them. They are deeply moving, and a reminder of the power of American cinema as a medium of transformation.

Dead Man

Dead Man, written and directed by Jim Jarmusch, stars Johnny Depp as a young man whose name happens to be William Blake, and Gary Farmer as a Native American called "Nobody." The film is another revisionist Western, but really it is in a class of its own. It is a film that allows the white man to see himself through the eyes of the Native American, but more than that: to somehow participate in his world, portrayed in the film as the target of deliberate destruction by the white man. It is the only Jarmusch film that deals with this subject, though Gary Farmer does appear again in a cameo in Jarmusch's *Ghost Dog—the Way of the Samurai*. In *Ghost Dog* Gary Farmer keeps pigeons, and when white gangsters shoot one, he simply repeats the line: "stupid fucking white men," which is taken directly from *Dead Man*.

That Kilpatrick, as half–Cherokee, and as critical as any commentator on stereotypical portraits of Native Americans in film, should rate *Dead Man* so highly is interesting, as other commentators have mixed feelings. Eric Wilson, whose quest to discover the "Gnostic" in film might make him well disposed to it, dismisses the film, saying "The hip western resembles the staid."[20] Gregory Salyer considers it to be "an ironic rumination upon sacrality, meaning and the future in light of mythology, technology and capitalism."[21] But Jarmusch himself does not consider it ironic; instead he wanted more directly to give the central Native American character complexity, instead of choosing between the two-dimensional polarity of early Westerns: brutal savage or noble savage.[22] Mary Katherine Hall, examines its credentials as revisionist Western, making the point that Jarmusch as a white man, however good his research and collaboration with Farmer, still makes films that serve a white audience.[23]

The film opens with William Blake on the long train ride from Cleveland to the city of Machine in the Wild West: he is starting a new job there. Each time he dozes off and wakes up again his fellow-passengers are replaced with rougher and rougher looking types. A man sitting next to him tells Blake not to expect anything in Machine except his own grave, and then points out: "Look. They're shooting buffalo." Jarmusch only shows the other passengers with their rifles at the window, firing away, but we know this to be a key madness of the white man in his determination to destroy the Native American. The same scene is illustrated more graphically in Kevin Costner's *Dances with Wolves*, when its hero stares in disbelief with the Indians he has joined at thousands of buffalo carcasses strewn across the plains. It was a deliberate Government policy, one we now regard as part of a deliberate genocide.

As his fellow-passenger predicted, the piece of paper promising Blake a job in Machine was worthless, and he runs into much worse trouble defending a young woman who has picked him up. As he rolls over in her bed he feels something hard under the pillow and pulls out a gun. "Why do you have this?" asks Blake. "Because this is America," is her reply. Her lover surprises them and shoots her through the chest. The bullet goes clean through her and lodges close to Blake's heart, and from now on he is dying. But first he manages to use the woman's gun on his assailant to shoot him dead, thus ensuring that a local posse will hunt him down through the rest of the film. Blake flees the town of Machine by night, and when dawn breaks he is found by a Native American called Xebeche,[24] who attempts to dig the bullet out of his chest with his knife. We are treated to the Indian's first monologue:

> Here's white man's metal next to your heart. I tried to cut it out, but it's too deep inside. A knife would cut your heart instead and release the spirit from within.... Stupid fucking white man.

But Xebeche is no saint, and gets mad when it appears that the white man has no tobacco. Meantime the wicked Mr. Dickinson, played by Robert Mitchum, is gathering together the meanest, nastiest posse of bounty hunters ever known to track down Blake. We return to Blake's new found Indian friend, who has prepared a poultice for his wound, still muttering "Stupid fucking white man." He chants a Native American song, presumably to invoke the spirits of healing. As night falls we see the posse set off in pursuit, and Xebeche engages with Blake in conversation. At one point he asks Blake: "Did you kill the white man who killed you?" Blake naturally responds that he is not dead. "What name were you given at birth, stupid white man?" "Blake. William Blake," he responds, and is astonished at the intensity of reaction this seems to create. Xebeche cannot believe that the white man's name is William Blake, but when Blake insists upon it, Xebeche takes it to mean that he is the great, dead, poet. This confusion is what drives the subsequent relationship between Blake and Xebeche, who tells him that Blake will now write his poetry in blood. He is now a killer of white men.

Xebeche soon reveals his own story, and why he is so obsessed with the white poet William Blake. He reveals that his name means "He Who Talks Loud, Saying Nothing," a name given to him by his own people after returning from England. Xebeche had been kidnapped by white soldiers, sold into slavery, but found that in England his ability to imitate his captors led them to giving him a white man's education. It was here that he encountered the "voice" of William Blake, a voice that spoke to him from the pages of a book in images he could understand. Somehow he made his way back to America, but his own tribe thought his story mere fiction, hence his name. So he prefers to be called "Nobody." Jarmusch is targeting almost every aspect of the white man's madness, and here he is mocking the desperation of Americans to be "somebody." As we have pointed out, the aggressive American competitiveness requires every citizen to strive for greatness, for success, or be a "loser." Even in 1876, when this film is set, Americans did not want to be losers, so Blake is astonished that Xebeche prefers to be called "Nobody."

Meantime the posse hunting down Blake are being portrayed by Jarmusch as collectively displaying every conceivable vice and madness known to man, including cannibalism. But Blake's image is on wanted posters throughout the region, and the posse gets worked up at Dickinson's betrayal:

he has offered them less than the reward money. The youngest of the posse gets shot dead by their leader Cole, the most determined of Blake's trackers, but Blake in the meantime is getting to kill a few more white men of his own. Jarmusch now takes us deeper into Indian territory, and into the world of Nobody. Blake watches him take peyote, but it is not even for William Blake, it is medicine to give the Native American sacred visions (prohibited to his Southern brothers by the "Spanish devils," we learn). Blake is hungry, but all that Nobody can tell him is that fasting is good for the vision quest, that the sacred spirits recognize those who fast. Nobody knows that Blake is dying, and he wants to give him a send-off in traditional fashion for this strange white man whose poetry so moved him, and which is now written in blood. Part of the preparations includes Nobody's own sacred rituals, and part includes the ritual painting of Blake's face. But Blake doesn't understand anything of Nobody's world, naturally. "You're a very strange man," he tells him, but in the morning Nobody is gone.

Blake is on his own now, weak with loss of blood, but warming to his new role as a killer of white men. Two marshals come across him: "You William Blake?" demands one of them, aiming his rifle at him. "Yes I am," comes the reply, and he adds: "Do you know my poetry?" Blake shoots them both, even murmuring a line of his namesake's poetry that he has learned from Nobody. A little later it is clear that Blake is taking on more of the Indian ways: he has lost his eyeglasses, and the diamond-shaped markings on his face place him better in the winter wilderness in which he travels. In one of the film's most moving scenes he discovers a recently dead fawn, and smears some of its blood on his forehead. He then lies down next to it on the ground, making clear the new bond he feels with the natural world, and his kinship with other dying creatures. As he drifts into sleep he watches the bare branches of the trees above him, framing the wild cloudy sky

But Blake is not to die with the fawn, and during the following night he comes across Nobody again, nearly shooting him by mistake. Next day they ride together, and Nobody explains to Blake what he is doing for him:

> I will take you to the bridge made of waters. The mirror. Then you will be taken up to the next level of the world. The place where William Blake is from. Where his spirit belongs. I must make sure that you pass back through the mirror at the place where the sea meets the sky.

Although Blake does not yet understand it, Nobody is planning a ritual sea-burial for him, such as is reserved for great warriors. They must first pass a white trading-post, which is the occasion for Jarmusch to point out to us more of the crimes committed by the white man against the Indians; and all the while they are being tracked by Cole. Blake is getting weaker all the time, and gets shot again as Cole gets close enough to fire on them. Nobody takes him down river in a canoe, passing Indian sacred territory, and further signs of the white man's slash and burn vendetta against the original inhabitants of the wilderness. A mature elk grazes on the bank; Nobody looks at it as if it were a sign; they pass a totem, and Blake looks at it, feeling the growing presence of the Indian consciousness around him. Nobody sings quietly all the while. Blake can barely walk as Nobody takes him into the settlement that they finally reach; he is absorbing the myriad foreign signs of a life that he as a white man was complicit in the destruction of.

He regains consciousness to find himself placed in the sacred vessel, a ceremonial canoe, with the artifacts appropriate to his final journey. Here is their last dialogue:

> NOBODY: I prepared your canoe with cedar boughs. It's time for you to leave now, William Blake. Time for you to go back to where you came from.
> BLAKE: You mean Cleveland?
> NOBODY: Back to the place where all the spirits came from ... and where all the spirits return. This world will no longer concern you.
> BLAKE: (holding up a twist of tobacco, smiling) Found some tobacco.
> NOBODY: The tobacco is for your voyage, William Blake.
> BLAKE: I don't smoke.
> NOBODY: Aho, William Blake.

Natural Born Killers and *U-Turn*

That the Native American "genocide" is deep within the American psyche is shown by how often the issue crops up in American films, not only revisionist Westerns, but in other genres too. Oliver Stone has twice made significant references to the Native American in films that have no semblance to a Western: in *Natural Born Killers*, and in *U-Turn*. In *Natural Born Killers* the young killers on the run (Mickey and Mallory) spend a night with a Navaho shaman, and kill him almost by accident: his is the only death that the couple ever expresses regret over, as Dawn Perlmutter points out.[25] Perhaps in Stone's mind, while all whites are implicated in the endemic mediafuelled violence of American society, the Native Americans are not. Mickey and Mallory stumble into the wooden dwelling of the old Indian and his grandson, and are initially polite, though anxious about the rattlesnakes that the old man handles. The old Native American is played by actor Russell Means, born an Oglala/Lakota Sioux Indian. He also appeared in *Last of the Mohicans*. (Means is politically active on behalf of his people, having founded the American Indian Movement,[26] and, interestingly, prefers the term "Indian" to the more politically correct "Native American.") In the film the old man sees the word "demon" light up on Mickey's chest, and also tells his grandson that Mallory is suffering from the "sad sickness." She is lost in a "world of ghosts"—or what we would call depression. Mallory understands that they themselves are the demons, beyond help, while Mickey, plagued in the night by his own nightmares, wakes up in a panic and shoots the old man. As he lies dying the old Indian tells us that twenty years earlier he had seen this demon coming in a dream, and was prepared for it. "I was waiting for you," he says in a moment reminiscent of Old Lodge Skins' resignation towards the destruction brought by the white man. Mallory screams at Mickey: "Bad, bad, bad, bad." He says it was an accident, but she tells him: "there are no accidents Mickey." He looks down in shame. "You are death," she yells at him, "you killed life! He fed us. He took us in there." "Well," acknowledges Mickey slowly, "that is a harsh indictment." And it is just about the only indictment of their murder spree that we hear from them in the film, while Dawn Perlmutter suggests that the old man's death leads to their "redemption."[27]

In *U-Turn* a character known just as the "Blind Man" (Jon Voight) plays a central role as the least crooked of the characters, though ultimately even he cannot be trusted. It is not explicitly stated, but the Blind Man appears to be a Native American. Jon Voight appeared alongside Native American actor Graham Greene in *The Last of His Tribe* (based on the life of Ishi, the last Yahi Indian), and his experience there may have helped make his delivery in *U-Turn*, coupled with the film's sharp script, very believable. *U-Turn* stars Sean Pen as Bobby Cooper, a small-time crook stranded in a small Southwest town after his car breaks down. He has to beat a deadline to pay back big-time crooks the money he owes them, or he will lose more fingers, and he is naturally desperate to get going again. He gets involved with Grace (Jennifer Lopez), whose husband (Nick Nolte) offers him cash to kill her. But they all, including the local Sheriff, double-cross each other until the bitter end. It is down to the Blind Man to provide a moral reference by which the scheming betrayal of the major characters can be juxtaposed. Cooper, having been told by a villainous mechanic that his car will take yet longer to fix, is nursing a soda in the town square, not knowing what to do next. Stone runs past us a kaleidoscope of images that represent small town dereliction and small-town mentality. It is bright sunlight; Cooper's brow is furrowed; he is sitting on a bench under an awning; his left hand still bandaged after the loss of the first finger. The Blind Man, trailing all the necessary junk of the derelict, comes up to him and they engage in conversation, but Cooper is not convinced, telling him that he sees a lot for a blind man:

> BLIND MAN: Just 'cos I ain't got eyes, don't mean I can't see. I see pretty good. You know we're all just eyes in the same head. Everything is everything.
> COOPER: (sharply) What?

BLIND MAN: Everything is nothing too.

COOPER: Yeah, well, maybe one day I'll have time to sit on a corner and spout wise.

BLIND MAN: Think you'll live that long, cocksucking motherfucker? ... Everybody's got a mother. You know that. Can't you understand that you don't rip up the mother? The mother earth and you just take everything? It's like the Cracker-Jack box, "the more you eat, the more you want."

COOPER: I've got things to do.

BLIND MAN: You don't see me stopping you.... (holds up a tin mug) Ain't you got a little something for the infirm?

COOPER: I'm a little short today. I'll catch you next time.

BLIND MAN: (pause) Your lies are old, but you tell 'em pretty good.

Now, granted, some of the Blind Man's ramblings are rather unedifying, while the more mystical points could just be "cod" philosophy[28] (the issue of cod philosophy in American film is discussed in the section on the New Age). But what is most striking in this exchange is the old man's parting shot. His philosophy was spurned, and he didn't even get some small change out of the encounter, but there is a gentle humor in his last remark (not adequately represented in the bare text of the script). The average down-and-out white man might well accuse the ungenerous passer by of lying, when told "I'm a bit short today." But, one might suggest, he is more than likely to follow it with a stream of invective; a "fuck you" dismissal which permits of no further exchange. What the Blind Man does, which is perhaps typical of many races that are at heart gentler than the white man, is to soften his accusation of lying with the admiration of doing it well. It makes him morally generous to Cooper, because the Blind Man implies that he himself is also an accomplished liar, or at least tries to be. It is absurd to make a generalization from a single moment in a film, but the aggression shown by the Blind Man is a gentler aggression, one that does not make *competition* so brutally stark the first and last resort as in the case of the American madness. The Native American as a warrior is no less capable of breathtaking brutality than an American: even to put it this way round is perhaps unfair. But there is something else at work which mitigates the aggression of the warrior, which balances it out, and that is the continued recognition of a web of relations in which ultimately the opponent of today *must* be honored as the friend of tomorrow, or of yesterday. In *U-Turn*, the Blind Man reaches out to Cooper with such a friendship, for no other reason than their common humanity. No other character in the film does that. In describing the laconic understated style of white actors like John Wayne or Robert Redford, Robert Pirsig says "... there was a warmth beneath the surface that you couldn't point to the source of."[29] Yet Pirsig is convinced that the source of this warmth is the Native American spirit; perhaps Stone drew on the same source in constructing the personality of the Blind Man.

Thunderheart

For the moment we are not however looking at the alleged sanity of the Native American, but at the alleged insanity of the white American. One of the last battles between Native Americans and U.S. Government forces took place at Wounded Knee, South Dakota, and there is now a memorial museum there. The United States government broke an earlier treaty regarding the Great Sioux Reservation of South Dakota, after Sitting Bull refused to cooperate in its sale.[30] The Reservation, an area that formerly encompassed the majority of the state, was "broken into small inlands around which would rise the flood of white immigration," which was in accordance with the government's clearly stated policy of "breaking up tribal relationships" and "conforming Indians to the white man's ways, peaceably if they will, or forcibly if they must."[31] Once on the much reduced reservations, tribes were separated into family units on small plots, forced to farm, raise livestock, and send their children to boarding schools that marginalized Native American traditional culture and language.

This is a good description of the process of cultural genocide, that is the forcible destruction of a culture's way of life, which in this case was intimately bound up with hunting. (The land allocated to the Native Americans in this case was unsuitable to farming.) The film *The Education of Little Tree* illustrates how Native American children were forced into Christian schools and exclusively educated in the culture of the white man. Little Tree is even given the name "Joshua" to deny his origins; the name chosen at the whim of his headmaster. A journalist called L. Frank Baum, later famous as the author of *The Wonderful Wizard of Oz*, wrote in the *Aberdeen Saturday Pioneer*:

> The Pioneer has before declared that our only safety depends upon the total extermination of the Indians. Having wronged them for centuries, we had better, in order to protect our civilization, follow it up by one more wrong and wipe these untamed and untamable creatures from the face of the earth. In this lies future safety for our settlers and the soldiers who are under incompetent commands. Otherwise, we may expect future years to be as full of trouble with the redskins as those have been in the past.[32]

In the film *Thunderheart*, directed by Michael Apted, the question of Wounded Knee is central to the story. A young white FBI officer Ray Levoi (played by Val Kilmer) is quarter–Indian, and, during his assignment to a reservation has flashbacks of the Wounded Knee massacre. After a raid in which he had attempted to protect the Indians sought by the FBI, he is joined in his car by Grandpa Sam Reaches, played by Native American actor Ted Thin Elk. He is an old man, reminiscent in his manner of Chief Dan George. Sam believes that the young Ray has been sent to help them and tells him that his people had been shot down at Wounded Knee because they were Ghost Dancing. Amongst the three hundred men, women and children killed by white soldiers as they ran for the "Stronghold" in the mountains was a holy man called Wakiyan Shante, Thunderheart. Grandpa tells Ray:

> It is his blood, the same blood that was spilled on the grass and snow at Wounded Knee, that runs through your heart like a buffalo. Thunderheart has come, sent here to a troubled place to help his people. That's what I am told. (chants) Ho Hecetu Yelo. Run. Run for the Stronghold, Thunderheart, run. The soldiers are coming.

Now it is bad enough that the Native Americans suffered a deliberate attempt at cultural genocide. And that Frank Baum, the creator of that all-American cultural landmark *The Wizard of Oz*, even demanded actual genocide, (though of course Baum was far from alone in his opinions). But many would now object to the reversal which sees white Americans appropriating Native American culture for the sake of Hollywood film-making. Hence it is a delicate issue that young Ray, in the film *Thunderheart*, is presented as in some way a reincarnation of a Lakota holy man, or shaman. Towards the finale of the story, Ray is driving with Walter Crow Horse (played by Graham Greene), and they start a conversation about Grandpa Sam Reaches. Crow Horse tells Ray that Grandpa's visions are strong, which prompts Ray to ask about visions. Crow Horse tells him that they can come in dreams, or during sickness, in the sweat lodge, or in the vision quest. Ray hesitantly tells him that he had a dream of being run down with other Indians and being shot in the back by white soldiers, and that he had driven past the place where it had happened. He had *seen* it.

CROW HORSE: Saw what?

RAY: The Wounded Knee memorial.

CROW HORSE: (turns in disbelief) You were running with the old ones. At The Knee?

RAY: It was just a dream

CROW HORSE: Who the hell are you man?

RAY: What do you mean?

CROW HORSE: You had yourself a vision. A man waits a long time to have a vision. Might go his whole lifetime and never get one. And along comes some instant Indian with a fucking Rolex and a brand-new pair of shoes, goddam FBI to top it all up, has himself a vision.

RAY: Sorry.

CROW HORSE: Ah, maybe it was just one of them, what do ya call 'em, fitful dreams?

RAY: Yeah. Fitful dreams.

CROW HORSE: (pause) Fitful dreams, horseshit. You had yourself a vision.

RAY: What the hell do you want me to do?

Broken Arrow, The Outlaw Josey Wales, and Dances with Wolves

There are of course many more films, including a whole series of revisionist Westerns, which paint a portrait of the American madness as seen through the eyes of the Native American. As mentioned earlier, *Broken Arrow* is perhaps the first of these. It was directed by Delmer Daves and released in 1950, starring James Stewart as Tom Jeffords, the man who talked to the Indians as his equal. He represents what could have been an American sanity, a simple incomprehension as to why these two races could not co-exist, but is the odd one out in a climate of fear and hatred. He almost gets lynched for being an Indian-lover.

The Outlaw Josey Wales is a much later offering, released in 1976, based on the book *Gone to Texas* by Forrest Carter, and directed by Clint Eastwood. As mentioned earlier, it contains a fine performance from Chief Dan George as an aging Native American who is losing his touch: first Josey Wales sneaks up on him, and then a young Native American woman does the same thing. But the dignity and humor with which Chief Dan George protests at this affront to his "power" is what is so endearing and which suggests a uniquely Native American sensibility. It poses the question: how come so many white American filmmakers keep drawing on this stereotype? And no film is perhaps more famous for doing so than Kevin Costner's *Dances with Wolves*. Costner and Eastwood in these two films play white men who have "gone over" to the Indians, or at least accept them as essentially good, because they have found in their own race only betrayal. In effect then we see the white man's madness, not so much through the eyes of the Native American, but through white men whose worldview has been changed by the Indian. Kilpatrick sums up the dangers in this:

> The main flaw of *Dances with Wolves*, however, remains the problem of appropriation of identity; John Dunbar is the white narrator of an Indian existence who, when the white men become so loathsome to him he can no longer stand being identified as one of them, shouts "I am Dances with Wolves!"[33]

Forrest Carter himself is an interesting case: born as Asa Earl Carter in 1925, he was a speechwriter for segregationist Governor George Wallace of Alabama. Under his pen-name Forrest Carter, he published Westerns and a fake autobiography, mentioned earlier: *The Education of Little Tree*, in which he falsely claimed to have grown up with Cherokee grandparents. What do we make of a man like Carter, who on the one hand belonged to white supremacist organizations, including the Ku Klux Klan and the White Citizens' Council, and who on the other seems to have undergone a transformation in later years into a promoter of Native American culture? It was only after his death that it was realized that they were one and the same man. Another example of a white man who took on a fake Native American identity is the famous case of Grey Owl. He was born in Hastings, England as Archibald Stansfeld Belaney, married an Iroquois woman Gertrude Bernard, and made considerable service to the cause of conservation. (There is also film version of his life, directed by Richard Attenborough, and starring Pierce Brosnan in the title role.)

The history of white America's "cultural genocide" against the Native American is nothing new on the world stage, it is just recent, well-documented, and to a small degree a living wound in the American mind. It can also be understood, as Benshoff and Griffin point out, as part of American identity building after independence: "... some defined American identity as 'not British' but even more quickly and repeatedly, American national identity was conceived of as 'not Indian.'"[34] But white English-speaking America also ruthlessly shut out the French and their culture, as is shown starkly in the film *Southern Comfort*. More than that, there is a wholesale betrayal of Nature as well as those cultures, like the Native American and the Louisiana Creole of the South, which live closer to Nature. Films such as *Southern Comfort*, *Deliverance*, and *The Blair Witch Project* all speak of this retreat from the natural world, the world which was at the heart of Native American consciousness. Though there is not space here to go into this issue, this retreat from Nature is another significant corner of the contemporary madness, also present in the American mind.

Having talked up the value of the revisionist Western in highlighting a peculiar madness of the American mind, it is worth pointing out that the critical distance possessed by these films is contested. Both the cultural conservatives, such as Medved, and the more left-leaning critics, such as Quart, find that the Native American in these films is romanticized as a polemical tool. The revisionist Western is not propaganda on the scale of the apocalyptical films discussed in the previous section, but perhaps a similar mechanism is at work: the subject matter is too cathected in the American mind to allow for real critical distance.

9

The New Age and Narcissism

KEY FILMS: *I Heart Huckabees, Waking Life*
ADDITIONAL FILMS: *What the Bleep Do
We Know!?, Indigo, Zelig*

In America the psychoanalytical culture segues into the New Age: a mishmash of shallow occultisms and non–Christian millenarianism. It is deeply self-absorbed, symbolized by its fascination with "synchronicity" or "coincidences"—the bible of which is the novel *The Celestine Prophecy*1 and its surrounding industry. One should not however paint a completely negative portrait of the New Age, as it is a spiritual movement existing outside of mainstream religion, and has its origins in Hellenic rather than Hebraic spirituality, and also in new spiritual movements at the turn of the 19th century such as Theosophy and Anthroposophy. Its existence is made possible by the secular guarantees of religious freedom in America, but it shares with the religious right a distrust of critical thinking. This leads however to the opposite of religious dogmatism: an uncritical acceptance of almost any spiritual idea. At its best the New Age presents a vision of open enthusiasm for the spiritual life, free of religious dogmatism and prejudice. At its worst it is both religiously and politically naïve. And it is very American.

Leonard Quart, in considering American films of the 1970s and how they represent American society says of that period: "The public began to distance itself from politics, expressing only cynicism about the rhetoric and programs that politicians proposed. By 1973 it was clear that the political passions and polarization of the sixties had died, replaced by a general sense of political alienation and apathy." He goes on to cite cultural critics such as Christopher Lasch and Tom Wolfe who "had called the 1970s a narcissistic era, the 'me decade,'" and adds: "To some extent this collective narcissism was partially brought on by the failure and collapse of the New Left and counterculture in the early seventies."[2] Lasch's work deals with narcissism as a broad cultural phenomenon, whereas the New Age is merely one expression of it.

Narcissism is a also close relative of nihilism, though the subject of nihilism, in particular its American form in which it is closely coupled to aggressive rage, will be dealt with mostly in the next chapter.

The films *I Heart Huckabees*, directed and co-written by David O. Russell, and *Waking Life*, directed and written by Richard Linklater, have been chosen here to represent some elements of New Age thinking and narcissism, and to show how these contribute to a uniquely American madness. Neither of them are explicitly New Age films like *What the Bleep Do We Know!?*, *Indigo*, and *Conversations with God*, which will also be discussed. What *I Heart Huckabees* and *Waking Life* show is how New Age ideas permeate the American mainstream in a way that does not happen in Britain and continental Europe. This chapter, by way of leading to the topic of nihilism, finishes with Woody Allen's *Zelig*, a comedy of the self-absorbed "psychologized" man who is narcissistic, but who does not quite attract a New Age label.

I Heart Huckabees

I Heart Huckabees is billed as an "existential comedy." (It therefore runs the risk of putting off both those who take existential questions seriously and those who want their comedy untainted by the difficult questions of life.) Protagonist Albert Markovski is troubled by "coincidences" in his life, which to most film audiences would be taken at face value, but for anyone exposed to New Age ideas is more significant. Albert leads a local coalition attempting to save an area of wetlands from development by a rapacious chain store company called "Huckabees." He wants to get to the bottom of the strange coincidence of repeated encounters with a tall African, and, through another strange coincidence, has come across the usually-secret business card of the "Existential Detectives." After the opening scene of the film where Albert recites poetry to a group in the wetlands he is hoping to save—and in which we also hear his inner, less gracious thoughts—he arrives for his interview with the Existential Detectives, a married couple called Bernard and Vivian Jaffe (played by Dustin Hoffman and Lily Tomlin). Vivian is quite stern with Albert:

> Mr. Markovski, we see a lot of people in here who claim they want to know the ultimate truth about reality. They want to peer under the surface of the "Big Everything." But this can be a very painful process, full of surprises: it can dismantle the world as you know it. That's why most people prefer to remain on the surface of things. Maybe you should go home. Let sleeping dogs lie.

But Albert won't take the brush-off, and negotiates a pro-bono deal with them. We are already in an odd situation though: therapists, like lawyers, don't work for nothing in the United States. What we are getting is the first indication that the film is constructed around Albert as the center of his universe, where "coincidences" must have significance for him, and where professionals find him so interesting that they offer their services for free. But the Existential Detectives deny that they are therapists, and are in fact a great comic creation, having the right to snoop into every aspect of their client's life, including whatever goes on in the bedroom or bathroom. Before long however the Existential Detectives extend their services to more key characters in the film, including Brad Stand (Jude Law) and Tommy Corn (Mark Wahlberg). Brad, a Huckabees executive, is on the rise as Albert is on the wane in the coalition to save the wetlands, and the plot revolves mainly around their antagonism. Tommy is a fireman whose existential questioning is so advanced that his wife is leaving him. But he has begun to doubt the seeming infinite wisdom of the Existential Detectives—or is that wisdom about the infinite—and is leaning towards their philosophical rival, a seductive French woman called Caterine Vauban (played by Isabelle Huppert).

Tommy is perhaps the film's most illuminating character in terms of the American mind, because he combines the existential anxieties that are very real to many of those with wealth and leisure—whether American or not—with a pumped-up level of personal aggression. His targets are various, and include the wasteful use of fossil fuels and other ecological issues, but he initially at least gives Albert time, warmth and friendship. He is "buddied" or partnered to Albert by the Existential Detectives, a typical therapeutic device. Tommy's problems are first played out in a scene where his wife is leaving him, unable to share in his existential quest that veers chaotically between the meaningful and the meaningless. Existential Detective Bernard arrives on the scene and is alarmed to find that Tommy's anxieties are caused by the book he is reading, the author of which is Caterine Vauban. Tommy's first really aggressive act is to punch out a friendly neighbor who dares to call Bernard a therapist, but it is so casually done that he turns and simply carries on with his cod philosophy (perhaps an example of poor emotional bracketing). Bernard is likewise unphased at this random violence, in fact it is just part of the chaotic scene. Such scenes litter the film, with people talking across each other and very little communication going on; in one sense this is natural to the genre of slapstick comedy.

But Bernard is alarmed at a quite different possibility: that Caterine Vauban is in America. Cut to a woman's legs in high heels below a designer jacket; pull back to reveal the alluring Caterine. She appears to be snooping on Bernard's partner Vivian, who appears to be snooping on an employee of Huckabees.

Even more mysterious than the pro-bono deal with Bernard and Vivian, Caterine intervenes almost by stalking Albert. She can't want to steal him as a client from the Existential Detectives for the fee, as there isn't any, so we are left with the conclusion that, again, Bernard's case is remarkably interesting. Granted, the point of any film or novel is to run the protagonist through a telescoped set of events in order to tell the story of a person reacting to life's more unusual twists and turns. But the focus on Albert goes beyond this requirement, and reflects a typically American self-absorption shown at one level in America's shrink culture, and, at another level, in a smaller corner of the American cultural landmass, the New Age. Early in the film we are in fact presented with a typically New Age psychotherapeutic device: the "isolation bag"—a black zip-up bag into which Bernard makes Albert climb. Normally this would be an isolation tank, in which the client floats naked in warm salty water in complete darkness (as featured in the film *Altered States*). The point is to allow the mind to freely associate in the absence of sensory input. Bernard's mind floats off to violent images: people from the past and present appear before him and in the end he is hacking them to bits with a machete. At the end of his first session Bernard says, "You gotta lot of layers in there, don't you?"

The film *is* a comedy however, and even if we can't be sure that its cod philosophy is actually the target of the satire, there are very funny scenes. It also takes a pretty accurate shot at the very American phenomenon of the chain-store (of which perhaps Wal-Mart is the real-life prototype), the kind of cheesy advertising used in its promotion, and the possibly unscrupulous methods used to acquire new sites for development. But Albert's second session in the zip-up bag yields only more aggressive images, this time centered on his arch-rival Brad. Albert again does what he knows best—in his fantasy at least—and chops him up with the machete. While the New Age promotes a fluffy-bunny, happy-clappy peace-loving image of the ideal self, the reality seems to be full of aggression.

Albert is none too pleased to see Brad in the office of the Existential Detectives, and even less pleased that Brad has been encouraged to write poetry. Their relationship is getting increasingly fractious. But Albert tries really hard to apply the existential philosophy of sameness to the situation. He swallows his anger and says to Brad: "We're the same Brad. It's all the blanket." (The blanket is Bernard's metaphor for the interconnectedness of the universe.) Nods of approval from his mentors: "That is wonderful Albert," from Vivian. "Oh, honey, he's got it," from a beaming Bernard. But Albert soon relapses when Brad lets him know that Albert no longer has a place in the coalition he founded. As the film progresses Albert has to confront an even more alarming existential notion: that he and Brad had been in all conceivable permutations of human relationship in their past lives. Albert is confronted by his own fantasy image of him suckling at Brad's breast, but shakes it off. This is of course another New Age staple, the shallowly conceived interpretation of Hindu and Buddhist ideas on reincarnation and karma. On a more prosaic level, the drama unfolds a reversal in the fortunes of the two rivals, so that towards the end Brad and Albert are reconciled through the common perception of Huckabees as an avaricious and ruthless corporate monster.

I Heart Huckabees is a film that, on the surface, beautifully portrays the "Mom-and-apple-pie" side of America. In cinematographical terms it is well shot with a light and airy feel, conveying urban and suburban affluence untainted by vandalism, litter, graffiti or any signs of poverty. But what Billy represents so well is the lurking bewilderment at the underlying contradictions behind the American dream. For example, in the chaos of his wife walking out on him, he reaches across their lawn, strewn with their possessions, and grabs his little daughter to tell her that mommy's sneakers are made in a dark and horrible factory, by girls just as young as her, for peanuts. He also rails that to use petroleum is murder, supporting his argument with details of life in the Arabian Peninsula. Billy is thoughtful, sensitive, and angry. It is not however the moral outrage of the average activist, but more a kind of all-pervasive testosterone-fuelled aggression, the expression of which has universal American cultural sanction.

When the Existential Detectives give a party, Billy offers to help Albert by creating a diversion so Albert can sneak into the office and look at his files. As Albert argues (rather childishly) with Brad, Billy takes the opportunity to confront Brad. Billy pushes him over and starts to dance with Brad's girlfriend. Billy then argues with Brad, and in his eyes is a steely aggression. Bernard's attempt to calm them down involves asking rhetorically, "Do you want to go backwards? Go backwards on all fours?" But Billy's aggression is not something in the human past, in Stone Age or Neanderthal times; it is deeply in the American present. It is the aggression that cuts through difficulties, takes risks, creates opportunities ... and doesn't much care who gets trampled in the process. Albert is discovered leaving the office with his stolen file, and the whole party stops. Horror! How could you! Billy moves out of the room with Albert, saying "Hey, Albert's got to do what Albert's got to do. Anybody think they know better?" He spreads his arms in a stance that expresses physical dominance. "Wanna take a shot?"

That's the American way of settling a difference: slug it out in the parking lot. And we have to admire Billy: he is afraid of nothing, and sticks up for the little guy. Albert contributes by saying "It's *my* coincidences." In this scene we have Albert's continuing adherence to an essentially New Age idea (the coincidences) backed up by Billy's male aggression. This partnership is uniquely American.

In the next scene they track down the Sudanese African of Albert's coinciden-ces, and are invited to the family which has hosted him as a refugee. They are church people, and this gives the film a chance to represent the hostility across the church / New Age divide. As in so many scenes in the film, what starts out as a potentially fruitful debate about values quickly descends into a shouting match, dominated in the end by Billy's method of confrontation. (Albert also displays an impressive turn of conversational aggression.) But really this scene is a gem in which the whole gamut of American social issues and preoccupations are run past us at dazzling speed. A whole film could have been made around the characters just sitting at the dinner table here, and the bewildering contradictions that their different worldviews represent. But we don't have time in the zany world of *Huckabees*, and so the encounter ends with rancor rather than understanding. And as they leave, the Existential Detectives report on their snooping: they had been at the window with their microphones and tape recorders throughout. But they were only interested in a passing remark over a cat, which seemed to hit a nerve with Albert. Otherwise they seemed to think he was making "progress," though based on what one can't imagine.

There are further twists and turns of the plot, and the wetland's future looks less and less secure as the Coalition battle it out with Huckabees. The wetland also becomes the scene for Albert to get intimate and muddy with the sexy French philosopher Caterine. That is if you think taking her doggystyle over a fallen tree trunk is "intimate." We can take it merely to represent the Freudian necessity for sexual obsession to be gratified in American culture, and a signal to Albert that he is somebody after all. Billy's self-confidence takes a knock at this development however, showing again how crucial sexual "success" is to the American male; he responds to their affair with predictable aggression. The really Freudian element of the film however (tying in nicely with Albert's very New Age self-absorbedness) turns out to be the issue of the cat. Thanks to Caterine's own patient existential detective work, she engineers a confrontation with Albert's mother in which it becomes clear that all of Albert's problems go back to the day his cat died. His mother apparently didn't give him her full love and attention over the issue, and hence this was at the root of his ongoing existential crisis, a parallel perhaps with the issue over the burnt sled named "Rosebud" in the film *Citizen Kane*.

I Heart Huckabees presents us with characters that are comic creations of genuine originality, pursuing at breathless speed a zany world of plots and sub-plots with an existential flavor. The speed at which developments unfold makes the film engrossing, but it is that very speed which ensures that the existential questions degenerate into cod philosophy. At the same time this is quintessentially American, the requirement to do everything in the fast lane. The pumped-up aggression ensures that existential questions become grist to the mill, almost as if the very cheek of these difficult questions demands a snarling response at break-neck speed. A resolution has to be forced as quickly as possible, as with all other issues that break through the surface tranquility of middle-class American life. In this film the question of Albert's existential crisis is "solved" by the discovery of the childhood trauma of the cat. But such questions do not yield so easily to this approach, whatever the well-intentioned psychotherapeutic and New Age gurus preach, and this creates frustration that in turn feeds into more aggression. Freud may initiate the process, but it seems Rambo has the solution.

Waking Life

Waking Life was a radical experiment by director Richard Linklater, using an unusual technique called "rotoscoping" for turning live-action filming into a cartoon effect. This gives the film a surreal atmosphere, well suited to its subject matter, and was used again by Linklater in the film *A Scanner Darkly*. The theme of *Waking Life* is the uncertainty that perhaps life is a dream, coupled with the tantalizing promise of what is known as "lucid dreaming"—the ability to consciously control our dreams. The film is no doubt a work of art in its visuals, its dialogue, and the choice of music, but it is not as art that we are considering it here.

Linklater has used *Waking Life* to explore existential questions in a similar fashion to *I Heart Huckabees*. While the questions may be posed more clearly in *Waking Life*, and in reference to specific philosophers and traditions, the speed at which the issues are run past us ensures that the film degenerates again into cod philosophy. More important however is what is probably quite unintended by Linklater: the portrait of typical young American— apparently free from any grounding necessity to make a living—who has succumbed to a quiet and pervasive *depression*. The protagonist of the film doesn't even have a name, and, despite the rotoscoping technique which completely hides the nuance of facial expression, it is obvious that the character is not happy. His mild depression is typical of any person wealthy enough not to have to struggle for the basics of life, but is uniquely American in his New Age shrink-culture searching. Interesting again, from a European perspective, is that while the protagonist himself is not in the least aggressive, there are a number of characters in the film who epitomize American, male, pumpedup aggression. Like Billy in *I Heart Huckabees*, they combine New Age beliefs with this quintessential American aggression, a combination guaranteed to fail in producing any existential answers. There is also a healthy dose of typically American paranoia about the media and about the political process.

The film starts with the protagonist as a child responding to the idea that "Dream is Destiny." He walks over to a car, but starts floating upwards, only restraining himself in his upturned position by holding onto the door handle. This image may well represent something positive: the ability to dream, to conceive of a different future, to break free of the constraints of a repressive society, and so on. But in the context of the film as a whole it could also represents a kind of despair or bewilderment. The character is *ungrounded*, and as such is prey to any kind of fantastical set of ideas. He floats off. We then cut to the protagonist on a train, looking out of the window. At his destination he makes a phone call, takes a ride in a hippy-style "boat-car," but doesn't know where he wants to be set down. A fellow-passenger decides for him, but the choice turns out to be a bad one: the central character is knocked down by a car on that spot. It is all a dream however, as we see him wake up and have breakfast. The central theme of the film, now made clear, is that he is never sure if he has actually woken up, or if subsequent events are still part of his dreaming.

The protagonist's first stop of the day is a philosophy lecture delivered by Robert Solomon at the University of Texas at Austin, on the topic of existentialism. This gives a possible clue to the depression of the central character: his mood is reminiscent of the hero at the centre of Jean-Paul Sartre's novel *Nausea*. Sartre's existential philosophy makes clear that nothing real is given to us by birth and society—it is up to us to forge our own identity, to wrest from an indifferent fate one's own individuality. This emphasis on the individual is expressed by another character we meet in *Waking Life*, a professor vividly animated and discussing evolution:

> And what is interesting here is that evolution now becomes an individually centered process, emanating from the needs and desires of the individual, and not an external process, a passive process where the individual is just at the whim of the collective. So, you produce a neo-human, okay, with a new individuality and a new consciousness. But that's only the beginning of the evolutionary cycle because as the next cycle proceeds, the input is now this new intelligence. As intelligence piles on intelligence, as ability piles on ability, the speed changes. Until what? Until we reach a crescendo in a way that could be imagined as an enormous instantaneous fulfillment of human and neo-human potential. It could be something totally different. It could be the amplification of the individual, the multiplication of individual existences. Parallel existences now with the individual no longer restricted by time and space.

This might well be exciting philosophy, at the cutting edge of human potential and scientific endeavor. Or it might be New Age junk-cod philosophy. But the propositions in this discourse are not so interesting in themselves as the assumptions behind them, that *intelligence* is all that counts, and that we should pile it up. "Intelligence" *could* mean the Native American wisdom and simplicity represented by Chief Dan George in the various films he plays in. But in *Waking Life*, as in many other Western cultural productions, "intelligence" is merely a kind of advanced computational skill, a dry intellectualism, floating free of any grounded experience of the wilderness, the sky, and the animals and forests ranged beneath it; floating free of the experience of the body. *Waking Life* represents the phenomena called here "cultural autism," dealt with in detail later on. A little later the protagonist accompanies a man, apparently in sound health and mind, who purchases a gallon of petrol for his jerry-can, asks for a match, and then sets light to himself on the pavement. It is a protest against the media portrayal of the "evils of the world," probably a reference to Norman Morrison, a Baltimore Quaker who committed an act of self-immolation in protest against United States involvement in the Vietnam War.

After further encounters the protagonist is sitting with a man in a bar: it is philosophy professor Louis Mackey from the University of Texas again. He is reiterating the point that the intellectual is the highest attribute and goal of the human being:

> When you come to think of it, almost all human behavior and activity is not essentially any different from animal behavior. The most advanced technologies and craftsmanship bring us, at best, up to the super-chimpanzee level. Actually, the gap between, say, Plato or Nietzsche and the average human is greater than the gap between that chimpanzee and the average human. The realm of the real spirit, the true artist, the saint, the philosopher, is rarely achieved.

But many people would far rather spend time in a bar with an "average" human than either Plato or Nietzsche, or perhaps also better enjoy the company of a chimpanzee. Plato's "great" intellect gave us the fascist and eugenicist philosophy of *The Republic*, and Nietzsche went mad, probably not as a result of terminal syphilis, but because, like the protagonist of *Waking Life*, he was lost in the dream-world of his great artistic and intellectual genius. He was ungrounded. His writings are no less contemptuous of the ordinary man than are Plato's, and, it could be argued, are in direct contradiction to what is great in American democracy: comradeship and the ordinary friendliness of the American people.

Linklater follows up the philosophy professor with a scene of quite random and meaningless violence: a man in a bar seems to be recounting either a dream or a real event in which he defends himself with a gun, only to demonstrate it in reality to the bartender. Splat! Blood covers the back of the bar. As the fatally wounded bartender struggles up, he draws out a gun from behind the counter and shoots the customer. Splat! Blood covers the carpet, and they both die. Why? And why is there a scene earlier in which a red-faced prisoner in a cell harangues us with the most appalling details of his disgust for the world and the torture he is going to inflict upon his captors once released? What is the relationship between this undercurrent of violence, and the philosophical and psychological questions under discussion? There is no emotional bracketing in the film around these events, thus trivializing the tragedy and violence in them, as in the self-immolation earlier. What the scenes help portray is the uniquely American madness, which touches every sphere of human endeavor with paranoia and extreme violence. Or is it that, in dealing with dreams, one is dealing with the unconscious, and there must automatically be extreme and sadistic violence in the unconscious? Is this the real fear, that the moment one allows the irrational unconscious to well up into the conscious mind we will be overwhelmed by rage, libido and the lust for murder? Is the American id especially to be feared because, as in *Forbidden Planet*, it can draw on vast reserves of physical power?

But *Waking Life*, if it is about anything, is about lucid dreaming, the ability to control one's dreams. It is when the protagonist is channel-flipping his TV, perhaps hoping to make sense of his dream-waking state, that the first mention of lucid dreaming is made. A serious-looking woman, perhaps another University professor, is giving us a lecture:

> ... venerable tradition of sorcerers, shamans and other visionaries who have developed and perfected the art of dream travel, the so-called lucid dream state whereby consciously controlling your dreams, you're able to discover things beyond your capacity to apprehend in your awake state.

It reminds us that the American New Age has appropriated some of the religious tradition of the Native Americans, in particular the "art of dream travel." But, for the protagonist of the film, as for so many New Age thinkers, lucid dreaming perhaps just represents a way of controlling reality that is denied to them in real life. Whereas shamans of all cultures had specific and social purposes in their dream travel (also called dream flight), the rootless depressed youths represented in this film merely do it for kicks. Later our hero meets another character, a typical Californian surfer-type with a bottle of beer, who is master of lucid dreaming and who teaches it to others. He says, "You know, cut all that fear and anxiety stuff and just rock and roll." This must be the ultimate form of escapism: floating free from the body and from any responsible and nurturing relationship with other human beings and the rest of reality. It is the American gated community of the mind, hermetically sealed from the living world, and also sealed off from the darker parts of the unconscious. True, the real world brings with it fear and anxiety, but we can see very vividly in *Waking Life* what price the apparent security of retreat: isolation unto death.

The film now gets into its stride, as the protagonist meets more and more bizarre characters spouting existentialist philosophy, and as he is more and more anxious as to how to wake up. In the last scene Linklater himself appears (rotoscoped of course), playing a pinball machine, and gives our hero the advice he needs: "Just wake up." (In the film *Open Your Eyes*, on which *Vanilla Sky* is based, the hero receives similar advice.) It is also a chance for Linklater to expound on yet more philosophy and mysticism, partly derived from a science-fiction novel by Philip K. Dick. So our protagonist wakes up. Or at least we see him in bed again, opening his eyes, and then walking outside in the "real" world. Or is it? This last scene is perhaps the most moving, in that it seems to confirm that the protagonist is simply suffering a profound depression, perhaps even a schizophrenic breakdown. His body language as he walks through the same rotoscoped world (beautifully painted, and always shifting around, slightly nauseating) is of melancholia, sadness, and depression, reinforced by the minor chords of the accompanying music. And the final image in the film confirms it: standing by the same car as in the opening, he begins to float upwards. He fails to grasp the door handle, and continues in his upward flight, floating free, hopeless. Poor young man! One's heart goes out to him.

What the Bleep and *Indigo*

Unlike *I Heart Huckabees* and *Waking Life*, the film *What the Bleep do We Know!?* is made by a New Age group for a New Age audience. It is amusing to note that after Britain's worst nuclear accident at the Windscale atomic plant in Cumbria, it was renamed Sellafield; that American religious fundamentalists have renamed themselves "evangelicals"; and that many New Agers now prefer to be called "cultural creatives." The makers of *What the Bleep* also prefer to be called cultural creatives (as they made clear at a private screening of the film in London), but the film itself is pure New Age. It is part documentary, dealing with the question of quantum theory, and part drama, in which a photographer called Amanda finds love and happiness. What makes it quintessentially New Age is that Amanda, played by Marlee Matlin, is cured of her loneliness by the revelation of quantum theory, namely that everything is interconnected. The film intercuts Amanda's story with interviews with scientists, theologians and philosophers. The revelation that the physics of quantum theory now tells us that everything is joined up to everything else is apparently a transforming experience for Amanda, who jettisons her anxiety pills and opens up to love again. She has a speech impediment born of deafness (as does the actress who plays her), and so is struggling anyway with a mild disability, but her new-found ability to love is more to do with the overcoming of painful memories of earlier romantic disappointment.

Now, it is a central New Age belief that physics-proves-mysticism. Certainly it is a more optimistic worldview that quantum physics might provide compared to the older "clockwork universe" of cold, mechanical forces and interactions. But it is bordering on insanity to suggest that a study of quantum theory is going to transform your love life. It is also just completely unscientific to suggest that quantum theory shows that one's mind can alter reality, which is the core message of *What the Bleep*. William Tiller (Professor Emeritus of Material Science and Engineering, Stanford University) and Miceal Ledwith (formerly Professor of Systematic Theology at Maynooth College, Ireland) seem to propose this theory, as their intercut interviews in the film indicate:

> WILLIAM TILLER: Most people don't affect reality in a consistent, substantial way, because they don't believe they can. They write an intention, and then they erase it, because they think that's silly ... I mean ... I can't do that. And then they write it again, and then they erase it. So time average, it's a very small effect. And it really comes down to the fact that they believe they can't do it.
> MICEAL LEDWITH: If you accept with every rudiment of your being that you will walk on water, will it happen? Yes, it will.

Amit Goswami (Professor of Physics, University of Oregon), who appears many times in the film, also insists on this idea:

> AMIT GOSWAMI: I choose that experience. And therefore, literally, I create my own reality. It may sound like a tremendous, bombastic claim by some New Agey ... without any understanding of physics whatsoever ... but really quantum physics is telling us that.

From the perspective of Upanishadic Indian philosophy, one might agree with Goswami. But not at the level of physics: most people probably *would* regard his claims as "a tremendous, bombastic claim by some New Agey." For example many thoughtful Christians object to the New Age as self-absorbed narcissism, and point out that a key Christian idea is summed up in the phrase, "Not my will, but God's will."[3] So it is odd that a theologian like Medwith should be supporting the claim that one's mind can alter reality, but even stranger that a scientist would want to believe it, or claim that quantum theory proves it. Actually, even as a lay person, one wouldn't want this to be true: just imagine that a neighbor for some reason had this power and decided they didn't want one to exist. It's a great relief that people's intentions take the classical route to manifestation in the world, i.e. through hard work and consistent effort. If my neighbor's deeply focused thought is to kill me, then I am glad that in reality quantum theory obstinately refuses to grant his passion. He is going to have to do it the hard way. (Of course, his next focused thought might be to give me a million dollars, but I'll just have to forego that.) But for the New Age, just as for Albert in *I Heart Huckabees* and for the protagonist of *Waking Life*, it is a core belief that somehow the world should revolve around oneself. It is a simple extension of the idea of lucid dreaming, where one can control the world of one's dreams, to the idea of controlling the real world.

The film *Indigo* is another specifically New Age offering, this time dealing with the subject of children who have special spiritual gifts. We learn from the film that they are called "Indigo children" because that is the color of their aura as seen by psychics. The film stars Neale Donald Walsch as Ray, the grandfather of the Indigo child Grace. Much of the film is about their developing relationship, but what should have been a showcase film for the genuine positives in New Age practice turns out to be a dismal illustration of American dysfunctional family life. It should also have been a vehicle to convey what millions of readers had received from Walsch's best-selling *Conversations with God* book series: a positive spirituality updated for the modern world. Walsch wrote the script for *Indigo* and took a lead role in it. The film's director, Stephen Simon, is known for other New Age films, including *What Dreams May Come* starring Robin Williams. The second partnership between Simon and Walsch, a film version of *Conversations with God*, actually works much better, possibly because the book series itself is probably unfilmable. Instead the film became a biopic of Walsch, in which he comes over as a man whose "frailties and errors" take him to the bottom of the social pile in America—and it is to the film's credit that it portrays this world unflinchingly.

Without meaning to, *Indigo* illustrates a number of aspects of the American madness so far identified, including aggression, Oedipal behavior and apocalyptical thinking. It was mentioned before that the New Age replaces Christian millenarianism with its own version: the imminent global transformation of consciousness, heralded by many "signs," which supposedly include the increasing numbers of Indigo children. Since the first accounts of Indigo children in the 1980s the idea has evolved to the next stage: "Crystal children." Either way, these children have been sent to assist in the transformation of the planet. Instead of the apocalypse as imagined in films like *The Rapture* or the *Left Behind* series, the New Age—as the term suggests— imagines a new age or heaven on earth, but depicted in more Eastern or esoteric terms. It may be that Walsch wanted to juxtapose that vision of peace and beauty with the life that average Americans experience in the ugliness of contemporary materialism, but he ended up creating a family whose lack of warmth and love are far from the average. Grace's mother is estranged from her father Ray, and her brother Stewart appears to be a violent drug-dealer who also cannot stand his father. The film opens with Ray and Grace arguing; she leaves to join her husband at some kind of meeting, which turns out to be a drug deal gone wrong; they are raided by the police and she gets a five-year prison term. Little Grace is cared for in a home, and Ray, her grandfather, doesn't bother to visit her. Grace's mother is told by her legal council that her husband Alex is suspicious that she hid the $50,000 that went missing in the raid, and he wants the information. There is concern that Stewart or Alex might kidnap Grace in order to get the information, so Ray is persuaded to abscond with the child.

Much of the film is then taken up with the journey that Ray and Grace take together, on the run from the police. Walsch has intended this as a journey of discovery as Grace's Indigo talents manifest themselves. This is where the film becomes just so much make-believe: Grace cures an old man of Alzheimer's; cures a young mother of breast cancer; knows what people are thinking; and knows events before they happen. Ray is of course bewildered by these manifestations, but is gradually transformed through the presence and spiritual gifts of the child. In the dénouement of the film Stewart does capture Grace at gunpoint, and a furious and aggressive interchange takes place between himself and his father: a scene of Oedipal rage. Grace eventually reveals where the cash went: it was stolen by a corrupt police officer. Ding-dong! Guess what? That same officer rings the doorbell and Grace denounces him. All is peace and light as her mother is released from jail.

What is striking about this film is that most of the characters in it are so alienated and lacking in ordinary human warmth and love as to represent nothing like the American reality, but instead the American nightmare of selfish individualism taken to the extreme. Perhaps this is the source of much New Age madness: the despair of this alienated existence cannot imagine a solution in terms of *ordinary* human warmth, but must posit a supernatural plane of being which will make the necessary intervention. And, because children and animals seem to be capable of the unconditional love that the New Age soul longs for, they become the focus for these supernatural imaginings. Because wealth has allowed American individualism to become such an armored and isolated existence, such a paranoid contraction of the spirit, only a miracle can break this down. Children appear to embody this miracle, at least until they grow up themselves and succumb to this alienation: "Shades of the prison house begin to close / Upon the growing Boy," as Wordsworth put it. Hence the Indigo and Crystal doctrines place on children not just the ancient and normal innocence that have always made them so important to adults, but occult and supernatural gifts.

At the beginning of the film Grace's mother says: "I don't know if it's just me, but there is something special about her. I mean, I know I am her Mom, and every parent says that...." If this is said in true self-awareness it would be fine, but the message of the Indigo and Crystal children is one that

places an unbearable burden and self-importance on them: they are told effect-
tively that they are here not just to redeem their parents but to save the human
race. One can't think of a worse start in life, and though the ideas are spreading
to Europe and beyond, they are uniquely part of the American madness.
This is not to dismiss the New Age in its entirety: there is much that
is valuable in it, and we *ought* to take an interest in the spiritual life of
children. But *Indigo* is such a poor film on all levels that it merely confirms
mainstream prejudice against the New Age. For a film that deals in a more
constructive and believable way with a child who redeems her community,
one might turn to *Whale Rider*. Its young female protagonist is also at odds
with her grandfather, a traditionalist Maori in New Zealand, but the journey
of reconciliation, involving as it does some issues close to the New Age sensibility, unfolds without recourse to absurd supernaturalism. *Whale Rider* is
everything that *Indigo* fails so dismally to be.

Zelig and the Narcissism of the Other-Directed Person

Cultural conservative Allan Bloom devotes a couple of pages in his *Closing
of the American Mind* to Woody Allen's film *Zelig* in order to critique
Riesman's idea of the other-directed person. In the film Woody Allen plays
Leonard Zelig, a man with a chameleon-like ability to take on the appearance
of the people he is with, whether Republican or Democrat, Afro-
Caribbean or Native American, or fat or thin. He is the ultimate caricature
of the other-directed person, and as such becomes—implausibly—a celebrity
who attracts a devoted psychiatrist, Dr. Eudora Fletcher (Mia Farrow), in the
cause of his cure. Long before *Forrest Gump*, this film used special effects
techniques to place Woody Allen in historical footage, including clips featuring
Scott Fitzgerald, the Pope, and Hitler. The film is played as a pseudo-
documentary, featuring cameo interviews with a range of actual cultural and
psychiatric figures, such as Susan Sontag, Saul Bellow and Bruno Bettelheim.
Earlier we made the point that Whitman's outgoing personality made some
of his verse seem narcissistic, but that he actually epitomizes the innerdirected
person. However Zelig, by his extreme other-directedness, and by
the continued plot device of making him a celebrity for being so, is the one
who is truly narcissistic. Bloom is scathing of the turn in the film that sees
Zelig cured by Fletcher and becoming properly "inner-directed"—to the point
where he disagrees about the weather and assails visiting psychiatric dignitaries
with a garden rake. Bloom says: "... Allen's inner directed man is simply
empty or nonexistent, forcing one to wonder how profound his creator's
understanding can be. Here is where we confront the nothing, but it is not
clear that Allen knows it."[4] (It is amusing then to see that Saul Bellow wrote

a laudatory introduction to Bloom's book, having participated in a film that Bloom castigates.)

Christopher Lasch is equally skeptical of Woody Allen, saying in the context of his films: "The confessional form allows an honest writer like Exley or Zweig to provide a harrowing account of the spiritual desolation of our times ... [but] the narcissist's pseudo-insights into his own condition, usually expressed in psychiatric clichés, serves him as a means of deflecting criticism and disclaiming responsibility for his actions."[5] This raises again the question of what genuine critical distance means in filmmaking. The films discussed here generally lack any critical distance: while *I Heart Huckabees* is an amusing satire on therapy, it merely parades its stereotypes; *Waking Life* has no insight at all into the possibility that its protagonist's lucid dreaming aspirations are the source of his depression; and *What the Bleep* and *Indigo* are the crassest of New Age propaganda. Surprisingly perhaps, *Conversations with God* has considerable dignity, coming from a more honest "confessional" than the other films provide for. But *Zelig*, like many of Allen's films, is confessional in a dishonest way, as Lasch points out. It therefore has no critical distance at all. This is not to say that it is not a well made and entertaining film: it is. But Bloom's point is that one cannot mask a nihilistic core—the nothing—by a narcissism parading as psychiatric insight. In the next chapter we tackle nihilism head on, and consider Bloom's idea that Americans can't really do nihilism properly, like the Europeans.

10

Nihilism, Alienation and Self-Destruction

KEY FILMS: *Zabriskie Point, Fight Club*
ADDITIONAL FILMS: *Fear and Loathing in Las Vegas,
Taxi Driver, The Conversation, American Psycho*

Nihilism is a kind of passive despair that finds no meaning in life. It is present in the philosophy of Existentialism, though this philosophy also proposes a way out through individualism. Nihilism can be understood as the inevitable accompaniment to wealth and leisure, where individuals of a certain class, having no daily necessity to wrest a living from the land or other constructive employment, lose their sense of purpose. There is also a very different kind of nihilism: that of the person or nation so frequently brought to the edge of death or destruction that they succumb to despair. When this despair is given a religious or philosophical underpinning then it can be thought of as a well-articulated nihilism, though very different from the nihilism of the wealthy. Parts of the Old Testament demonstrate such a nihilism, born out of the sufferings of the Jewish people over centuries. The author of Ecclesiastes, a former Jewish king known as "the Preacher," had known wealth, but writes a despairing nihilism easily understood by any downtrodden or unlucky peoples: "Vanity of vanities, saith the Preacher, vanity of vanities, all *is* vanity." He finds the stillborn more fortunate than the living; the day of death better than the day of birth; and grief better than laughter. (That an Old Testament prophet must have a deeply depressing outlook is borne out by the prophet who appears at the beginning of *Left Behind*: he seems to drag himself about, and has to summon up his prophecy by a considerable effort of will.)

In *Macbeth* Shakespeare has contributed his own vivid statement of nihilism: "Life's but a walking shadow, a poor player that struts and frets his hour upon the stage and then is heard no more: it is a tale told by an idiot, full of sound and fury, signifying nothing." T. S. Eliot wrote an early 20th century English kind of nihilism, spouted as we saw by the insane colonel Kurtz of *Apocalypse Now*. The American nihilism draws on this rich inheritance of cultural imagery, but is naturally the nihilism of the rich. This is a despair that cannot be assuaged by hope, by the possibility of a future freedom and material plenty, because that is enervatingly present. At best the present prosperity and freedom of the American citizen—the envy of the world—can be negated or overlooked by imagining a future utopia blissfully free of the difficulties, compromises and paradoxes of contemporary democracy. In this nihilistic form of imagining, any perceived or actual weakness in the current system is not a partial defect to be overcome as part of a general working towards a better future, but a symptom of a total decay, depravity or hopelessness. And the American solution?

Blow it all up.

Where the "Preacher" of Ecclesiastes recommends a trust in "God" and a moderate enjoyment of labor and the food and drink it brings, the American nihilism is mostly full of armored, pumped-up aggression. It is a nihilism of the fast lane. It is fast-talking, fuelled by drink or drugs; its images include that of the fast car and the quick buck, though arrived at by counter-culture means rather than through the pursuit of the now-loathed "American dream." As in *I Heart Huckabees*, or in New Age productions, the pressure to get a quick solution makes American nihilism very different from the slow timid despair of the English or the cultured flamboyant philosophy of the French and Italians. The journalist Hunter S. Thompson embodies much of the American nihilism: both its positive, engaged, counter-culture attacks on political sleaze and cultural superficiality, and its negative, cynical, self-destructive tendency. He wrote the novel *Fear and Loathing in Las Vegas*, made into a film of the same name by Terry Gilliam, and shot himself at the age of sixty-seven. His suicide note reads as follows: "No More Games. No More Bombs. No More Walking. No More Fun. No More Swimming. 67. That is 17 years past 50. 17 more than I needed or wanted. Boring. I am always bitchy. No Fun—for anybody. 67. You are getting Greedy. Act your old age. Relax— This won't hurt."

Allan Bloom insists that nihilism must have a high-culture basis: if it can't trace its philosophy to Hegel, Nietzsche or Heidegger, then it must be an empty nihilism. He says "Although nihilism and its accompanying existential despair are hardly anything but a pose for Americans, as the language derived from nihilism has become a part of their educations and insinuated itself into their daily lives, they pursue happiness in ways determined by that language."[1] He continues: "No wonder the mere sound of the Existentialists' Nothing or the Hegelians' Negation has an appeal to contemporary ears.

American nihilism is a mood, a mood of moodiness, a vague disquiet. It is nihilism without the abyss."

We start with two iconic films of American nihilism: *Zabriskie Point* and *Fight Club*, which respectively document typically '60s and '90s American despair, and wonder if they represent "nihilism without the abyss." We will then look at *Fear and Loathing in Las Vegas*, *Taxi Driver* and *Crimes and Misdemeanors*, and also revisit *The Conversation* and *American Psycho*.

Zabriskie Point

Antonioni's *Zabriskie Point* is in essence an import of the European mind into America. Antonioni, an Italian director, chose a subject that is very American, the student life of late sixties campus protest. The film was released in 1970, and follows a student who flees from a campus riot, hijacks a light aircraft, and meets up with a young secretary in the desert. They make love in the desert, poetically imagined by Antonioni as fully peopled with copulating couples, after which the male protagonist returns the plane. He is shot dead by the police, and in her sorrow the young woman imagines the blowing up of the desert hotel in which she is supposed to have been assisting in a business conference. The finale lovingly depicts this destruction, played over and over again in slow motion.

Antonioni's imaginings may have a deeply European source in the existentialism of French and other Continental writers, but he captures well the hidden darkness of the hippy days of student revolt. The campus events he portrays as fiction had a direct source in the shocking reality of the University of Wisconsin student protests that marked the beginnings of serious activism against the Vietnam War in 1963. Local police —fuelled it seems by contempt of the students' indolent middle-class lifestyle, and by hatred of what they saw as "unpatriotic" opinions—quashed a sit-in in such a brutal fashion as to politicize a whole generation. But the students who emerged out of this experience to lead the anti-war movement were not nihilists: they had a cause they believed in. In contrast, the nihilism in *Zabriskie Point* is that of the young, relatively idle person who could not constructively engage with either side of the debate, and who retreated into narcissistic sex and then violence. There is no "first blood" here, as in *Rambo*, no actual transgression against them that justifies such complete disengagement (discounting the shooting of the male protagonist, an improbable narrative device). "Let's blow everything up" is instead a petulance of the spoiled rich kid aimed at a world the complexities of which would take too much effort to comprehend or reach an accommodation with.

Fight Club

A more contemporary American nihilism is portrayed in *Fight Club,* released in 1999, and featuring an ending where major banking corporate headquarters are blown up, fuelling speculation that the 9/11 attackers had been inspired by the film. The protagonist even refers to "the controlled demolition thing," (a 9/11 conspiracy theory) and the site as "Ground Zero." The British would-be terrorist, Dhiren Barot—given a forty year sentence in 2006 for plotting the destruction of landmark buildings in the U.S. and U.K.— labeled one of his computer files "Brad Pitt," quite possibly a reference to the film's star. *Fight Club* was directed by David Fincher, also responsible for *Seven* and *The Game.*

The film opens with protagonist Jack speaking off-screen as we watch him mumble on-screen: he has a gun forced into his mouth. He tells us: "The Demolitions Committee of Project Mayhem wrapped the foundation columns of ten buildings with blasting gelatin. In two minutes, primary charges will blow base charges, and those buildings will be reduced to smoldering rubble. I know this because Tyler knows this." Tyler Durden (played by Brad Pitt) is a bizarre character that Jack meets on a plane who will have a profound effect on Jack's life. But this opening scene is actually the end of the story, and we then cut back to where it all started, in Jack's exploration of New Age-style self-help support groups—group psychotherapy which helps him sleep but ultimately fails to give him purpose. He becomes addicted to the groups, but is a fake: he neither suffers from testicular cancer or tuberculosis, nor is he recently bereaved. Imagine his alarm when he discovers a fellow cruiser, another fake addict to group meetings: Marla Singer (played by Helena Bonham Carter). In a surreal comic episode, they agree to carve up the local self-help groups between them, so as to avoid the further embarrassment of exposing each other's fraudulence. So far, so New Age psychobabble: it could be a noir version of *I Heart Huckabees.*

We now meet Tyler Durden, fellow passenger on yet another dull flight that Jack takes as part of his insurance work, and the film lurches into a very different surrealism. Jack is struck by Tyler's weirdness, but it is only when he returns from his trip to find his flat a smoldering ruin that he thinks to call him up and ask if he can stay a while. Tyler agrees, but then asks Jack to hit him. Jack is naturally bewildered, but Tyler is serious, and so they begin a bare-knuckle fight in the parking lot. Bruised and bloodied, Jack shares a beer with Tyler afterwards and says simply: "We should do this again sometime." They go back to Tyler's place, a derelict house in an abandoned industrial area of town. And they do indeed do it again before long, this time attracting a group of onlookers. The idea of the "fight club" is then born, and snowballs, first in their home town and then across the country. The rules of Fight Club become legendary: "The first rule of Fight Club is ... you *don't talk* about Fight Club. The second rule of Fight Club is ... you don't talk about Fight Club." As a secret organization it provides Jack with everything he was seeking from the support groups, except that it swaps talk for pain.

Jack's anarchic life in Tyler's ruined house and the nights at Fight Club begin to change him: he becomes assertive at work, and takes no trouble to hide the bruises on his face. The fact is that the film is offering the American male a deeply alluring prospect: a way of life that is elemental, that cuts through the artificiality of materialist society, and which allows for masculine aggression to flow in an almost Nietzschean way. They become supermen, unconstrained by feeble morality, reminiscent for example of Frank in *Blue Velvet*. It becomes difficult to draw the line between joyous lunacy and true insanity. But over time Tyler Durden's vision becomes more extreme and Jack is dragged into the next phase of the venture: Project Mayhem. It offers a natural extension to the adrenalin-high of bare-knuckle boxing: a sustained program of attacks on the visible targets of decadent affluence. TV stores, shopping malls, and ultimately banks will be the targets. Jack is now also deeply troubled as to the identity of Tyler Durden, and we as an audience begin to suspect his true nature.

Jack is mostly blossoming under this new regime, and blackmails his boss to give him his salary without having to work for it. Or rather, his work will be not to expose the things he knows about the insurance scams his company is involved in: a "work" he can pursue at home. It is this scene that begins to tell us what is really going on: Jack has put the proposition to his boss, and to convince him that he means it he begins to act in a very scary way. He starts to beat himself up. His boss just stares at him, as the blood flows from Jack's face and he smashes into furniture in the mock fight. He is on his knees in front of his boss, having covered the older man's hands in his own blood, when security guards burst in and stare at the sight, drawing the obvious conclusion. "Please don't hit me again," sobs Jack, faking his distress, and we guess the rest: he gets the deal he wants. Jack has rebelled against his identity as a worker in insurance, just as Lester in *American Beauty* disowned his persona in advertising, and Bateman in *American Psycho* found no meaning in corporate finance. Millions of Americans in well-paid but boring jobs can surely relate to this.

Project Mayhem gains momentum now, while throughout this the strange Marla hangs around and becomes the lover of Tyler, much to Jack's annoyance. He is not jealous: he just can't stand her. In the next stage of escalation, Tyler effectively builds a barracks and recruits misfits of all kinds to be his army, building up to their final act of resistance. Life is lived as an extreme adrenalin rush, where everything transgressional has to be experienced, including a car crash deliberately initiated by Tyler. Jack weathers this fine, having never lived through this particular situation before, but things get out of hand when one of their gang is shot in a particularly outrageous stunt, and Tyler disappears. Jack now gets alarmed, but not before receiving another clue as to the identity of Tyler Durden. Marla turns up that evening and asks if she can come in. "He's not here," replies Jack in a surly manner, swigging from a vodka bottle. "What?" says Marla, uncomprehending. "He's not here!" insists Jack. "Tyler's not here anymore! He's gone away!" Marla stares straight at him, and then turns to leave.

Things begin to really fall apart now, and Jack flies all over the U.S. to track down Tyler Durden, only to find that Fight Club and the Project Mayhem initiatives are everywhere. He is received almost as royalty, or as a military commander, but cannot find Tyler. But eventually all the clues fall into place in a conversation with a wounded bartender, his head held in a bizarre neck brace:

WOUNDED BARTENDER: How have you been?
JACK: You know me?
WOUNDED BARTENDER: Is this a test, sir?
JACK: Yes ... it's a test.
WOUNDED BARTENDER: You were in here last Thursday night.
JACK: What?
WOUNDED BARTENDER: You were standing right where you are now, asking how good our security is. It's tight as a drum.
JACK: Who do you think I am?
WOUNDED BARTENDER: Are you sure this isn't a test?
JACK: No, this is not a test.
WOUNDED BARTENDER: You're Mr. Durden. You're the one who gave me this.

The bartender shows him a livid scar on his hand, a rite of initiation that Jack had been through, apparently at the hands of Tyler Durden. But now we know that Tyler is just Jack's alter ego (or the other way round), that Jack had just been beating himself up (so finding no trouble in scaring the hell out of his boss), and that Marla was Jack/Tyler's lover, also scared to death that Jack had denied that he was there, while standing in front of her, plain as day. This is one of those moments in a well-constructed film where an audience is required to absorb the remaining drama while also re-framing the entire story up to that point. Jack is insane. He has to confirm it with Marla, who has clearly suffered from his Jekyll and Hyde behavior over the entire period. Yes, there is only one person here, not two, and his name is Tyler Durden. But in that moment Tyler appears in the room, and we know that Jack is still delusional, arguing only with himself. And the argument takes us to the bitter end, or the beginning rather, where Jack imagines that Tyler has forced a gun into his mouth, and makes him wait for the explosions that will destroy the banking headquarters. Of course Jack is alone in the room, imagining it all, as the detonations rip through the basements of the tower buildings and one by one they fall, a perfect picture of controlled demolition.

So, *Fight Club* is a clever film, crafted by David Fincher to the same standard as *Seven*. Predictably, critics on the conservative side bemoaned its attack on American values. Many young men apparently took only the fight scenes from it as significant, and there was a spate of copycat bare-knuckle scraps around America. But digging under the gloss of this film we find a truly American nihilism, in which the protagonist cannot even believe in the negative values of subversion. He only *imagines* the destruction he would like to heap upon the urban excess and meaningless he finds around him, just as Bateman only *imagines* that he is a serial killer. But most tellingly his violence is directed at himself, and is expressed as he punches himself in the face, and at the end of the film when he shoots himself in the mouth. Jack cannot even sign up to any real protest movement, as in *Zabriskie Point*; he hasn't any element of U.S. foreign policy or war to object to; he simply doesn't care about anything but himself, and then not much. It is the madness of a culturally dictated self-absorption that cannot express its negative energy through commitment to New Age ideals (however shallow), or political ideals (however lofty), or even the psychotherapeutic ideals of healing. It simply implodes, a madness brought about in a society so wealthy, and so removed from the impact of its wealth on the world's poor, that there is no plausible goal to work towards, only destruction. Its course runs from meaninglessness to fake adrenalin high to suicide.

That the film is significant can be judged from the considerable critical reaction to it. Paul Watson calls it "political indigestion."[2] Speaking broadly from a Left position, he calls for a new critical vocabulary to deal with the nihilism in the film, suggesting that the political indigestion over the film is due to a failure of the older Left-Right critical debates. We saw in the introduction that Giroux and Szemen attacked the film for not properly challenging capitalism, while Watson points out that "the socioeconomic advantages of being born a heterosexual white male in American society" fail to be apparent in such films. He classifies them as "male hormone movies" or "angry white male films," which include *Magnolia* and *Falling Down*. Alexandra Juhasz in turn calls them "feminist" films because they show masculinity in crisis: "Tyler exposes Jack to the deep reaches of this effeminization: he knows the meaning of the word *duvet*, he's never been in a car crash, and most significantly, and from whence *Fight Club* is born, he's never been in a fistfight either."[3] The Left's dismissal of the film can be summed in the characterization "defeat in the face of contemporary capitalism";[4] the classical cultural conservative's dismissal as "nihilism without the abyss"; and the religious cultural conservative's dismissal as part of the "myth of the alienated artist." Who, ask critics like Medved, would want to make such a film in the first place? But a criticism rooted in the idea of catharsis finds that the film is well-constructed to evoke compassion: Tyler—"Ikea Boy"—represents affluent successful America as a society that "can no longer remember what it is like to be inundated by desire," to use Lasch's memorable phrase.[5] Tyler's tragedy is real, even if his abyss has no high culture grounding. But: "Nihilism and despair amongst the rich?" asks the Right, "How ghastly!" And: "Compassion for the rich?" asks the Left, "How ghastly!"

Fear and Loathing in Las Vegas

Hunter S. Thompson invented what is known as "Gonzo" journalism, the origins of which term are a bit obscure but may mean "last man standing after a drinking marathon." Anyhow this is most apt for the characters in the film *Fear and Loathing in Las Vegas*, though their mind-altering favorites go far beyond alcohol. The film is a part road-trip/part drug-trip hotel-room-trashing weekend binge with the excuse of journalism behind it. Johnny Depp plays Hunter S. Thompson, a.k.a. Raoul Duke, accompanied by his attorney Dr. Gonzo, who keeps him supplied with a veritable encyclopedia of drugs. Two counter-culture Americans goof off as they parody the American dream, leaving unpaid bills and a trail of destruction. As they leave Las Vegas behind Duke muses: "We had abused every rule that Vegas lived by: burning the locals, abusing the tourists, terrifying the help. The only chance now, I felt, was the possibility that we'd gone to such excess that nobody in the position to bring the hammer down on us could possibility believe it." *Fear and Loathing*'s nihilism belongs to the '60s, to the era of the Vietnam war and hippy revolutions: its protagonists are naïve and childish. If our transgressions are this extreme, reasons the adolescent, then the authorities won't even believe we did it. Like in *Zabriskie Point*, their nihilism is the product of affluence, and also disillusion with a specific war. The journey from *Fear and Loathing* to *Fight Club* is from adolescent naiveté to the heights of urban sophistication; from the time of Timothy Leary to the time of 9/11. *Fear and Loathing* is about the nihilism of drug-taking, inspired by Leary's exhortation: "Tune in, turn on, drop out." To drop out of the mainstream is one thing, but a genuine counter-culture replaces mainstream values of materialism with activism, religion, voluntary simplicity, eco-lifestyles or any of a host of meaningful oppositional stances. Duke and Gonzo believe in nothing, however. Their empty hedonism merely illustrates Dr. Johnson's dictum, boldly displayed at the beginning of the film:

> He who makes a beast of himself gets rid of the pain of being a man.

Fear and Loathing ends with a diatribe against Leary and his LSD legacy, but this and the Johnson quote bookend what is perhaps a pointless ordeal of film viewing (despite Depp's almost endearing rendition of Duke). Perhaps Hunter S. Thompson himself is better represented by the bookends than what lies between them, but as a record of a truly American nihilism *Fear and Loathing* is useful. (A better representation of Thompson's delightfully anti-establishment invective is portrayed in the film *Where Buffalo Roam*, though Thompson himself hated it.)

Taxi Driver and *Crimes and Misdemeanors*

Although *Fight Club* is clever, it is not psychologically subtle. *Fear and Loathing* is neither clever nor subtle: its true strength is a very American crassness. For a truly subtle portrayal of American nihilism and alienation we turn now to consider *Taxi Driver*, an early Martin Scorsese film written by Paul Schrader. Its hero, Travis Bickle, is a "hollow man" who gets a job as a New York taxi driver because he cannot sleep at night. T. S. Eliot's "hollow man" would be an English vision of Travis's alienation, but in one version of the script the film starts with a reference to Thomas Wolfe's' "God's Lonely Man," a more American archetype. Such a man feels alone because only he can see the world's evil. Travis, superbly played by the young Robert de Niro, loathes the decadence of night-time New York: "The animals come out at night. Whores, skunk pussies, buggers, queens, fairies, dopers, junkies. Sick, venal. Someday a real rain will come and wash this scum off the streets." This is early in the film and we are set up for the idea that Travis will be that rain, a righteous torrent which has an undercurrent of American Christian apocalypse in it.

Travis conveys many aspects of the American madness for us, but in a subtle, understated way that is truer to the thoughtful American, rather than to the mainstream. (The script is in fact a partly autobiographical account of Paul Schrader's own journey through depression.) *Taxi Driver* is indirect because we are set up to understand Travis as a Lee Harvey Oswald-type character,[6] and at one point he is primed to assassinate a presidential candidate. Instead he takes vigilante-style revenge on a local pimp and whorehouse manager in the bloodbath that marks Travis's cathartic resolution. Travis represents again a truly American alienation and nihilism, because he is uneducated and uninformed (almost to the point of implausibility, and in contrast to the deeply cultured reality of Schrader's own mind). His descent into loneliness is matched by his very American obsession with guns. But this is no Rambo-style weaponry and the flaunting of it: rather he obsessively hides the guns and knives about his body, practicing their deployment over and over again against the imaginary low-life he has grown to loathe. Travis has an aggression that is not, for a change, pumped-up, armored, and cartoon-like. But the subtlety of his character, his reserve, and the total atmosphere that Scorsese builds up is perhaps even more disturbing as a portrait of the American madness than any cartoon-style violence. Although it is only hinted at in the ending of the film, it seems that Travis's murder spree has resolved his existential crisis: he seems relaxed, smiles occasionally, and may even finally get the girl. It is an American rite-of-passage.

But how come a vigilante-style killing in New York leads to no police charges against Travis? Is it justified, as in *Seven*, because the victims "deserved it?" How does he become a local hero, feted in the papers, read by the woman who spurned him, and who only now appears willing to take him seriously? Is this the ultimate American dream, the ultimate rite of passage, that initiating a bloodbath is the only way to be taken as a "somebody"? That appearance in the newspapers turns the sexual and social failure into a man to admire? *Taxi Driver* is a film that was received with universal critical acclaim, but few seem to ask these questions. It seems that the cartoon-style violence of Rambo is acceptable because it is escapist fantasy, while the quiet man's violence of Travis in Scorsese's film is acceptable because it is high culture. And the question of where art ends and life begins is made stark here by the fact that John Hinkley, the would-be assassin of President Reagan, claimed he had been inspired by the film. The interleaving of filmic fiction and real-world American-style violence does not end there however: the character of Travis was based in turn on Arthur Bremer, the man who shot Governor George Wallace in 1972. (And Forrest Gump was right there to boot.) Prior to the shooting, Bremer's diary holds this entry: "It is my personal plan to assassinate by pistol either Richard Nixon or George Wallace ... to do SOMETHING BOLD AND DRAMATIC, FORCEFULL & DYNAMIC, A STATEMENT of my manhood for the world to see." It is hard to find a better statement of the American way out of nihilism: prove your manhood by murder. John Hinkley was obsessed with Jodie Foster who plays the teenage prostitute in *Taxi Driver*, and prior to his assassination attempt wrote this note to her: "Over the past seven months I've left you dozens of poems, letters and love messages in the faint hope that you could develop an interest in me. Although we talked on the phone a couple of times I never had the nerve to simply approach you and introduce myself. The reason I'm going ahead with this attempt now is because I cannot wait any longer to impress you." Hinkley was suffering a deep depression at the time, and was fascinated by Lee Harvey Oswald: the culturally sanctioned solution, it appears, is celebrity murder.

Kolker objects, saying of Bickle's murder spree: "The sequence could be considered one of the more cynical moments in contemporary cinema,"[7] and goes on to explain it as a ploy to attract audience attention at a specific point in film history. Given the wider oeuvre of Schrader, over a long career, we suggest otherwise: incongruous violence is a trademark that also appears in *Affliction* and *Light Sleeper* amongst his other films. The strangest response to this issue in *Taxi Driver* comes from the interdiscipline of film and religion, where two authors independently pursue the thesis that the violence is in *itself* redemptive. Christopher Deacey comments on the violence that it could be said to "constitute a baptismal, cleansing bloodbath.... Only by engaging with, and confronting, the 'filth' that has suffused the city can Travis's redemptive mission be fulfilled, in a manner analogous to—albeit ontologically different from—Jesus'...."[8] David John Graham in a similar vein asks: "The notion of redemptive suffering is probably a familiar one; can redemptive violence be as valid?"[9] It is worth recalling that Christianity was founded on the idea that Jesus's sacrifice was to suffer the violence meted out *against* him—as Gibson is so keen to show us. If even theologians can miss the central point in the defining narrative of their discipline, then we might suspect that the American madness on film has far-reaching influence.

The Conversation and *American Psycho*

The theme of *The Conversation* is surveillance, and so it is a useful record of American paranoia in a country which thinks, rightly or wrongly, that its premiere position makes it a continuous target to enemies from without, and from subversives within. But this brooding *film noir* conveys more than a paranoid or legitimate fear of surveillance: it also conveys an alienation or nihilism much influenced in its portrayal-contra Bloom—by European culture. Its protagonist, Harry Caul, is played by Gene Hackman, and seems to have a non-existent or difficult emotional life. His fastidiousness in creating an invisible persona means that he does not give out his phone number, not even to his girlfriend. His only "friends" are other operatives in the surveillance industry, who laud him as the best "bugger" on the West Coast; his only real passion is for the electronics that let him do his job. He could be Roquentin from Sartre's *Nausea*, or almost any other anti-hero of surreal Existentialism. But he is also any American male imprisoned within his brittle self-constructed and armored identity, and his descent into despair is instructive. Quite simply, the tables are turned on him—he becomes a bugger bugged. His entire constructed persona is annihilated as he becomes the subject of surveillance; one could say that his masculine prerogative to be the remote observer of others is undermined as he becomes the passive subject of that surveillance. And Coppola creates a great filmic image of this at the end of *The Conversation*, when Caul methodically rips his flat bare to find the device that is listening to him. He fails to find it, and is left with a scene of chaos, his inviolable sanctuary desecrated by himself in his desperate search. And, just like the anti-hero of *Nausea*, he is left a "reduced figure" as Kolker puts it,[10] left only with the possible and remote consolation of "art": he takes out his saxophone and plays in the ruins.

But Patrick Bateman perhaps best represents the ultimate American nihilism. As the all–American psycho he serves us better than Harry Caul, who operates at the margins and disappears from them without trace. Bateman's nihilism is an insanity, the course of which is directly caused by affluence on a scale available to millions in America, and previously only known to emperors. In this world of money all human experience has been reduced to a *price*; all that is nourishing to the human soul has been hollowed out by its status as an object. The exemplar of this is women: Bateman pays for prostitutes to return to his flat where he murders them with appalling brutality, because as *objects* they can never satisfy him. In this desperate downward spiral, their murder confirms their status as objects, just meat to keep in the freezer. He is alienated from the possibility of love because he believes that love is a commodity like all the others he deals with: its value is its scarcity-value. Hence his rage at what he is culturally programmed to understand as the source of love—the sex-relationship, the woman—when in reality love is that which is least like an object, has no material source, and has no limits. Where Goethe's character Faust cannot even seduce a peasant girl without the help of the devil, Bateman cannot even act out his rage without fantasy. He is doubly stymied. He starts the film by telling us:

> There is an idea of a Patrick Bateman. Some kind of abstraction, but there is no real me. Only an entity ... something illusory. And though I can hide my cold gaze, and you can shake my hand and feel flesh gripping yours, and maybe you can even sense our life-styles are probably comparable, I simply am *not there*.

This can hold its own with any expression of European existentialism, but as the quintessentially American psycho Bateman is emasculated even of the reality of murder (because he only imagines it), or the consolation of high culture (because high culture is not commodifiable). He is a fantasist in a culture of empty materialism; his is an uncultured nihilism that makes him, ironically, a completely tragic figure.

11

The Intellect and Cultural Autism

Key Films: *A Beautiful Mind*,
Artificial Intelligence: A.I.
Additional Films: *Rain Man, In the Cut*

The U.S. is curiously ambivalent about intellectual achievement. On the one hand its popular culture is anti-intellectual, as epitomized in the song "A Wonderful World," sung for example by Art Garfunkel:

Don't know much about geography, don't know much trigonometry
Don't know much about algebra, I don't know what a slide rule is for
But I do know one and one is two and if this one could be with you
What a wonderful, wonderful world this would be
What a wonderful, wonderful, wonderful world.

The character Forrest Gump in the film of that name also represents the widespread approval for the good-natured person of low I.Q., who nevertheless succeeds in life. When Ronald Reagan won against Jimmy Carter, and George W. Bush won against Al Gore in Presidential elections, there may have been a "Forrest Gump" factor in each case: Reagan and Bush having an easy folksy charm, with Carter and Gore being clearly more intellectual. On the other hand the term "rocket science" epitomizes America's pride in its science and technology. When an American wants to explain that something isn't really difficult they reach for the sarcasm, "It isn't rocket science." Rocket science, by implication, *is* really difficult.

America and the U.K. have a cultural skepticism towards the intellect that perhaps continental Europe does not (Ian Drury and the Blockheads summed it up for a British audience in the popular song "Clever Trevor"). A skepticism towards high-flown phrases and beautiful language is important if behind them there might lurk intolerance, prejudice, sexism, racism or fascism. Hence reservations regarding Western cultural icons such as Plato, Goethe and Nietzsche—of the kind voiced by Popper—or acknowledging that racist ideas lurk behind such a universally acclaimed work of popular culture such as *The Wizard of Oz* are far more than mere "political correctness." It means that the highest intelligence, manifest in either science or the humanities, needs all the closer scrutiny because of its aura of genius and its ability to persuade using advanced logic or high aesthetics. And part of that is a recognition that genius is often accompanied by an emotional impairment, now recognized in the terms "Asperger's syndrome" or "high-functioning autism." We will use the joint acronym AS/HFA for this condition.

The literature on AS/HFA shows an ongoing debate about whether, for example, there can be a clear distinction between Asperger's syndrome and high-functioning autism, but often acknowledges that the film *Rain Man* (described shortly) was a watershed in public awareness of the issue.[1] There is general agreement that autism involves a triad of impairments: social difficulties, communication difficulties, and restricted or repetitive activity;[2] while within AS/HFA there may be normal or above normal intelligence and language skills; that these may mask social difficulties; and that repetitive behavior may be part of artistic or scientific activity. One account suggests that "many higher-functioning autistic individuals have particular islands of ability such as unusual memory ..."[3] and goes on to list the kind of skills exhibited by Raymond Babbitt in *Rain Man*. The term "islands of ability" is useful here, indicating the possibility of genius within a personality that is not rounded, specifically being poorly developed in the emotional and empathetic domain.

Individuals such as physicist Albert Einstein and artist Andy Warhol have been considered as suffering from Asperger's syndrome on the basis of impairment of social interaction. Obsessive behavior is another symptom; for example Warhol famously insisted on always wearing the same make of green cotton underpants (Raymond Babbitt also obsessively required a particular brand of underwear from K-Mart[4]). However, since *Rain Man*, it is possible that the term "Asperger's" has gained a popular currency beyond its clinical definition. British popular singer and electronic music pioneer Gary Numan—known for his dystopian lyrics—was asked in an interview about Asperger's syndrome. He replied "It was suggested I had it when I was younger but no one knew much about it then. I've read a lot about it since and I fulfill some of the diagnostic criteria but not others. I probably only have a mild form."[5] It is also commonly reported on the Internet that director Stephen Spielberg has been diagnosed as an adult with Asperger's syndrome. In a well-meaning book called *Different Like Me: My Book of Autism Heroes*, a series of well-known and successful public figures are cited as suffering from autism, including Einstein, Andy Wharhol, Wassily Kandinsky, Piet Mondrian, Alan Turing, Lewis Carroll, Isaac Newton, and Immanuel Kant.[6] The issue is now publicly debated, and may even have reached the point where celebrity cachet attaches itself to the term, beyond the world of careful clinical research and deliberation.

In Richard Hofstadter's 1964 essay on the paranoid style in politics he says: "When using the expression 'paranoid style' I am not speaking in a clinical sense, but borrowing a clinical term for other purposes."[7] Similarly, some of the public debate around HFA/AS is clearly borrowing the terms from the clinical literature to describe high-functioning individuals with poor emotional capability. The relatively new idea of "emotional intelligence," popularized by the psychologist Daniel Goleman, is part of this move.[8] Christopher Lasch, as we saw earlier when adopting the term "narcissism" to describe a broad cultural movement, was keen to keep the clinical roots of the term to prevent it becoming so wide as to be virtually meaningless. Here we are going to suggest the term "cultural autism" to cover cultural productions such as cinema, and the reception to them, where there is clearly artistic and technical intelligence at work, even if emotionally clumsy or incongruent. It is intended as a shorthand for "HFA/AS-like attributes" which are *unintended* in the films, and largely *unnoticed* in the critical response to them. Hence an obscure film about autism may not show "cultural autism" at all, whereas highly regarded films may exhibit these traits with no critical exposure of them. The lack of comment would then be due to the fact that contemporary culture itself, to some degree, exhibits these traits.

Examples of directors whose films show cultural autism in this sense might include Steven Spielberg, Robert Bresson, and Jane Campion. Of these, only Spielberg is American, Bresson being French, and Campion being Australian. What is common to the films of all three directors is a kind of "emotion-by-numbers," an emotional dissonance in the characters and their actions. The actors may be highly skilled in conveying a particular emotion, but they are scripted and directed to do so in ways that are unconvincing in the setting. For example a character may show no emotion at the injury or death of another, or may over-emote at something quite trivial. We saw earlier that Stephen Prince had defined the term "emotional bracketing" as a technique used in the Production Code era to signify a violent act that could not then be shown explicitly, and we have been using it in the context of all transgressional situations. We can now see that it is useful in the definition of filmic moments that exhibit cultural autism: they have poor emotional bracketing.

An example—to briefly step outside American cinema—is in Jane Campion's film *Holy Smoke*, when a group of people (including characters played by Harvey Keitel and Kate Winslet) pass a young mother playing with her children by a truck. The kids jump off the tailgate into her arms, and she lowers them to the ground, but when she sees the group passing by she turns to gawp at them. Meantime her boy, who is playing at Batman, dives off the truck. She is so absorbed that she fails to put out her arms, and he misses her and hits the ground. There is a brief pause and one of the group screams; then cut to another scene. Why? What purpose did this whole scene serve? We don't know if the boy broke his limbs, or what the scream was intended to convey, or what was so wrong with his mother that her deepest instincts, to protect her child, were negated by the mere sight of Harvey Keitel in sunglasses. Or was it that—in American terms—the mother and children are "trailer trash," and so who cares? In Tom and Jerry, we expect one to hit the other repeatedly with a frying pan, with no resulting brain damage; the laws of nature are suspended. Clang! It's funny. But in *Holy Smoke* the basis is of realism, where people can be hurt physically, and, especially, emotionally. The child is allowed to fall to the ground. Splat! It's not funny, and it doesn't fit: it's poor emotional bracketing.

But what is the particularly American style of cultural autism? Can we find it in the works of Spielberg, for example, confirming his own apparent diagnosis of Asperger's? A cultural autism that is specifically American would have to be located in the exaggerated impetus in the American mind for competition, and a paranoia that others will get ahead of us. It is this that elevates the "rocket scientist" or any person of high I.Q. over the common masses. Being "smart" is the opposite of being a "loser," Forrest Gump not withstanding. Perhaps Spielberg's films also grow out of the inevitable downside of a shrink culture: the continual subjection of the world of emotion to rational examination. His obsession with the world of children could well be part of the cultural autism in his films, as it is the child who seems to us as emotionally whole. (We suggested earlier that *Indigo* focuses on children for the same reason.) The innocence of the child is deeply attractive to the American mind, as a contrast to the scheming unreliable falsity of adulthood. Freud tells us that our conscious personality is a mere sham, vainly trying to keep the lid on the unconscious. As David Banner tells his son, the Hulk: "You're nothing but a superficial shell, a husk of flimsy consciousness, ready to be torn off at a moment's notice." So perhaps Spielberg continuously juxtaposes the "genuine" world of the child with the "false" world of the adult, because he finds the world of mature adult emotionality something of a mystery. In Spielberg's *Schindler's List*, the one use of color in the film—a very dramatic device—is to pick out the red coat of a child.

In the sanitized, competitive, "Pleasantville" kind of world that Spielberg's films mostly inhabit, the prize of course must be the very emotional maturity which is known intellectually to be the goal. (The film *Pleasantville* is discussed in the next chapter.) And so a calculating intelligence is brought to bear on the emotional, and hence it always appears, often subtly, to be "emotion-by-numbers." Al Pacino once said in an interview "actors are emotional athletes," and so they can turn on emotion according to the dictates of the script or the instructions of the director. But, like in any work of art, emotions as elements of the greater composition can be harmoniously placed, dissonantly placed, or just subtly misplaced. When an entire culture fails to notice the subtle or even gross misplacements of emotional performance in a film, then it has to be considered "autistic" in the sense used here. We will look at the films *A Beautiful Mind* and *A.I.* to show how the intellect and science are elevated in American culture, and then consider *In the Cut* and *Rain Man* to show the more subtle dimension of cultural autism.

A Beautiful Mind

A Beautiful Mind was directed by Ron Howard, and stars Russell Crowe as John Nash, a mathematician who won the Nobel Prize. The film opens in September 1947 at Princeton University, host at that time to Albert Einstein. The math class is addressed by their tutor: "Mathematicians won the war. Mathematicians broke the Japanese codes and built the A-bomb. Mathematicians ... like you. The stated goal of the Soviets is global Communism. In medicine or economics, in technology or space, battle lines are being drawn. Who among you will be the next Morse, the next Einstein?" This speech neatly sums up for us an American competitiveness directed towards its Cold War enemy, Russia, and the cultural elevation of the intellect in that context.

On the lawn we meet John Nash's classmates, who apparently include the one who broke the Japanese code, helping themselves to punch. Nash is shy, with eyes mainly cast downwards. This might remind one of what is supposed to be a popular joke in engineering circles. Q: how can you tell an extrovert engineer? A: because he stares at *your* shoes when he talks to you. Nash perfectly illustrates this through the film, rarely making eye-contact with anyone, a tell-tale sign of autistic traits. But while Nash may be socially retiring, when he speaks about mathematics he can be aggressively confrontational. Faculty member Martin Hansen mistakes him for a waiter, and admits "It was an honest mistake," by way of apology. Nash responds: "I imagine you're getting quite used to miscalculation. I've read your pre-prints, both of them. The one on Nazi ciphers and the other one on non-linear equations, and I am supremely confident that there is not a single seminal or innovative idea in either one of them.... Enjoy your punch." Naturally the whole group is stunned by this show of contempt.

Nash also has a sense of humor: "Despite my privileged upbringing I am actually quite well-balanced: I have a chip on both shoulders," he confides to his roommate. "Maybe you are just better with the old integers than you are with people," comes the reply. Nash tells us that: "My first great teacher told me I was born with two helpings of brain, but only half a helping of heart." "Wow, she sounds lovely." "The truth is, I don't like people much. And they don't like me." Nash is a loner who is immensely ambitious: "Do you know, half these schoolboys have already published.... I cannot waste time memorizing the weak assumptions of lesser mortals," he says, and skips class in order to develop his own ideas on gaming theory (which would eventually lead to his Nobel prize).

Nash is predictably clumsy with the girls. At the college bar with an attractive blonde he manages this: "I don't exactly know what I am required to say in order for you to have intercourse with me but could we assume that I've said all that? I mean, essentially we are talking about fluid exchange, right? So could we go straight to the sex?" Nash gets the slap he deserves. He isn't doing any better in class either, mainly because he doesn't deign to attend. His record so far doesn't make him eligible for the placement he so badly wants, and this disappointment spurs him to extreme efforts. It pays off. His next encounter with the authority of Faculty is quite different, and his work is recognized as a breakthrough.

Five years later Nash seems to have secured the assignment of his dreams, at the Pentagon. It is at the start of Cold War paranoia, and he is frustrated that his ideas are not being followed up. He lands up teaching at MIT, letting his class have no doubts about his feelings. Nash may be shy at one level, but at another he is hell-bent on establishing himself as the alpha male. He enters the classroom saying sarcastically: "The eager young minds of tomorrow." A pneumatic drill starts up outside the window, so he strides over to shut it. When a student protests: "Can we leave one open professor, it's really hot, sir," Nash merely says: "Your comfort comes second to my ability to hear my own voice." He throws the textbook in the bin. "Personally, I think this class will be a waste of your time, and what is infinitely worse, my time." He starts writing equations on the board, but is interrupted when Alicia, the only female student, opens the window again. "Excuse me, excuse me ..." she shouts to the workmen, and sweetly negotiates a 45-minute delay in their work. The window stays open. Nash, as alpha male, has to regain the dominant position, and does so by saying: "As you will find in a multi-verbal calculus, there is often a number of solutions to any given problem," and returns to writing on the blackboard, "... as there are to this problem." Nash subsequently returns to the Pentagon, saying "McCarthy is an idiot, but unfortunately that doesn't make him wrong." He gets the job of decoding messages in newspapers and magazines, routing orders for Russian portable nuclear bombs. Nash gets so excited that he misses the next class. Alicia walks into his office, commenting on his absence, and to give him her solution to his class exercise. It is elegant but "ultimately incorrect." She asks him to dinner. "You do eat, don't you?" At their date, his eyes wander off Alicia towards shadowy figures lurking in the hallways of the elegant function they are attending: an early sign of his paranoia. Outside, his chat-up line seems to have improved: "Pick a shape," he says. "What?" "Pick a shape, any shape. An animal, anything you like." "Okay..." she responds. "An umbrella." He moves behind her, his eyes on the starry sky, and reaches down to her right hand. Raising it up, he traces out the shape of an umbrella that he can read into the stellar configurations. However fanciful this might be in terms of Nash's actual life, the film makes the point very well here that Nash's acute intellect has a particular genius: the ability to spot patterns in deeply complex and confusing information: again this is typical of HFA/AS. It also gets him the girl.

His work for the Pentagon carries on in parallel with his dating Alicia; both seem to go well. But Nash soon reverts to his previous style of interaction with women, and confesses that the Platonic activities they are engaged in for the sake of convention are not what he wants: it is sex that he is after. Alicia is not so offended however. His former college roommate and his niece also turn up, completing what is now a pleasant work and social life for Nash. He proposes to Alicia in his own inimitable style, and she accepts. But their marriage is soon overshadowed by his bizarre behavior. His Pentagon work suddenly leads him into a fearful car chase and fire-fight: the shadowy figures who have obviously had him under surveillance have made their move. He comes home to his newly-wed wife many hours after leaving his office, in a state of shock, unable to share his problems with her. He cannot talk to her. His paranoia kicks in very visibly now: he is unable to stand in front of his class, and peers round doors as he goes. He tells his Pentagon contact that he can't go on, his circumstances have changed as Alicia is now pregnant. But the Pentagon makes it clear: if he quits working for them, they will quit working for him, which means that they will no longer protect him from the Russians.

He returns home and shouts at Alicia for leaving the light on: he is desperate to turn off the lights in the house; his eyes are staring. "You have to go to your sister's" he insists; peering through the blinds he sees the sinister black automobile in the drive. His attempts to keep a lid on his paranoia finally end when he is giving a public lecture to a large audience. Seeing the men in black enter the back of the hall, he trails off and slips away, running across the quadrangle. But the men chasing him are a psychiatrist and his aides, and not the Russians that Nash believes them to be. After sedation with Thorazine he wakes up in a psychiatric hospital.

It is we, the audience, who are now in for a shock. This is a well-made film which now reveals that Nash has fantasized much of what we have seen, including characters such as his roommate and niece, whom we took to be a real part of the historical story. Likewise the Pentagon and all his military work. He is diagnosed as a paranoid schizophrenic, with hallucinations that include his roommate Charles. Alicia finds this hard to accept, as John Nash had talked repeatedly of Charles, his college roommate. The psychiatrist presses her to give any account of actually meeting Charles or seeing a photo. "This is ridiculous!" she says. He turns to her and says: "I phoned Princeton. According to their housing records John lived alone." This moment is a great filmic device, because even though we are gripped by the drama of Alicia's slow realization, we have at the same time to rewind the film in our heads, disentangling what was real from what was unreal (just as in *Fight Club*). We get it. There were no men in black, no visit to the Pentagon, no secret assignment, no secret drop-off, no car chase with flying bullets, and no reason to obsessively read newspapers and magazines, to tear out fragments and paste them over a huge notice-board with arrows and red markings. Nash is mad.

Alicia helps John confront his delusions, but progress is slow. He starts to cut himself in his bleak white-tiled cell: we realize that he is bloodily searching in his arm for his imaginary electronic "implant," the electronic device that gave him access to his imagined secret drop-off. His real treatment now begins: electroshock therapy vividly dramatized in his shackled, quivering body. John eventually returns home and is on medication. His sheer brute intelligence is one defense against his delusions: intellectually he knows about his illusions, but at the same time his medication makes it harder to think. Life for Alicia is not easy with her young baby and a man in many ways just as unsuited to adult life. There is a poignant scene in bed where he resists her sexual advances. "Is it the medication?" she asks, but his slight nod is no comfort to her: she goes to the bathroom and breaks down in a rage against her situation. Next evening we realize that he is only pretending to take his medication: he is absorbed again in the "codes" that he perceives in the newspapers he is studying. A sound in the garden disturbs him, and he is encircled by Pentagon military personnel. He is shown into his garden outhouse, full of code breakers and their equipment; oscilloscopes and radar, maps and hanging light bulbs. But John this time is fighting the illusion ... unsuccessfully it turns out, for now. It is 1956, and John leads a double life, on medication apparently in his home, but back at work in his garden outhouse.

Alicia inevitably stumbles into his workshop, though it is of course no code breaker's electronic haven replete with Pentagon staff. Rather it contains the familiar manic cuttings from newspapers and magazines with string connecting the words circled in red that spell out the routing codes in Nash's fevered mind. She rushes back into the house to grab the baby, who she feels is now threatened by his madness. Nash's familiar set of delusional characters crowd into his brain and he attempts to prevent Alicia's desperate flight. But he has made a breakthrough: he realizes that the little girl he sees, niece of the imaginary Charles, never gets old. He has used his logical mind to punch through the illusion.

John Nash then asks his old rival Martin if he could hang around the Faculty, as it would help if he had a routine and familiar places and faces, but to start with it goes badly wrong. His friend rescues him from a delusional moment, but they have patience with him, and he returns to a routine after attempting to dismiss his imaginary friends. He audits another professor's course, in the same teaching room that he started out in. He works in the library and becomes a familiar dotty figure on campus, mocked at times, but otherwise much helped by the familiar surroundings. By 1978 he has aged but is apparently stable, and able to communicate at least in the language he understands best: mathematics. He begins to hold his own with a new generation of enthusiastic young mathematicians, and asks if he can teach again. Coming out of his classroom in March 1994, a stranger meets him in the corridor to tell him that he is being considered for the Nobel Prize. Nash's "Equilibrium" theory has made such an impact on economics and law that his work now has widespread recognition.

What is clear from the film is the high and fond regard that American culture pays to such a character, in a fictionalized account at least. In reality, those having to deal with his lack of social skills would often just reject him, but in the afterglow of a Nobel Prize award he becomes a cultural icon. He is a "winner," not a "loser." While at most levels this film shows critical distance regarding its subject matter, it doesn't challenge the status of intelligence per se, and neither does it make any link between his emotional underdevelopment and the broader question of "emotional intelligence" as proposed by Goleman and others. It is true that Nash's diagnosis is schizophrenia, not HFA/AS, but this is just where a broader cultural framework is necessary, beyond the immediate clinical literature. Bleuler, the Swiss psychiatrist, used the term "autism" in adults to describe schizophrenia, leading apparently to the use of the term "childhood schizophrenia" for autism in the young for some time.[9] This shows how mutable such terminology is and how hard it is to prevent leakage across diagnostic boundaries. Keeping outside of the clinical niceties however, the point here is that *A Beautiful Mind* conforms to an ideal of mind that indicates *cultural* autism, as we define it. Nash's mind can only be called beautiful from a very narrow achievement-oriented perspective.

Artificial Intelligence: A.I.

A.I. was originally a short story by Brian Aldiss, and was worked on by director Stanley Kubrick for many years. He had discussed it with Steven Spielberg, who took it on after Kubrick's death at the wishes of his widow. Spielberg wanted to remain faithful to Kubrick's vision, and so undertook the completion of the script himself, involving hundreds of small changes. But *A.I.* is a quintessentially Spielberg movie, exhibiting two key features: the obsession with children, and what we are calling here cultural autism. In the film we are in a future world after global warming has flooded coastal cities, causing millions to starve; but, thankfully, mega-prosperity still holds a bit further inland. There is a shortage of resources of course, and the Government has taken the obvious step to conserve them: they "introduced legal sanctions to strictly license pregnancies, which was why robots, who were never hungry and who did not consume resources beyond those of their first manufacture, were so essential an economic link in the chain mail of society." Now, science fiction always requires the suspension of disbelief so that an implausible constraint on society, or new opportunity, can be the prism through which to examine a familiar human dilemma. But the idea that a robot would consume *no* resources at all is an absurdity that surely only an autistic mind would entertain: we are now being told that even leaving a TV on standby is contributing to global warming—what to say of a robot? However, let us swallow our disbelief.

Dr. Hobby of Cybertronics Corporation takes up the theme: "To create an artificial being has been the dream of man since the birth of science. Not merely the beginning of the modern age, when our forebears astonished the world with the first thinking machines: primitive monsters that could play chess." This gets a laugh, as the assembled staff think back to those days. Hobby has an idea, which he pronounces to the class in classic though subdued mad-scientist tones: "I propose that we build a robot child, who can love. A robot child who will genuinely love the parent or parents it imprints on, with a love that will never end." Note that love is already defined in terms of the biology of chickens—"imprinting" is apparently what chicks do to anything that moves. For Dr. Hobby this robot child is an addition to their range of "mechas" which already serve all of mankind's needs (or at least for those with sufficient cash). It would be more than a child substitute mecha, it would be:

> a mecha with a mind, with neuronal feedback. You see what I'm suggesting is that love will be the key by which they acquire a kind of subconscious never before achieved. An inner world of metaphor, of intuition, of self-motivated reasoning. Of dreams.

Only an engineer can speak this way! The "subconscious" is the difficult, unprogrammable, slippery stuff of emotion, but by programming the robot with "love," all this difficult stuff would somehow emerge. Ridiculous! A survey of the computer science literature on artificial intelligence—a project that almost defines cultural autism—tells one that this is bunkum. But let us swallow our disbelief again. One of his staff, or students, challenges him: one might make such a thing, but "isn't the real conundrum—can you get a human to love them back?" Hobby has an answer: "Ours will be a perfect child caught in a freeze-frame—always loving, never ill, never changing." Isn't this the perfect illustration of what the autistic mind demands of family life? Did not Einstein's marriage collapse because of his inability to cope with the chaos of childhood, a chaos that he also fought tooth and nail to eradicate from quantum theory? Is not the inability to cope with unpredictability and change central to the diagnosis of autism?

Twenty months later we meet the couple destined to be those parents on which Hobby's creation "David" will imprint. Their own son is comatose, and may not recover. It is perhaps during the first period of their relationship with the mechanical child, when Henry brings David home to meet Monica, which provides the creepiest part of the film. At bedtime David reveals that he does not sleep, but he can lie quietly and not make a peep. How marvelous that the child goes to bed in such a model of engineering orderliness! But Monica is too freaked out to help David into the pajamas he holds outstretched for her. The next day it is she who cannot respond emotionally to his cute smile, as he pops up everywhere round the home as she does the housework. Finally she shuts him into a closet and leaves him there for a while. When she relents he just asks chirpily: "Is it a game?"

In the evening Henry is home (it seems that despite all the robots in the world, Daddy still goes to work and Mommy stays at home and does the ironing), and they sit round the table at supper. David of course does not eat, as he consumes none of the planetary resources. The awkwardness is palpable. David then begins to imitate their eating and drinking, with his empty glass and plate. As suddenly as in a horror film David bursts into laughter at the spaghetti dangling from Monica's mouth. Dad joins in, almost hysterically, and the ice is broken. Monica tucks David up in bed, and the next day Monica gets out the "Imprinting Protocols." These remind her of an awful fact: that once imprinting has taken place it is "permanent, indelible and unalterable," and if they ever want to get rid of David he would have to be destroyed. Now, in real life, who could possibly enter into such a Faustian pact?

Martin, their real son, recovers from his coma and returns home with space-age prosthetics, triggering a mutual jealousy. David is now started on the road to win Monica's love (not, interestingly, Henry's, pointing again to the Oedipal nature of American society), but the competition between the boys escalates so badly that the parents eventually decide to get rid of David. In a scene of complete maudlin sentimentality Monica drives David back to Cybertronics to be destroyed, but relents at the gates and leaves him to his fate in the woods. At this point the story turns from what was a standard scifi genre to a fantasy adventure more akin to *The Wizard of Oz*. Just like the Tin Man, David must find the Wizard to give him a heart, though in David's case it is the Blue Fairy who will turn him into a real boy, upon which his Mommy will love him. But the Blue Fairy is drowned in a Manhattan funfair.

Aristotle wouldn't have liked it. Spielberg then comes up with one of the most spurious *deus ex machina* scenarios in dramatic history: David spends 2,000 years staring at the Blue Fairy in her drowned world until aliens wake him up and take him in hand. Through his mind they reconstruct the extraordinary world of human achievement, and out of respect they do everything to make him happy. Unfortunately the equations don't allow for them to bring back his Mommy until Teddy, his mechanical sidekick, produces a hair from her head. Using her DNA she is brought back to life, but an obscure technicality means that they can only do it for one day. But it is the happiest day of his life! For the autistic person, perfect love can only last a day. Any longer and all the complicated and bewildering mood-changes and contingencies of actual human love would inevitably intrude.

David, as a boy who never grows up, stands for a peculiarly male autistic mindset. This mind is competitively gadget-obsessed, and conceives of love as a scarce commodity that can be programmed into a million-dollar machine, or reconstructed scientifically from Mom's DNA. The American psycho, Patrick Bateman, kills the women who are the source of love, whereas the autistic technocrat cultures women from their DNA—like so much yogurt. Love is a commodity that is bought, sold, bio-engineered, or its absence raged at in imaginary murder.

But perhaps science fiction naturally tends to the culturally autistic. Think for example of both the Russian original of *Solaris* and its American remake, or all of the sci-fi Spielberg films. So what about Spielberg's non-science fiction films? Taking perhaps his most celebrated "serious" film, *Schindler's List*, one finds the same emotional dissonance at work. *Schindler's List* is an important film and very successful in what it sets out to do: to portray the Holocaust through the story of a German who helped to save many Jews. It may well tell the story in a historically accurate and powerful manner, but it is completely flawed in its emotional bracketing. To give just one example: there is a scene in which the little girl in the red coat is walking through the streets as Schindler looks on from horseback on a hill. As his eyes follow her we see Nazi soldiers ransacking Jewish apartments, and then a group of Jews rounded up and shot in cold blood. All that Schindler manages to express at the horror and contradiction of the scene is mild concern. He could have been thinking that there was too much litter around, or, tut-tut, it was time those trees in the park were pruned. Yet he has to make a turning point in his allegiances, from the Nazi regime to the Jewish victims, and this would be the point in the story where it happened. So perhaps he is hiding the horror and anguish overcoming his soul, because he is a public figure. But if that were the case we should cut immediately to a scene where we could share his private outpouring of emotion, an anguished re-evaluation of his entire moral universe. We don't. While Spielberg tells in the most arresting of imagery the outward course of Schindler's story—and with it the dreadful fate of the Jews—he fails dismally to show us the inward and profoundly emotional course of Schindler's conversion. Likewise his portrait of the Nazi camp commander Goetz is a clumsy caricature, giving us no insight into the true squalor of his fractured moral universe. (The Greek-born French director Costa-Gavras does no better in his portrayal of Nazis in his 2002 film *Amen*: perhaps the subject matter is ultimately beyond film.)

Wheeler Winston Dixon considers Spielberg to show a "distressing lack of depth" in *Schindler's List*,[10] while citing Lloyd Kaufman, head of Troma Pictures: "*A.I.* represents a kind of 'emotional pornography' ..." and "pointing out the flaws in *A.I.* is like saying you hate love or children or teddy bears."[11] More specifically we can say that the lack of critical distance in *A.I.* represents a very American cultural autism, where only the few—like Dixon and Kaufman—are prepared to resist its assumptions.

In the Cut and *Rain Man*

Brilliant mathematicians and child robots are perhaps unsuitable cases for illustrating the more pervasive and less extreme aspects of cultural autism, so we turn now to *In the Cut*, a thriller whose heroine is an ordinary college teacher, Frannie. *In the Cut* is a Jane Campion film released in 2003, and stars Meg Ryan as Frances Avery. Although Campion is Australian, this film is set in America and its theme is serial killers, so it usefully embodies many elements of the American madness. Campion, like Spielberg, is a gifted artist, though with a more subtle eye for mood and cinematography, and she attempts to deal with more complex issues. *In the Cut* is based on the novel by Susanna Moore, written, the author tells us, to explore sexuality in a way that she finds lacking in male authors. The end result of a female writer, female director and female star is so profoundly autistic (in the sense used here) as to explode the notion that autism might be a male preserve.

Tellingly, Frannie is interested in words: she is a writer and teacher of English literature, and jots down a word early in the film: "disarticulated." This is the word that detective Malloy (Mark Ruffalo) uses to describe the dismemberment of a murdered prostitute, parts of whom were found outside Frannie's flat. But Frannie had witnessed a sexual act between the murdered girl and a man with a tattoo on his hand just like Malloy's (though she saw neither face), and so we are set up for a journey in which Malloy and Frannie strike up a relationship based on a profound contradiction. To start with Frannie just has masturbatory fantasies about him and his tattoo: is this about the eroticization of murder? In another shot she is in Malloy's car looking at a photo of the severed head of the victim: the camera briefly catches a glimpse of her legs. She shows no response to the picture, just as Schindler shows no response to the murdered Jews as he gazes down on them from his Olympian heights. Now, we know that she is hiding the fact that she went to the bathroom and witnessed a woman perform fellatio on a man displaying Malloy's tattoo, but her unemotional response to what must be one of the most gruesome images a human being can endure is simply not believable. No gasp, no sign of revulsion, no turning her head away, no demand to be let out of the car. Nothing: she is emotionally dead, living in an emotional vacuum.

Frannie's half-sister Pauline has got the clap, and Frannie, in a roundabout way, recommends giving up men and confining herself to masturbation, despite the fact she has just made a date with Malloy. In the bar he is only a touch more subtle than John Nash with his chat up line. Malloy tells her earnestly: "I can be whatever you want me to be. You want me to romance you, take you to a classy restaurant, no problem. Or I can be your best friend and fuck you, treat you good, lick your pussy ... no problem." But he gets no slap: Frannie just changes the subject. They are then joined by another officer who sums up his philosophy towards women: "All you need are two tits, a hole and heartbeat." Malloy contributes: "You don't even need the tits." Patrick Bateman would be in good company here—after all this *is* about serial killers. When the officer comes back with "You don't even need the heartbeat, pal," Frannie walks out into the rain, and then walks home slowly in her high heels, only to get attacked and then bounced off the bonnet of a taxi as she runs away. Malloy turns up and comforts her somewhat, in a remote professional way, asking about the assailant. They land up in bed. Afterwards Frannie is most impressed, it seems, with his sensitive attention to her genitals. She finally challenges him as to whether he was the man with the prostitute, but he swears it wasn't him. Later in a café with Pauline, Frannie begins to cry.

Frannie's ex-boyfriend John (Kevin Bacon) now turns up. He wants her to look after his dog; he is having panic attacks; he will have to go on anti-depressants; and when she finally tells him that she doesn't want to see him any more he gets aggressive in the way that only American males know how. "Fuck!" he shouts, just like the young men in *The Blair Witch Project* when they get lost in the woods. The world, it seems, is nothing more than a continual affront; its unwillingness to conform to expectation elicits an infantile rage summed up in the bellowed: "Fuck!"

Like *Seven* and *Silence of the Lambs* this film juxtaposes murder with high culture. Not only is Frannie a writer and teacher of literature, she keeps reading "Poetry in Motion" on the subway, short poems that appear to her like *haikus*, perhaps offering her clues to her alienated existence. She reads: "I was like one blind, not afraid of the dark." Is an autistic culture also one that is blind, and pathologically unafraid of the "dark," its alienated cultural productions? Does not a film like this represent an endemic insanity, one which we *ought* to fear?

As we might anticipate, Frannie visits Pauline, only to find her, inevitably, murdered, dismembered in her own shower. Frannie is finally properly distraught, and clutches the bloody head of her half-sister, wrapped in a plastic bag, sobbing. We suspect all the time of course that Malloy is the killer, and that Frannie must also suspect him: after all she accuses him of being a liar over his marriage. We also get a Freudian glimpse into why Frannie might be so distant in her emotions, as she tells Malloy after the murder that her father—separated from her mother by now—had left her alone for five days in Geneva. It hadn't occurred to him that she wouldn't be all right. Just like Albert in *I Heart Huckabees*, Frannie offers an analytical explanation, a single traumatic event in her past. She asks Malloy: "did you kill her?" He says no, and sends her home to be alone in her apartment. Surely no police force in the developed world would send the sister of a just-murdered woman home alone, without offering police protection from the still-at-large serial killer, counseling, or a woman police officer to stay with her, or ascertain what close relative she could stay with. Absurd. Autistic. It is not a plot device; it serves no purpose. It is just poor emotional bracketing.

In her flat Frannie drinks herself numb, and plays in her mind the romantic fantasy of her mother and father skating on a lake where he had originally proposed to her. In her mind, this well-worn image now turns into horror, as her father runs over her prone mother on the ice, cutting her legs clean through with his skates. On the return run he is aiming at the neck, but the imaginary scene is interrupted.

Later on Frannie has sex again with Malloy. She has bound him with his own handcuffs to a heavy pipe and straddles him on a swivel chair. "Will I like this?" he asks, to which she says, "I don't know." "I like it in the cut," he says as he enters her, presumably meaning "cunt." One presumes it is a play on words, linking sex and wounding; the vagina as a wound, and sex as inevitably leading to laceration and then murder. But she achieves her climax, as does he, and there seems to be a real moment of tenderness between them. She won't release him immediately. "It makes me very nervous to be in handcuffs," he says, growing anxious, but then she finds what she thinks is the clue that conclusively identifies him as the murderer, and runs out with his coat.

His detective colleague, Rodriguez, picks her up as she stumbles, distraught, in the street, and takes her to a lighthouse. "I've read that," she says, a literary reference to Virginia Woolf. But he has imprisoned her, and she finally realizes that it is he who is the killer, not Malloy. They happen to both have the same tattoo; they belong to the same exclusive police club of which it is a mark. As Rodriguez forces Frannie to kiss him in preparation for her dismemberment, he says: "Will you marry me?" Rodriguez wants the woman without the heartbeat. But she shoots him with Malloy's pistol that she has found in his coat; at the same time we cut to Frannie's dream sequence of her parents skating, the romantic story her mother had told of their engagement. The point of this shot is that marriage has become an ideal that she and Pauline desperately longed for, but is irrevocably tainted as a concept, first by the separation of their parents, and now, by association, with gruesome murder. Marriage means death. Bloodied, she returns to the handcuffed Malloy and they embrace, and we are left with the hope that they might salvage a real relationship out of all this.

A feminist reading of *In the Cut* might say that "disarticulation" is about denying women their voice (the chance to be articulate) and that Rodriguez is the epitome of male violence that dismembers the woman and leaves her without a heartbeat. More than this: *marriage* itself is nothing short of disarticulation. No problem: art is all about constructing powerful non-literal images to convey a point or social message. But one can see an autism in this that has Frannie and Pauline believe in such a perfection of marriage that nothing in real life can live up to, and so romance becomes an amputation. Real marriages and real relationships are messy compromises and don't last for ever. It is autistic to hold aloof from real relationships while dreaming of a perfect one. Spielberg's vision of perfect love is experienced by a robot, reconstituted from DNA, and, most tellingly, lasts for only a day. In a single day, he hopes, no reality can seep in; the single honeymoon day is the perfect relationship. Its mirror image is the equally autistic idea of eternal romantic love, an impossible ideal which means that Frannie and Pauline are doomed to disappointment.

The question remains: is there real critical distance in *In the Cut*, or is it unknowingly a perfect example of cultural autism, as we would suggest? To argue for real critical distance would be to argue for the film as *irony*. Is it bitter, feminist irony? If so, it would have to be a double irony, in that the females in the film are represented as the parodies of real women as would be constructed by the men in the film, themselves already parodies. The conversation in the bar between Frannie, Malloy and Rodriguez might be construed that way. But, because there is not one person in the film whose emotional life is authentic, the irony must go further and be an indictment of society as a whole. But if American cultural life is already to some extent autistic, then the argument either way becomes a circle, which can only be broken by pointing to the existence of the *clinical* work on autism. And this shows overwhelmingly that society as a whole is not autistic: it is a small proportion of individuals. The fact that some of those suffering from a mild HFS/AS-like condition are cultural producers—perhaps disproportionately—skews *culture*, not society. "Cultural autism" then becomes a little like the "paranoid style" of Hofstadter which he compares as a term to the baroque or mannerist styles in art history.[12] These become terms usefully applied to a historical moment in a sector of cultural production or politics.

On the other hand *Rain Man* and a series of other films such as *I am Sam* and *Snow Cake* are films specifically about an autistic person—in the clinical sense. *Rain Man* is interesting because it *also* portrays the more subtle and endemic kind of cultural autism under discussion here. It does so in the two main characters: brothers Raymond Babbitt (played by Dustin Hoffman) and Charlie Babbitt (played by Tom Cruise). At the start of the film Charlie is unaware that his autistic brother is cared for in an institution, but is rudely awakened to the fact of his existence when he finds out that it is Raymond, not himself, who will inherit his father's $3 million estate. Charlie is the one of interest to us here, as the point of the film is to show how a so-called "normal" person may be as undeveloped emotionally as those with a diagnosed condition. The key characteristic of all those who might be placed on the autism spectrum is the inability to empathize with others. Yes, for a high-functioning autistic like Raymond Babbitt or John Nash, there may well be other obvious symptoms such as obsessive behavior, but it is the problem with empathy that is the defining characteristic. The fictional Raymond Babbitt was inspired by the life of Kim Peek, considered to be suffering from "savant syndrome," another way of describing high-functioning autism. It is the inability to empathize, regardless of its origins, that is of interest here in exposing a facet of the American madness, and it is in the so-called "normal" brother that it represents something at a cultural level, as opposed to within the tiny minority of clinically diagnosed autistics.

Charlie is into cars and money, and is angry not to receive his share of the inheritance. Also, it seems that he cannot relate to his girlfriend. He tracks down his brother and takes him off in what effectively becomes a fraternal road movie involving a series of encounters where Charlie grows up and into the role of a caring brother. Where his loving girlfriend had failed to break through Charlie's armored personality, the vulnerability of Raymond, and his infuriating obsessional behavior, succeed. Charlie has, at the start of the film, some elements of the American madness, though in a mild form compared to other film characters that we have examined. He is aggressive, armored, emotionally undeveloped. When the doctor in charge of Raymond tells Charlie that his brother is autistic savant, that he "can't express himself or understand his emotions," we understand that Charlie has the same difficulties, but on a different scale. Charlie is merely impatient however when pressed as to the point of his questioning. "What's the fucking point? Why didn't anyone tell me I had a brother?" Over the course of the journey, which was for Charlie initially a way to secure his part of the inheritance, his defenses soften, and in the end he not only offers to be Raymond's guardian, but regains his estranged girlfriend.

In contrasting a diagnosed autistic with a "normal" person—one we could characterize as suffering from a *cultural* autism—*Rain Man* is knowing and intentional. *In the Cut*, *A.I.*, and many other Spielberg films, it is argued here, show this cultural autism in an unintended fashion. *Taxi Driver*, *Indigo*, and countless other films are ultimately heartless, and this fact should make us ask questions about our culture and society. "Autism" is a word that derives from the Greek for "self" and is related to solipsism, the idea or philosophy that one is at the center of the universe. The uniquely American version of this derives from the extreme competitiveness which locks one into a lonely, solipsistic world of armored defensiveness, made all the more isolating through wealth and the technologies purchased by wealth.

12

Virtual Reality and Saccharine Fantasies

KEY FILMS: *The Matrix trilogy, The Truman Show*
ADDITIONAL FILMS: *Lawnmower Man, Pleasantville*

One indicator of madness in an individual is a retreat from reality into a fantasy world. It appears sadly normal to take for granted all those material comforts that wealthy nations provide for their citizens, including such basics as electricity, sewerage and running hot and cold water. There is a simple lack of interest in how these things are provided, and the real economic (for workers and other countries) and environmental costs. These impacts are too far upstream or downstream for the consumer to notice. But this endemic indifference to the true reality and consequences of the American (and Western) lifestyle is just one element in a stance that so easily takes the citizen towards a completely escapist fantasy lifestyle. Film and TV, as well as novels and comic books, provide the material for that fantasy: here we pick out just two elements, virtual reality and "saccharine fantasy."

True virtual reality (VR) involves technologies known as "full immersion," where the user dons head-up computer graphics displays and suits that provide navigational input and kinesthetic feedback.[1] These have been surprisingly slow to enter the marketplace, which gives hope perhaps that the human imagination is still powerful enough to do without this technology. On the other hand a more pessimistic conclusion might be that the requirement on the user to interact with the VR environment has lessened its appeal to the terminally lazy, as the thoughtful techno-prophet of VR, Jaron Lanier, pointed out at the birth of the technology. But the public knows about VR mainly from films and TV, including such works as *Tron, Lawnmower Man, eXistenZ*, the *Matrix* trilogy and Oliver Stone's made-for-TV series *Wild Palms*. These generally represent VR in a state of sophistication far in advance of what is technologically possible, so they already represent a fantasy about a fantasy, as it were.

Predicting the future is a precarious profession. Of course it would have been deeply embarrassing to have been amongst those who predicted that heavier-than-air planes wouldn't fly, but there are probably more embarrassments all-told, amongst the technological optimists than amongst the pessimists. A good example is when the latest professor of robotics comes on TV to tell us that robots will be able to do the housework "real soon now," as one can find such predictions going back forty years. The professors of robotics retire, take their pensions, and still no sign of it. There is no robot in the world that could negotiate the route from the average front door to the average kitchen sink without tripping over, and even if it got there, it would have no idea how to do the washing up. The chances are it would drop and smash the very first dirty plate. Or take the case of the scientists building Britain's first nuclear power stations: they went on TV to say that the plant would produce "electricity so cheap we won't need to meter it." To date nuclear electricity is more expensive than any conventional source, and is only commercially viable because decommissioning costs are unknown and therefore not calculated into the true cost of the energy produced.

So it should be no surprise to find that the introduction to the film *Lawnmower Man* states this:

> By the turn of the millennium a technology known as VIRTUAL REALITY will be in widespread use. It will allow you to enter computer generated artificial worlds as unlimited as the imagination itself. Its creators foresee millions of positive uses—while others fear it as a new form of mind control.

The film was released in 1992, but VR is no more in widespread use in the new millennium than washing-up robots are. But what is it in the American madness that VR films point to? We suggest that VR involves the same dynamics as the appeal of lucid dreaming: control. In virtual reality the body is left behind, cocooned and possibly even fed intravenously, while every conceivable thrill can be engaged with in complete safety. All penalties of the real world—including exhaustion, hunger, injury, and death at the physical level; defeat, humiliation and subjugation at the psychological level—can be excluded from the gameplay. Although true VR represents a technological and artistic challenge for the maker, and a potentially mind-expanding experience for the user, its pathology is the same as any extreme escapism. Once the user is accustomed to acts of god-like power and effectiveness in the virtual world, the real world, with its decreasing scope for adventure and increasing dull uniformity, seems unattractive. Addiction is the inevitable outcome for the vulnerable, as in drugs and gambling.

The films that in one way or another deal with VR generally have violent content or are dystopian, as are many computer games. But there are a slew of films that deal with an idealized perfect America, a fantasy so sugary as to deserve the epithet "saccharine." These saccharine fantasies, such as *The Truman Show* and *Pleasantville*, may be constructed to show how false these dreams really are, but there is no doubt that the worlds they represent are part of a truly American escapism. The *Matrix* trilogy and *The Truman Show* have been chosen to represent respectively VR and saccharine fantasy, and we then consider *Lawnmower Man* and *Pleasantville* to support the argument.

The *Matrix* Trilogy

Few recent films and their sequels have sparked so much written commentary as the *Matrix* trilogy: *The Matrix*, *The Matrix Reloaded*, and *Matrix Revolutions*, written and directed by the Wachowski brothers. These writings largely focus on philosophical, metaphysical and religious implications of the work, particularly around the question of what is really real. How would we know whether we lived the reality we perceive, or whether we are "brains in vats" fed a continual and convincing computer simulation? For this is the central conceit of the films: that "they" have imprisoned the human race in vats in order to suck the life energy from us, while keeping us sane through VR pumped directly into the brain. Versions of this conundrum have been circulating for centuries (going back in various guises all the way to Descartes), but *TheMatrix* poses it in a radically new and dramatically exciting way. Though for a trained scientist the premise is more than usually hard to swallow (no organism can produce a surplus of energy over input), the metaphor is not bad: even the Romans were accused of providing bread and circuses to keep the masses under control. As it turns out, the image of the Romans is a good one, as their military machine would have appeared as inexorable to those conquered by it as the "machines" that repress the good people of the Matrix.

The voluminous writing on the *Matrix* films is justified by the editor of *The Matrix and Philosophy: Welcome to the Desert of the Real* as a way of bringing "the reader from pop culture to philosophy."[2] The subtitle of the book makes reference to a phrase from Baudrillard, whose text *Simulacra and Simulation* was a "key source" for the *Matrix* trilogy, as Catherine Constable tells us.[3] In her paper "Baudrillardian Revolutions: Repetition and Radical Intervention in the *Matrix* Trilogy" she goes on to remind us that Baudrillard's book appears early in the first *Matrix* film, and that it was recommended reading for the cast members. She also defends the films' credentials as upholding Baudrillard's position, which can be summed up in two principles: that simulation is no longer the representation of the real—it is "generation by models of a real without origin or reality"[4]—and that this is the fault of Capital. But the sensibility of Baudrillard's essays and the sensibility of the films are worlds apart: the *Matrix* films may pose as antinomian revolutions of the people against oppression, but the "real" remains as the goal of revolution, while Capital is never mentioned; indeed the films are an orgy of capitalist production, product placement (without brand it is true, but "designer"-styling nonetheless), and liberal optimism. Baudrillard in contrast is a true pupil of the masters of suspicion for whom Capital is reified as the ultimate evil, and from which there is no escape, not even to the vantage point of the viewer of spectacle, because Capital has made the viewer into the spectacle. It is no surprise then that Baudrillard disowned *The Matrix* as unfaithful to his thought.[5]

A huge range of other philosophical sources have been brought to bear on the films in various edited collections and monographs. For example, in Peter B. Lloyd's *Exegesis of the Matrix* he suggests a visible presence of the perennial philosophy in the films, mentioning specifically Plotinus and the Neoplatonist idea of the demiurge.[6] In a different kind of film studies critique Eric Wilson says: "Films like *The Matrix* and *The Truman Show* have deployed Gnostic myths of the second and third centuries to explore the idea that the physical world is an illusion concocted by a tyrannical maker."[7] Not all analyses are sycophantic: John Shelton Lawrence lambastes the films as fascist and an example of the political poverty of Joseph Campbell's monomyth.[8]

While all of this is interesting, here we examine only how the *Matrix* films represent an ultimate escapist fantasy, and also how they document other elements of the American madness, including paranoia, aggression, and particularly the apocalyptic. There are also hefty doses of New Age narcissism and cultural autism on show. In fact the only elements of the American madness not recapitulated in these films are the sexual and Oedipal—a geek film can't deal with either sex or the unconscious.

The key character in the series is Neo, epitome of "geek-chic." He is a computer programmer who makes money on the side with programs that he sells as if they were hard drugs, to users who have obviously moved up from mere cocaine. The disks are kept in a space hollowed out in *Simulacra and Simulation*, open at the essay "On Nihilism"—in *noir* films this is where the gumshoe would have kept his gun, though the book would have been chosen from a different canon. Neo is played by Keanu Reeves, who also plays the protagonist in *Johnny Mnemonic*, a VR-themed film based on a short story by William Gibson. (Gibson wrote the defining cyberpunk novel of virtual reality, *Neuromancer*.) In the *Matrix* trilogy, Neo is plucked from obscurity by a key figure in the "Resistance"; is told that he may be the "One"; and does indeed become a god-like figure who saves the human race from enslavement by the machines. Morpheus is the captain of the fighting ship, the Nebuchadnezzar, a kind of earth-bound spaceship that navigates through the dismal, dark, and inhospitable real world left after some kind of apocalypse. Its crew, which includes love-interest Trinity, operate consoles that give them access to the virtual world inhabited by the enslaved humans of the Matrix. These enslaved humans are kept bottled in vast farms, in order to extract energy for the machines which now run the physical world, and which have designed the virtual world, a playground designed to keep humans passive. Initially everything that happens to Neo is merely part of the virtual world, the Matrix, but when Morpheus sends Trinity into the Matrix Neo is persuaded to join the Resistance. He is rescued from his "vat," unplugged from the Matrix, and plunges into the dark dystopian reality of the human world. The film trilogy follows his initial training, the many sorties into the virtual world of the Matrix, and his final heroic acts leading to liberation.

The point about a VR simulation is that anything can be made to happen—actually a deeply boring prospect. In fact the enslaved inhabitants of the virtual world of the Matrix are fed a fantasy based on late 20th-century city life close to the reality. But there is fun to be had if some of the usual limitations of reality are transcended just enough to ensure that the hero and heroine can engage in a plausible fight with near-normally-endowed enemies. What *TheMatrix* also provides are super-enemies who are a real match for Neo and Trinity. Gravity is one of the first victims of the film, as it is in *Crouching Tiger, Hidden Dragon*: it must be an enduring fantasy of ours, to fly. Neo merely bounces around the room in the first film, but in *The Matrix Reloaded* he can take to the skies—does "the Superman thing," complete with billowing cape. But this flying is not for any aesthetic enjoyment; it is an essential part of his strategy, as is the ability to stop bullets with mind-power, an essentially New Age idea worthy of *What the Bleep*. Another example of the "virtual" in VR is when Trinity needs to hijack a helicopter: she gets mission control, the good ship Nebuchadnezzar, to download a helicopter-flying program into her mind. She has this much expertise at least: she knows it is a V-212 helicopter ... or did she read that off the engine cowling? In *Reloaded* she requests a program to hot-wire a motorcycle, and so on. Why bother to learn anything the hard way when you can just download the program? (Such instant routes to martial competence are well satirized in the film *Team America* in its "montage" sequence.) Trinity's sudden helicopter skills are reminiscent of Zelig's flight from Germany in which his "other-directed" mentality is so developed as to turn him into an instant flying ace, despite having no previous piloting experience.

This is perhaps the most insidious part of the VR fantasy in the *Matrix* series: the facility to acquire skills in moments that would usually take a lifetime. These may be martial-arts skills, weapons skills, helicopter-flying skills, but above all they are looking-cool skills. The *Matrix* trilogy depicts a world where everything is faked by malevolent authorities to keep human beings enslaved. The paranoia usually directed to everything Federal in America is now extended to the whole of "reality," and focused on the "Agents," men in black modeled on the long film and TV tradition of FBI baddies, real or imagined. Nothing can be trusted, and all technology can be used to bug, listen, eavesdrop and betray the unwary. Perhaps deeper than any culturally located paranoia, such as the American paranoia about all things Federal, is the fear that existence itself is malign. Given the Western fixation on a creator "God," then what if "God," the author of all things, is just using us to extract electricity, to amuse himself, whatever? What if he is a Gnostic demiurge? So we look on with interest at the scene in *The Matrix Reloaded* where Neo finally meets the "Architect," the creator of the Matrix program. It's no fun to meet your Creator and have him tell you that: "Your life is the sum of the remainder of an unbalanced equation inherent to the programming of the Matrix." Makes you feel kind of small. The Architect continues: "You are the eventuality of an anomaly, which, despite my sincerest efforts I have been unable to eliminate from what is otherwise a harmony of mathematical precision." Or perhaps it's nice to know that one is the grit in the oyster! The Architect also lets on that he will succeed in destroying "Zion." He is confident because he has already destroyed it six times over.

Hollywood has provided its heroes with ever more implausible weapons, culminating perhaps in the ridiculous gadgetry of the *Men In Black*. The *Matrix* designers have gone to town, not so much in the absurd size of the weapons as in the styling. This is as much about the way that bullets fly, leaving visible swirls in the air, as in the weapons themselves. But perhaps the most nauseating conception in *The Matrix* is of Neo as the "One" ("Neo" is of course an anagram of "One" and also means "new"). It must be every nerd's wet dream to be have a woman as stunningly beautiful as Trinity track him down (through one's computer, naturally, as that is where one spends all one's time), and announce that she represents a heroic, almost mythical, resistance leader (Morpheus) who has intuited that one is the "One." We already know that Neo has purportedly left his friends and family in his quest to find "something"—but we suspect that actually he just doesn't have any friends or family. So his transformation from a computer geek nobody to the chosen One of the Resistance—wow! Later he also gets to kiss Persephone, another stunningly beautiful woman, as the price he must "reluctantly" pay for access to the "Key." Geeks never had it so good.

Morpheus cannot be one hundred-percent sure of his intuition however, so Neo has to visit the "Oracle," a Hollywood stereotype of a clairvoyant, such as those played so well by Whoopi Goldberg in *Ghost* or by Zelda Rubinstein in *Poltergeist*. The "mystic" is, by this stage in U.S. film culture, a caricature of a caricature: she has to be ordinary yet eccentric, insightful yet confusing, and preferably from an ethnic minority so you couldn't mix her up with other Hollywood stereotypes. Julia Roberts and Nicole Kidman don't get to play "mystics" of this type. The Oracle, surrounded by weird spoon-bending and levitating kids, knows everything about Neo.

SPOON BOY: Do not try and bend the spoon. That's impossible. Instead only try to realize the truth.
NEO: What truth?
SPOON BOY: There is no spoon.
NEO: There is no spoon?
SPOON BOY: Then you'll see that it is not the spoon that bends, it is only yourself.

In *The Matrix* we find cod philosophy's natural bed-fellow: cod mysticism. The cod philosophy of *Waking Life* and *I Heart Huckabees* is augmented by a populist cod-mysticism in *The Matrix*, making it not so removed from the New Age. What it also effectively has in common with *Waking Life* is lucid dreaming: the possibility of *control* in a virtual or dream world that is unavailable in real life. But, in *The Matrix Reloaded*, Neo has doubts about the Oracle. She isn't human, is she? She could be part of the system, simply another device to control the population. It is right and proper for a geek, inheritor of the scientific worldview, to question "mysticism." But the Oracle has enough New Age psychobabble to assuage Neo's doubts: she tells him that ghosts, angels, vampires and aliens are all manifestations of the "system that's assimilating some program that's doing something they're not supposed to be doing." She speaks Neo's language: the mystical arises through bugs in the software. Also, it helps that she now addresses him as the "One," and that she is always baking cookies. But if Neo does not fulfill his destiny then Zion will fall: a modern retelling of the ancient Messiah story.

It is not until the third *Matrix* film, where "Zion" is almost overwhelmed by besieging machines, that we realize how uncannily the scenario echoes a much more ancient siege: the one at Masada. "Zion" is the name given by the Wachowsky brothers to the heavily defended rebel community, a name that caused difficulties for the film across the Arab world. Zion is only mentioned in *The Matrix*, but *The Matrix Reloaded* begins with the threat to Zion from tunneling machines and "sentinels." A quarter of a million of them, one each for every man, woman and child of the Resistance. We first see Zion as the Nebuchadnezzar enters it after a mission; the vast underground cavern is the reverse-image of the technological polish of the Matrix. Instead of vast shiny machines, it has vast rusty machines; instead of the latest technology it has conspicuously clumsy cogwheels. Welcome to the Resistance. It has a "Council," and it meets in a "Temple." It has a vast population of different ethnic groups and orphans living in harmony—and in poverty. They regard Neo as the Messiah, and ask him to watch over their sons and daughters serving on the rebel ships.

It is the following scene, where counselor Harman addresses the people of Zion, that the parallel with first-century tragedy of Masada is made most clear: instead of the vast steel-clad interior where the Nebuchadnezzar lands, we are now in a natural cave formation, big enough to hold thousands. The anxious population is told of the enemy at the door, and to remember those who have been lost in the struggle so far. Harman introduces Morpheus to thunderous applause. He tells them: "The machines have gathered an army, and as I speak that army is drawing nearer to our home." The religious overtones cannot be missed. After his triumphant speech there is feasting, drumming and what appears to be ritual dancing by torchlight. Geek-chic is gone, and the rust-browns of earth and rags have taken its place; the scale of it is massive. Only the techno-beat of the music and the sexuality of the dance make us think of something modern: the disco, the rave, the night-club, and the inevitable orgiastic coupling. What young person could resist signing up to the Resistance?

In the third part of the trilogy the enemy "diggers" have to be battled in the Dock (the entrance to Zion), or, if they break through, then at the entrance to the Temple, which is an effective bottleneck. The film now presents almost Biblical images of inundation, of being overwhelmed by massively superior numbers, of soldiers, of locusts, of machines, of swarming things, of "sentinels." Despite a reprieve in which the Dock is wiped clear of its swarming attackers, the rebels are forced to abandon this strategic defensive position, retreat to the "Temple," and await their salvation at the hands of the Messiah, Neo. The machines re-group and the humans have less than two hours to stave off destruction. Neo, now blinded in a confrontation with a clone of chief enemy Agent Smith, is flying with Trinity into the heart of the Matrix. He then finally encounters the ultimate power, amusingly named "Deus ex Machina." It gives him virtual access to "program Smith," so that the final fight between good and evil can take place, personified in the two men. A user posted this comment on the Internet Movie Database regarding *The Matrix Revolutions*:

> Another thing I do not understand is why the humans want to be free? The Matrix is a much better place to live than the real world, which is dark and cold and only hospitable under the ground. The people here have reverted to a new religion and to wearing horrifically unflattering clothing. Why would they choose this life of

constant turmoil and darkness over the life of at least supposed happiness in the Matrix?[9]

This comment unwittingly gets to the heart of issues surrounding *The Matrix*. Wealth has brought America unheralded abilities to control Nature, its resources, and human society, and it is natural for the American mind to see virtual reality (or lucid dreaming) as the ultimate extension of that power. So why not offer them a virtual world such as the Matrix? Why indeed should one choose a dark cold world underground and have to wear horrible clothes and eat awful food? In fact one of the Nebuchadnezzar's crew makes exactly that choice: he betrays them so that he can exchange the slop he eats on ship for wine and steak in the virtual world. Also telling for the secular culture that produces and consumes entertainment like *The Matrix* is the comment: why revert to religion? But surely the most extraordinary question—asked by a generation who have succumbed to escapist fantasy—is, why would humans want to be free? Why should they willingly choose the real over the unreal?

The Truman Show

In Peter Weir's *The Truman Show* Truman Burbank (played by Jim Carrey) is an insurance salesman in the town of Seahaven—"the Best Place on Earth," according to the local newspaper. So why would he want to go to Fiji? And why are his attempts to book a flight there made so furtively? And why does he search in vain for a Sylvia Garland? Or is it Lauren Garland? The great thing about *The Truman Show* is that we know the answers to these questions, whereas Truman does not: he lives in a TV show revolving entirely around him, and he doesn't know it. The show's creators have gone to great lengths to make sure that he won't want to leave Seahaven: for example his failure to make a short ferry crossing due to nausea suggests that he is certainly not up to doing so by sea. Seahaven represents the American Dream come true: it is typical of thousands of wealthy small towns across America, and in its sealed-off nature is also a metaphor for the "gated communities" that increasingly shut out what wealthy Americans don't want to encounter: poverty, social deprivation and glimpses of other ways of living. But Truman, born into this most saccharine of reality shows, is getting itchy to leave, and Fiji is a place such that you "can't get any further away before you start coming back." He illustrates where Fiji is to his friend using the visual aid of a golf ball, innocent of fact that all the citizens of Seahaven are paid actors whose job it is to talk him into staying.

In a perfect world nothing unusual happens, so each day is much like the last. It's not quite *Groundhog Day*, but we get the point: the American Dream could easily become the American Nightmare of anodyne boredom. Truman does have his own demons, to do with a sailing tragedy in which his father died. And was the tramp on the street his father, mysteriously returned? The unexpected is quickly quashed in Seahaven. His mother's script is smartly rewritten to gloss over the awkward encounter with the tramp, as Truman bursts to tell his story to her. His wife is also primed with the right response. And she caps it brightly with "I made macaroni!" Product placement is everywhere in Seahaven.

But we have flashbacks in which Truman meets the mysterious woman he wants to find: Ms. Garland. She is an actress who wants to tell him the truth (and got fired for her trouble), but only manages a few words before her "folks" turn up. Truman is more interested in the romantic angle, so he isn't quick enough to probe her story. As she blurts it out her "father" bundles her into the car and explains her weird story with a single word: "schizophrenia." Dad makes sure that Truman can't find her again: "We're moving to Fiji."

From time to time glitches in the show appear and after enough of these Truman gets spooked and starts to run around rather bizarrely. Entering a building he presumably has no normal business with he strides towards the lift, watched by perturbed set officials, and, as the doors open, it reveals the rear of a stage set: there is no building there. Even the makers of the Truman show can't afford to fully kit out his world. What he actually sees is nothing like the interior of a lift, but the tea and sandwich area for the actors. They hastily pull a screen across his field of view, but Truman is seriously alarmed now. It makes no sense.

But Truman is living out a paranoia that we could all potentially slip into, if we took the lucid dreaming of *Waking Life*, or the virtual reality of *The Matrix*, seriously. If we think that the world revolves around us, then it wouldn't be hard to start reading this into innocuous events around us. Truman of course isn't reading anything *into* the events around him, but attempting to read *out* the true meaning of them. But when he attempts to explain his experiences to his vending-machine-stockist friend, it comes over as classic paranoia. "I'm definitely being followed," whispers Truman.

Truman can't book a flight to Fiji. "It's the busy season." His bus to Chicago mysteriously breaks down. "Sorry son." On a wild impulse he takes off in his car with Meryl, but traffic mysteriously piles up ahead of him. Impasse. He relents, and appears ready to drive his anxious wife home, but changes his mind and roars off again: the set manager has been unable to keep up, and Truman succeeds in crossing the bridge out of Seahaven (despite his gut-wrenching fear of water). Out of town a fake forest fire fails to stop him, but Christof, the creator of the series, has an ace up his sleeve: an emergency at the Seahaven Nuclear Power Plant. Truman is ready to give up and go home, until the police marshal accidentally slips up: "You're welcome Truman." By showing that he knows Truman's name, the actor has gone beyond the bounds of improvisation: he has given the whole game away. How on earth, if he was a complete stranger, could he know Truman's name? Truman makes a bid for freedom, running into the woods, pursued by "nuclear safety workers" in their silver radiation suits. He is overcome and deposited home with Meryl.

Poor Meryl! How much is she paid? Truman is disturbed and trying to come to terms with these developments and all she can offer him is "Mococoa," a drink she eulogizes about. Is it scripted? Is she really scared of him when he cries out, quite naturally, "What does this [all-natural cocoa drink product] hafta' do, with anything? Tell me what's happening!" He advances on her, and she picks up her latest kitchen gadget to hold him at bay. "You're scaring me," she says. "You're scaring *me*, Meryl," he replies in that comic-sinister manner that is the trademark of actor Jim Carrey. "What're you going to do? Dice me? Slice me? So many *choices!*" Things are getting out of hand, but there is a knock at the door and it is Truman's best friend, Marlon. Meryl runs to him sobbing: "Oh my God. How can anyone expect me to carry on under these conditions? It's unprofessional!" Clearly the actress who plays Meryl can't take any more. They may have a script framework to adhere to, but there are limits to how much one can improvise in such unforeseen circumstances.

Marlon tries to bring Truman round, to stop him thinking that the whole world revolves around him. "Everybody seems to be in on it," says Truman. This is prime time viewing: the nation is transfixed. We get to see Christof feeding the deeply emotional lines that Marlon is mouthing, via—one assumes—earphones. Everything is at stake, and Marlon pulls out all the stops, reminding Truman of their school days together, their friendship. But it is going to take more than that; as a nation holds its breath, an old man walks over the bridge towards them, the filming orchestrated to perfection by Christof. It is Truman's lost "father." The studio congratulates itself, as we see ex-cast member Lauren watching in disgust, knowing the trick played on the man she once tried to warn. Truman is lost in the emotion of the reunion. Lauren stares at her TV as Truman is later drinking a cup of something. The text moving across the screen says: "Truman drinks Mococao— world's finest cocoa beans, grown on the upper slopes of Mt. Nicaragua."

The film now takes a step back and explains to us how people from the outside world have broken in from time to time to expose the sham to Truman, including the mysterious Sylvia Garland. We understand that the actor who played his father was not pleased at being written out so many years ago, and this had prompted him to sneak onto the set. In a master-stroke Christof decided to both pacify the actor and fool Truman by writing him back in, hence the latest developments. But will this distract Truman from his quest for the truth?

Apparently not: Truman returns to his routine, or so it seems. Christof has turned round the crisis, increased viewing figures and, presumably, sold a lot of *Mococao*. Mock cocoa, mock marriage, mock life, all of it is superior to the real thing in Christof's inverted values. But Truman plays a trick: he tapes snoring sounds, and mocks up the shape of his body under the duvet. Actually he has sneaked off and taken the most fearsome option: he sails off in a boat. This is heroism at its best, and it pits his will directly against Christof's. For the first time in thirty years the show goes off air: a technical fault, the screen says. But the graphic, just a still frame apologizing for the fault, is earning higher audience ratings than ever before, as audiences stay glued to the set. Christof now pits his god-like control of the elements against Truman's will. The fugitive has tied himself to his boat as the computer-controlled winds howl, a storm rises, and in the end Christof's last weapon is deployed: giant waves. The Father is about to destroy the Son. And it is back on air. Audiences around the world stare in disbelief at the drowning Truman: he struggles, and all appears lost. But he has won in the battle of wills; no father can actually go through with it. Bad weather is turned off at a stroke of the computer interface, and Truman slowly emerges to view. He raises sail, and heads out into calm sunlit seas.

Until "Crash!" as his boat is brought to a jarring halt. He stares incredulously at what ought to be the sky, and steps up to the concrete painted wall that bounds his world. Beating his fist against it he is crushed, defeated, as the whole world watches him on TV. Turning slowly, he finds a walkway along the painted join between sky and sea, and steps that lead him to a door that might open to freedom. For the first time in his thirty years Christof speaks, god-like from the heavens to his child. "I am the creator ... of a television show," he begins. He explains to Truman the nature of the show, and then presses on him the idea that the outside world is no more representative of the "truth" than Seahaven.

Truman has a choice: what will it be? He chooses reality. And we are glad because, unlike in *The Matrix*, we know that however grubby, real life will be preferable to the constructed anodyne pleasantness of Seahaven. An American sanity prevails in this film, while usefully cataloguing many of the American madnesses, the underbelly of the saccharine fantasy that the American Dream has become. To be sure Truman's decision is not a difficult one: the fantasy of Seahaven was not his but Christof's, and he was a prisoner of it. In VR films the constructed reality may be one of one's own choosing, making the protagonist's decision to face the real world much more difficult (as we will see later in the film *Vanilla Sky*).

Lawnmower Man

Pierce Brosnan, long before his Bond outings, plays scientist Dr. Lawrence Angelo in *Lawnmower Man*, a science-fiction film that was no great success, but usefully illustrates further issues for us around VR. Angelo's character and working environment are based on the real life computer scientist and composer Jaron Lanier, mentioned earlier, and who represents a far greater cultural and philosophical acuity than the film does. Angelo has been working on chimpanzee intelligence and aggression enhancement for the military, but loses his best animal. He wants to try his technology, which involves big machines that whirl its occupants around, on a human subject: "The potentials for human advancement are endless!" he says, "Virtual reality holds a key to the evolution of the mind, and that's my focus."

Meanwhile Jobe Smith, a Forrest Gump-type of character, has built his own big machine—a supercharged lawnmower. Back to Angelo: he has a VR machine at home and is off on a little trip. His wife isn't keen on the thing and unplugs him, much to his annoyance. "Falling, floating, and flying?" she asks, "So, what's next, fucking?" The equipment has nothing like the sophistication of the VR installations imagined in *The Matrix*, and the computer animations now look laughable. Virtual sex doesn't look that likely. But the real world doesn't attract Angelo as much as it does his wife. Like many semi-autistic high-achievers, he doesn't really want to be around people. She tells him: "I'm young, Larry, OK? And I'm not going to become a recluse just for you. I'm into reality reality, not this artificial reality." And so she leaves him.

Angelo is now on his own, desperate to continue his research, and is gazing at Jobe (played by Jeff Fahey). Angelo gets him playing a VR flying game with the neighbor's little kid, who beats the pants off him.

ANGELO: You know, Jobe I have other, different games. I even have one that could help make you smarter.
JOBE: I was born dumb.
ANGELO: But, you would like to be smarter, wouldn't you?
JOBE: I don't know.
ANGELO: Well, if you were smarter, people wouldn't be able to take advantage of you. Do you understand what I mean, Jobe?

So Angelo gives him "nootropic" drugs and plugs him into his experimental machine, one only tested on monkeys before. Jobe responds far better than Angelo could have hoped and soon he can beat the neighbor's kid at the flying game. Just as rapidly his self-confidence and aggression are also on the rise. Angelo's research is back on track, but he has gone as far as he can with the equipment at home: he asks to continue it at the research lab. Jobe is going into the Big Machine. Before long he can master Latin in a mere two hours, and his sex appeal rockets. There is just a nagging feeling that something isn't quite right, but they press on, and, without Angelo's knowledge, the original aggression-enhancement drugs are used on Jobe. Along with aggression, Jobe acquires psychic powers: the ability to control things with just his mind. He confronts Angelo and tells him:

> It's not new. I realize that nothing we've been doing is new. We haven't been tapping into new areas of the brain. We've just been awakening the most ancient. This technology is simply a route to powers that conjurers and alchemists used centuries ago. The human race lost that knowledge and now I'm reclaiming it through virtual reality.

Jobe has surpassed his mentor in intelligence and it is he who now insists that the program must go on. Angelo must submit to his mind control, though he fears for Jobe's sanity.

Jobe has become Frankenstein's monster, and Angelo has become Faust (to mix up the literary sources). Like the Hulk, Jobe is the property of the military, which sees in his new powers only an awesome weapon. This is the truly American contribution to all the old stories of esoteric powers, occult gifts, and monsters of the irrational: the inevitable linking of increased intelligence and physical strength with rage and military power. In the *Alien* film series for example, the monster is always being saved from destruction at the hands of sane characters like Ripley by the military who want to exploit its raw power and aggression as a weapon. The Hulk is placed in a tank so his gene-bending moment of transformation can be isolated and developed into a controlled weapon, and poor Jobe is wanted for just the same reason. Jobe, like Frankenstein's monster, has to die, though not before he becomes the monster id of cyberspace, the cyberChrist who believes that he is an omnipotent "God." *Lawnmower Man* shows, more explicitly than the *Matrix*, that the American mind sees in all technology, including a VR technology that does not yet exist, a means to power and domination.

Pleasantville

The counterpoint to virtual worlds as a means to power is the desire for an escapist reality that is perfect, anodyne, and saccharine. Christof's Seaview is one such creation; Pleasantville is another. In the film *Pleasantville*, the imaginary world is again a television show, but this time there is a more fanciful entry to it. David and Jennifer are teenage siblings very different in their temperaments: he is geekishly obsessed with the *Pleasantville* TV program, and she is expecting a date. As they squabble over what channel they will watch, they accidentally break the remote control. The ring at the door is not Jennifer's date, but a mysterious TV repairman who is so impressed with David's grasp of Pleasantville soap history that he gives them a "special" remote, which magically transports them into the TV. They are now characters in the soap opera, living in black and white, and free from all the "nasty" things of real life, including sex. This doesn't suit Jennifer at all, and neither does the high-fat diet. The fact is that they are transported to an idealized 1950s of soda stores, burgers and jive music, and perfect picket-fenced suburban homes. But the presence of David and Jennifer from the real world acts as a subversive influence on Pleasantville, symbolized by the gradual "infection" of their monochrome existence with raw color.

There is an intriguing reference in *Pleasantville* to two books: *The Adventures of Huckleberry Finn* and *Catcher in the Rye*. When the young pair arrive books contain only blank pages, but Jennifer's partial recollection of the story of *Huckleberry Finn* fill in some of the pages, as if by magic. David then completes the story and other books come to life in the same way, leading to panic amongst the good citizens of Pleasantville and an orgy of book burning. Statistics are kept by the American Library Association on attempts by American conservatives to ban books from public libraries, and these two are high on the list. Apparently *The Adventures of Huckleberry Finn* was the fifth most challenged book in the period 1990–2000, while *The Catcher in the Rye* ranked thirteenth. Interestingly, the book *American Psycho*—on which the film is based—ranked sixtieth. *Pleasantville* gives us an interesting glimpse as to how classic American literature of a certain type is a threat to American saccharine fantasies: a glimpse into the madness of the American mind that prefers the virtual to the real. Cocooned by its wealth, America is paranoid about literature that might break into the gated community of its mind and force it to confront reality.

Neo and the "Me Generation"

Writers on *The Matrix* think that these films might lead an audience from popular culture to philosophy, as we saw. But can such films act as the nursery slopes for real philosophy? A similar question might be: can New Age practices become the nursery slopes for real religion? Or are both so sanitized of the real toughness and energy of philosophy and religion respectively, so bowdlerized, popularized and trivialized as to represent a completely wrong start? Are not the *Matrix* films just adolescent escapist pap? Does Neo represent anything more than a narcissism of geek-chic escapist violence for an other-directed generation?

Probably not. But understanding the critical success of these films requires a certain patience with popular culture. Pat Mellencamp writes: "I felt defenseless in front of *The Matrix*—and I am a film professor long familiar with disavowal (the use of 'it's only a movie' to quell anxiety)."[10] The reason for this defenselessness must lie in the film's exuberant imagination and high production values. Stacey Gillis, editor of a collection of *Matrix* essays, quotes Joshua Clover: "It's a visual object, and much of its meaning must reside there."[11] Mellencamp also talks about the film's considerable energy and artistic invention, that it has "an auteur imprimatur."[12] One could then argue that its status as art gives a certain kind of critical distance. We are not to take Neo seriously, because he is beautiful, he wears beautiful clothes, and he kills only "programs"—we should therefore understand the huge critical response as *homage to art*, in which it is legitimate, for example, to deliberate whether the films are "Buddhist" and decide ultimately no, because "programs" are sentient too, and Buddhism abhors harm to all sentient beings.[13] But this is more homage than moral philosophy, as the conclusion was obvious from the outset.

All of this makes sense in an "other-directed" culture, in Riesman's terminology. Escapist fantasy as a shared culture—just as much as popular music—helps allow the other-directed urban masses find a reciprocal identity, especially—for the young—if the fantasy is nominally transgressive. But the "inner-directed" person wishes to act on the world stage with the deepest understanding of the laws of Nature, because real-world agency, not escapist fantasy, is her milieu. Benjamin Franklin represents this in the public sphere, while Whitman represents this on the stage of the ordinary citizen: he was everywhere involved with soldiers, carpenters, cab-drivers, ferry captains, and even at times Presidents. But he was not the least interested in fantasy or the fashionable appearances of things, as we shall see.

PART THREE

The American Sanity on Film

13

The Unique Strengths of the American Mind

Unparalleled in the annals of fiction, American cinema has generated portraits of madmen and women painted in such vivid colors as to be etched
on humanity's collective consciousness. Is there one amongst those we have
examined who stands for the complete American paranoia, the complete
American madness? Is it Colonel Jack Ripper, paranoid about his "precious
bodily fluids"; Fox Mulder, paranoid about aliens; Jerry Fletcher, sharing with
Ripper his paranoia about fluoride in the water; or Harry Caul in the ruins
of his flat, unable to find the bug which spies on him? Is it in the military
madness shown by John Rambo or Colonel Kurtz? Or in the lust for killing
of Hannibal Lecter, John Doe, or Patrick Bateman, the all–American psycho?
Is it Mickey and Mallory who are the all–American natural born killers? Is it
David and Bruce Banner in their Oedipal struggle, or Kevin Lomax and John
Milton acting out the same father-son madness? Is it in the sexual obsession
of Bill Maplewood in *Happiness*, Lester Burnham in *American Beauty* or Frank
Booth in *Blue Velvet*? Is it one of the few women in our selection, Sharon,
whose belief in the "Rapture" brings her to murder her only daughter? Or
Buck Williams whose equally insane belief in the Apocalypse requires him
to conceive of the Secretary General of the United Nations as the Antichrist?
Is it one of the countless white men like General Custer who are satirized in
the many revisionist Westerns, those films which portray the Native American
as the truly sane? Is it all those characters like Albert in *I Heart Huckabees*
who uncritically pursue New Age psychobabble, or Zelig the human
chameleon? Is it the schizophrenic hero of *Fight Club*, Tyler / Jack, whose
nihilism is all in the mind, or is it Raoul Duke whose nihilism is drug-
induced? Is it Travis Bickle, the taxi driver who turns vigilante killer? Is it
one of countless film characters whose emotional impairment suggests an
autism at cultural level? Or is it amongst those who retreat from the world
into virtual reality or saccharine fantasy?

It is, of course, all of them. When taken together we have here a composite portrait of the American madness, drawn for us through the unforgettable imagery of the most compelling medium in the world: American cinema.

If the composite picture drawn here of the American madness was an affliction in every American mind, then other nations should recoil in horror, and American citizens should commit themselves to the insane asylum en masse. That would be ludicrous. This picture of American madness is of course an extreme, to which very few unfortunate individuals are driven. But, we suggest, when Americans *do* go mad, as individuals or through collective action, their insanity manifests itself along the contours we have outlined. The world should not forget the My Lai Massacre of 1968 in which American troops massacred civilian women and children in Vietnam, or the Abu Ghraib torture and abuse of prisoners by American soldiers in Iraq in 2004. The English insanity is quite different, for example: it is more timid, class-ridden, and conformist, while being less overtly aggressive or religious. The Arab insanity includes a paranoia of the "victim;" the German insanity includes a worship both of Nature and of high culture; the Latin insanity displays flamboyance. And so on. Each culture has its landmark horrors to mark its excesses. These are not so much stereotypes as potentially useful guides to understanding cultures on the world stage. And as America so dominates the world economically, militarily, and culturally, it becomes essential to understand the uniquely American madness.

However, after such a relentless presentation of the pathological in the American mind, we now provide the balance by considering what is uniquely great about it. All weaknesses exist in the context of specific strengths; all pathology exists in the context of a particular organic fitness. However much we may weary of the U.S. Government's bluster about democracy, it remains nevertheless a key element of the American genius, alongside which we can count its entrepreneurial "can-do" spirit. Walt Whitman perfectly expresses, in poetic terms, the source of American democracy as a comradeship and a deep-rooted love of the ordinary person and ordinary setting, and the primacy of those things over religion and philosophy:

I see reminiscent to-day those Greek and Germanic systems,
See the philosophies all—Christian churches and tenets see,
Yet underneath Socrates clearly see—and underneath Christ the divine I see,
The dear love of man for his comrade—the attraction of friend to friend,
Of the well-married husband and wife—of children and parents,
Of city for city, and land for land. ["The Base of All Metaphysics"]

Whitman epitomizes the expansive nature of the American vision, an expansiveness in the positive sense of inclusiveness and generosity of spirit, perhaps summed up in these lines:

I pass death with the dying and birth with the new-wash'd babe,
and am not contain'd between my hat and boots,
And I peruse manifold objects, no two alike and every one good,
The earth good and the stars good, and their adjuncts all good.
["Song Of Myself," v.7]

In "Song of Myself" Whitman lists the religions of old, but finds them wanting in a true appreciation of the greatness of ordinary life. He finds himself "discovering as much or more in a framer framing a house," meaning that the work of the carpenter, and the carpenter himself, are more important to him than all the scriptures. He finds the "well-married man or the well-married woman" more sacred than churches, and everywhere celebrates the ordinary man and the ordinary woman. Whitman is ultimately sane, not because there are no traces of aggression, competition, sexuality and religiosity in him—there are—but because his immense vision of America is not tainted by speed. He is not seduced by the fast lane, by superficial excitements, by appearances, but clings instead to a Nature-wisdom which draws its sanity from the slow-growing, and from the seasons:

One lesson from affiliating a tree—perhaps the greatest moral lesson anyhow from earth, rocks, animals, is that same lesson of inherency, of what is, without the least regard to what the looker-on (the critic) supposes or says, or whether he likes or dislikes. What worse—what more general malady pervades each and all of us, our literature, education, attitude towards each other, (even towards ourselves,) than morbid trouble about seems, (generally temporarily seems too,) and no trouble at all, or hardly any, about the sane slow-growing, perennial, real parts of character, books, friendship, marriage—humanity's invisible foundations and hold-together? (As the all-basis, the nerve, the great sympathetic, the plenum within humanity, giving stamp to everything, is necessarily invisible.)[1]

We see here proof that Whitman is not in favor of the "other-directed" mentality and its "morbid trouble about *seems*." And one could argue that film is not primarily a medium for "sane slow-growing" things: *I Heart Huckabees*, for example, degenerates into cod philosophy because of the speed at which it races through its existential questions. But there are many films that are slow-paced enough, or have slow-enough scenes, to reflect Whitman's "sane slow-growing, perennial, real parts of character, books, friendship, marriage." Actually, America's cars drive more slowly than in Europe, and its phones ring with a more measured tone than in Britain. It is vast and spacious, and its best history is that of a nation accommodating to all races and religions, though its worst history, signs of its potential madness, is not accommodating at all. American films deeply reflect the best and the worst of the American mind.

Sanity, even in individuals such as Whitman and Franklin who receive almost universal acclaim, is a mixed bag. One of Franklin's biographers talks of "the hodgepodge nature of great men in whom genius mingles with banality and in whom a perfect understanding of human means contrasts with a circumscribed view of human ends."[2] This might be fitting for Franklin, whose many very American and admirable traits were mixed with a certain amount of self-interest. For Whitman, what is "hodgepodge" in him is more psychological: his means of dealing with the transgressive was rather like that of Blake's, writing very dark inversions of his positive writings.[3] He never meant them for publication, however.

So where in America's films can we find the sanity that Whitman represents, a sanity of the slow-growing ordinary fundamentals of life, not forgotten in the aggressive haste for competition, sexual conquest, or escapist fantasy? Not forgotten in the madness of Apocalyptic or nihilistic thinking? Not forgotten in frenetic intellectualization or the empty pursuit of existential philosophy? Where are the inheritors of Franklin's Enlightenment values, including his Deism? Actually, everywhere. Many of the films chosen here to portray elements of the American madness also resolve themselves in depictions of America's best sanity. Other films tuck their sanity away behind their dramatic obligations to the filmgoer. Kubrick's *Eyes Wide Shut*, mentioned much earlier, is an example where the ending provides a poignant recognition of what is important in marriage. The couple's journey to that point illustrates a sexual aggression in the American mind, and also perhaps the decadence of American's wealthy and powerful people, but the ending is a refutation of all that madness. One might say, why go such a long way round to celebrate the "sane slow-growing, perennial, real parts of marriage?" But to make that objection is to ignore both the very human necessity for drama, and also the cathartic possibilities in peering over the abyss. We will explore these cathartic possibilities and the American sanity in general through the following films: *One Flew Over the Cuckoo's Nest*, *The Fisher King*, *Groundhog Day*, *The Apostle*, *Vanilla Sky*, *21 Grams*, and *Snow Cake*.

14

Filmic Journeys into Sanity

Key Films: *One Flew Over the Cuckoo's Nest,*
The Fisher King, Groundhog Day, The Apostle,
Vanilla Sky, 21 Grams, Snow Cake
Additional Films: *Eyes Wide Shut, Open Your Eyes*

One Flew Over the Cuckoo's Nest

It may seem odd to choose a film about a man in a mental hospital to explore what is deeply sane in the American mind, but the protagonist of *One Flew Over the Cuckoo's Nest* suits the purpose. In the film Jack Nicholson plays Randle Patrick McMurphy whose own assessment of his shortcomings is simple: "I fight and fuck too much." McMurphy might seem a rather unsavory character, having been arrested five times for assault and currently serving time for statutory rape. His defense is: "She was fifteen years going on thirty-five, and she told me she was eighteen." It *could* have been an honest mistake. And five fights? His doctor has to agree that this isn't really a reason to put a man in a mental ward. The central device of the film is that a person we would all normally take to be sane has somehow been shunted around a criminal justice system that cannot cope with him, to the point where he is "under evaluation" in the mental wing of a prison. The film is intended as an indictment of the psychiatric profession at the time of its writing, in the late 1950s / early 1960s, but it certainly does not deliver to us a conventional hero of American culture. McMurphy is a man at odds with society, so we have to see him as an anti-hero of some kind. What we can show however is that he exhibits not one of the "madnesses" detailed so far; rather that he shows what the counterbalancing sanity looks like in each case. Above all he is free from paranoia of any kind, perhaps even to his detriment.

The author of the novel *One Flew Over the Cuckoo's Nest* was Ken Kesey, considered to be the link between the "beat generation" of the fifties and the emerging hippie culture of the 1960s. He mixed with writers and poets such as Jack Kerouac, Allen Ginsberg and Timothy Leary, all of whom owed much to the vision of Walt Whitman. The film version was immensely successful: in recent film history only one other film has won all the major awards, and that was *Silence of the Lambs*. Both deal with the darker sides of life, but where Hannibal Lecter points to significant elements of the American madness, Randle P. McMurphy embodies much of its sanity. Actually, the head-to-head comparison is not that good because Lecter is the grotesque place-holder in the film designed to set off the very plausible, and very sane, Clarice Starling. But McMurphy is a better emblem of American sanity than Starling, because he embodies many Whitmanesque characteristics, including *bon-homie* (or comradeship as Whitman called it), expansiveness, generosity, and above all the common touch. Starling is caught up in her ambition, but McMurphy lives day by day with no grandiose or even commonplace goals.

His sanity is contrasted in *One Flew Over the Cuckoo's Nest* with the insanity of the psychiatric system at the time, personified in Nurse Mildred Ratched. She rules her ward with an iron adherence to routine, and from the start she has no idea how to cope with McMurphy. His sheer personal warmth and maddening spontaneity both infuriate and attract her. Jack Nicholson is perfect in the role of McMurphy, having a natural glint in his eye that is both a universal male "come-on" and at the same time something very American in its brash confidence. Whitman talks in one of his poems of a stallion "with eyes of sparkling wickedness"—an image which fits McMurphy well if we understand that this "wickedness" holds no malice or grudges. He is irked of course by the constraints to his freedom, belonging, like all of Whitman's inheritors, to the open road. But, one suspects, he makes do wherever he finds himself with what is on offer, and in the mental ward it is with the other inmates he builds up moving relationships. Nurse Ratched accommodates him to some extent at the start, but his friendly though determined assault on "routine" increasingly makes an enemy of her. Actually we should see not see her as evil personified: there are many staff nurses like her in mental hospitals, and she, like them, is simply trying to do her job well as defined in the system of the day. It is the *system* that represents a collective cultural insanity across the developed world, or, to be more charitable, a doomed experiment in psychiatric treatment arising inevitably in a materialist culture. Poor Ratched is just the messenger.

A key relationship that McMurphy strikes up is with the dumb giant of a Native American, Chief Bromden (played by Native American actor Will Sampson, who also appeared in *The Outlaw Josey Wales*). McMurphy won't accept that his deaf-and-dumb condition is any bar to the warmth of human communication, and gets him involved in basketball. On the day of a bus outing for the best-behaved inmates, McMurphy stands on the Chief's shoulders, and, in broad daylight, climbs over the high fence to freedom. But instead of making a run for it, he drives the bus off before the staff can get on board and takes his new friends on a fishing trip. Kesey's idea here is to show that the warmth and patience of a single friendly man can do more in a day to rehabilitate most psychiatric patients than all the high-falutin' psychiatric interventions can do in years. McMurphy gives each man a fishing line, or the helm of the boat; encourages them; tells them they "can do it," and—lo and behold—they rise to the occasion. He is not of course a complete philanthropist: while they are busy he goes below deck with his girlfriend. But when they return to dock the police are waiting, and McMurphy is returned to his ward. Naturally the staff are now wary of him, but his friendships with the gang are deepening, particularly with Chief. After a disruptive episode McMurphy discovers—to his great delight—that Chief has been shamming his deaf-and-dumb routine in order to escape the insanity of the outside world, the white man's world in which the Native American has no place. McMurphy is punished however with his first, though ineffective, dose of electroshock treatment.

McMurphy now decides to escape again, but not before he puts on a party for his friends. He bribes the ward orderly, who opens a window for McMurphy's women friends to enter with drink and party records. Naturally, McMurphy gets too drunk to remember to climb out of the open window, and is discovered next day by nurse Ratched, lying by an empty bottle on the floor. Her outrage is not just at the trashed ward, but is moral: the youngest inmate finally got laid that night (set up by McMurphy), and Ratched is scandalized to find the young woman in bed with him. Her scorn and condemnation is too much for the vulnerable young man, who then commits suicide. McMurphy's reward is a second dose of high voltage, this time sufficient to turn him into a vegetable. Twice he could have escaped, and twice he made his friends a priority, so that in the end he is crushed by the system.

The sanity of McMurphy is the indictment of not just the psychiatric system, but of the whole madness of American society. But he shows none of the archetypal American madnesses: he is not paranoid; is only aggressive when called to be; is oblivious to Freudian or New Age cod psychology; is only normally sexual; holds no bizarre religious beliefs; befriends the Native American; shows no sycophancy towards intellectual theories or high culture; shows no trace of nihilism; and does not indulge in escapist fantasy. He does not even *escape* when he could; instead he puts his friends first. McMurphy's is the tragedy of the *ordinary* man, making the film and other fiction of this genre a genuine updating of Greek tragedy for the modern world.

The Fisher King

We turn now to a film where the protagonist is far less appealing than McMurphy, to start with at least. *The Fisher King* was directed by Terry Gilliam, the only American member of the otherwise British Monty Python team. The film stars Jeff Bridges as Jack, and Robin Williams as Parry: two men brought together by tragedy. Jack is a cocksure loudmouth disk jockey reminiscent of some of the protagonists previously discussed: a bit of Patrick Bateman, a bit of Kevin Lomax, a bit of Tyler Durden. The film is deeply sane however, because early on Jack has to face the consequence of his glib unfeeling radio banter. We watch as Jack undergoes a somewhat telescoped moral development, catalyzed by his chance encounter with Parry. It is not plain sailing however, making this film a quite realistic portrait of a man painfully struggling with the image suddenly presented of himself, one that is deeply American, and deeply unlikable. The film is made all the more poignant as his unwitting moral benchmark is a woman: as in *Groundhog Day*, Jack's progress is charted by the litmus test of a woman's love.

In a very American cinematic image, Jack discovers that his cynical repartee has so depressed one of his regular phone-in clients that the man took a gun and fired indiscriminately into a yuppie restaurant. Jack is all primed for a career hike, a move from mere radio to the glorious heights of television, when he hears his own thoughtless witticisms played back to him from that very instrument. It is the television news, and he is being blamed for pushing the man over the edge to random murder and then suicide. Jack has no way out: he is human enough to feel responsibility for this dreadful occurrence, and the shock is etched on his face as he watches the Channel 7 News. "Few will soon forget this lonely man who reached out to a world he knew only through the radio, looking for friendship and finding only pain and tragedy," the reporter tells us of the lone gunman. "Fuck," is Jack's final terse response, and he disappears into a downward spiral of self-loathing.

Three years later he has a more down-market girlfriend (by his media-industry values at least), who loves him very much and puts up with his "moods." At this point Jack has merely become the inversion of self-absorbed success, i.e. he wallows in self-absorbed failure, and doesn't notice that his girlfriend, Anne Napolitano, is in a seriously one-way relationship with him. She gives and he takes. When she tells him: "You said you liked that we didn't have to think all the time. That we could just be together and not think," his sarcastic response is: "Suicidal paranoiacs will say anything to get laid." Jack goes out and gets drunk, and is about to be beaten up by young thugs when he is rescued by Parry, a down-and-out who appears to be some kind of king of the hobo underworld. Jack's slow climb to self-respect—the ground of which is of course respect for others—has begun in the company of this bizarre character.

The Fisher King is full of zany images, including an extraordinary vision of a flaming red knight on horseback (a Pythonesque image if ever there was one), which appears whenever Parry is having a relapse into his own madness. Robin Williams has a quintessentially American hyper-active, even slightly insane delivery in most of his films, and so one might ask why choose this film to represent a truly American *sanity*. It is because, amidst all the very real description of American failings, there is a deep self-awareness and a movement towards Whitman's "sane slow-growing, perennial, real parts of character, books, friendship, marriage." It is a Greek tragedy in which Jack's hubris causes his own downfall, but in which he undergoes a redemption by confronting the emblem of the pain he has caused. That emblem, as it emerges later in the film, is Parry, whose mental breakdown was caused by being witness to his beloved wife's murder at the hands of a lone gunman in a restaurant— the very man tipped over the edge by Jack's unfeeling wit. And so the two men, one lamed by bereavement and the other blinded by pride, gradually heal each other, and in doing so prove the depth of American sanity. Robin Williams is, of course, totally over the top in the role of Parry, but represents the American sanity precisely because his screen persona is so much larger than life: a Whitmanesque expansiveness. One has to add that Medved seems to display a complete lack of imagination when he characterizes Parry as a "homeless and delusional psychotic" and the Oscar nomination of his portrayal by Robin Williams as part of "honoring ugliness."[1] We saw that theologians are capable of ascribing "redemption" to films such as *Taxi Driver* where no thoughtful person could possibly describe Bickle's rampage as anything but cold-blooded murder, while the religious right it seems are incapable of discovering the genuine article when thrust under their nose. If Parry and Jack were not initially bound together in the "psychotic," then what would their eventual mutual deliverance mean as redemption?

Groundhog Day, *The Apostle*, and *Vanilla Sky*

If one is on the lookout for specifically American pathologies of the mind, then one can find it in countless American films: quite naturally the selection here has been somewhat arbitrary and personal, even if the taxonomy as subdivisions lends rigor to that choice. But likewise, once one is on the lookout for a quintessentially American *sanity*, one can find it everywhere. So, for each of the ten categories of American madness outlined here, one can find films that show its corollary, its corresponding sanity. The first two selected here featured, ironically, mental patients. We now look at some that take us away from that theme: *Groundhog Day*, *The Apostle*, and *Vanilla Sky*.

Groundhog Day has this in common with *The Fisher King*, that its hero starts out as a deeply egotistical media-industry presenter, this time a weather forecaster. But here the woman is to be won, rather than already committed to the man and hoping for his transformation. *Groundhog Day* stars Bill Murray as Phil Connors, the arrogant weatherman, and Andie MacDowell as his producer Rita whom he falls in love with. Its central device is even more surreal than in *The Fisher King*: on location in Pennsylvania Connors wakes up every day in his hotel room at 6:00 a.m., only to discover it is yesterday. He is condemned, it seems, to forever repeat this particular day, which happens to be a local festival celebrating the supposed ability of the groundhog to predict the arrival of spring. His calamity is quite different to Jack's in *The Fisher King*, but he undergoes a similar moral development, a journey from male, self-absorbed, cynical egotism to decent human being, the benchmark of which is Rita. This is a feel-good movie, and it has been suggested that it could have been made by Frank Capra, whose films, such as *It's a Wonderful Life*, set the early American standard for uplifting movie fare.

Interestingly the director of *Groundhog Day*, Harold Ramis, tells us that he began to get an inkling of the film's impact when someone told him that "Buddhists love this movie." He then met a yogi who told him that the film wholly expresses yoga philosophy, and received letters from Jesuits and fundamentalist Christians, all saying the same thing. In the chapter on the apocalypse and armageddon, a pathology of the Christian mind was highlighted that has found expression in a very American madness, but religion more generally represents something deeply sane in America. Criticisms from the Left simply cannot recognize this because Marx's complete rejection of religion cut off such discourse at its root. The religious response to *Groundhog Day* is indicative of the broader sanity of religion, because there is no overt reference to religion at all in the film. What makes it speak to the religiously-minded is simply the moral development of its central character, from jerk to loving human being. Of course religion does not begin and end with the question of moral development, and indeed we can find moral development framed just as well in a secular, humanist context. But this film speaks to a sanity that recognizes what the development into a mature human being looks like, even if it does not necessarily involve the religious trappings of "redemption."

A film that does overtly deal with fundamentalist Christianity, and shows the potential sanity of it, is *The Apostle*, starring Robert Duvall as the "Apostle E.F." He is known by this strange name because he is on the run from the police and cannot reveal his real name. The first part of the film would confirm for religious skeptics all their worst fears: a preacher apparently out of control and yielding to a fit of rage that sees his opponent in hospital and eventually dying of his injuries. It is again a story of an ordinary man, in the public eye for a different reason this time, confronted by a disaster of his own making, who redeems himself slowly and through his own efforts. In the second half of the film EF rebuilds himself and a small dilapidated church, amongst strangers. It opens to a congregation of just six people, but Duval (who personally experienced Southern fundamentalist Christianity as he grew up, and also wrote and directed the film) gives a wonderful performance as the preacher genuinely in love with his religion and able to communicate its power to ordinary people. Those who are viscerally atheist and allergic to all outward signs of religion will probably recoil from the scene, and there is little one can present by way of argument to explain the reality and sanity of it to them. But those broadly in favor of religion (and anxious that Americans have been falsely portrayed as succumbing en masse to the kind of Apocalyptical madness shown in the *Left Behind* trilogy) can be reassured that *The Apostle* illustrates a very American religion of the ordinary people.

Religion *can* be escapist fantasy, but it doesn't have to be. The rush to escape into lucid dreaming, virtual reality, or saccharine fantasy may be very American, but in fact there is plenty of self-awareness left in the American mind to distinguish between reality and fantasy. The film *Vanilla Sky* does this very well, dealing, as did the original *Open Your Eyes*, with a man retreating into virtual reality after being horribly disfigured. Tom Cruise, as the protagonist David Aames, spends most of this film with his face a complete mess. His love interest is two-fold: Penélope Cruz as Sofia and Cameron Diaz as Julie; he loses both in the end. In this story he must struggle with the monsters of his unconscious, as the saccharine fantasy of his virtual world—designed to insulate his ego from the reality of his disfigurement—implodes on him. (These are just the monsters of the unconscious that the lucid dreaming of *Waking Life* attempted to banish.) He is offered total control of reality, an American madness that expresses itself in the military insanity of Colonel Kurtz, or the retreat into VR of *The Matrix*, but David ultimately realizes that his conscious mind cannot marshal that world according to conscious plan. In the very end of the film he chooses to return to cold reality, one in which he will have to negotiate for what he wants with a thousand other egos just like his, handicapped further by the revulsion of response to his disfigurement. Like Truman he is offered the choice between saccharine fantasy and cold reality, and chooses the hazardous path of real life. It is an indictment of the New Age that Stephen Simon, mentioned earlier as producer or director of films such as *What Dreams May Come* and *Indigo*, learns quite the wrong lesson from the film. In one scene Aames is contacted within his virtual reality world by a representative of the company that instantiated it, in order to explain his situation to him. The representative tells Aames that he lives in a world completely of his own creation, commenting on which Simon writes:

> ...Aames flippantly says, "Well, if that's true, I wish all these people would just shut up!" Whereupon, every person in the bar immediately falls silent and just stares at David. *Never in film has there been a better envisioned example of the notion of each individual creating his/her own reality!* [Simon's italics][2]

21 Grams and *Snow Cake*

Earlier, we used two films about mental patients to illustrate the American sanity. Now two films about the aftermath of car crashes further illustrate it. The car crash is the great leveler, one might say, and a feature of modern life in the developed nations. America suffers about a hundred fatalities on the roads each day, Britain about nine. The statistics are appalling; for example the deaths in 9/11 are about the same as one month's road deaths in America, but of course the collective cultural response is utterly different— with the result that Federal spending to reduce certain road deaths is minute compared with Federal spending to reduce deaths from possible terrorism. Yet for the citizen who suffers bereavement through road accidents the pain of loss is no different—is perhaps even worse because of the lack of collective mourning.

In *21 Grams* Jack, an ex-convict attempting to go straight through his newly-adopted Christianity, runs over and kills a father and his two daughters. Panicked—as any ex-con might be through long experience of the law— he fails to stop his truck and give the help that might have saved their lives. Cristina, the wife and mother now bereaved, initially fails to press charges once Jack turns himself in, instead asking that her husband's heart be donated for transplant surgery. The recipient is the very ill Paul (Sean Penn). After the operation Paul tracks down Cristina and falls in love with her. When he tells her that he has her husbands' heart she feels betrayed; it puts in question his motivations and the very meaning of love at a time when she already feels absolute fury and emptiness at her loss. Paul, a mathematician, has just separated from his wife after he fails to agree on artificial insemination to help her get pregnant. Cristina needs him and his gentleness towards her, but as her emotions turn full circle she decides that Jack must be killed, and gets Paul to agree to it. Paul—whose transplant is not going well and is increasingly ill again—buys a gun, but cannot go through with the shooting, and in the end Paul shoots himself (to avoid the pain of his illness) in the motel room he has rented with Cristina, now pregnant by him. The whole complexity of this— including Jack's agonies of conscience and his marital break-down—is told in a non-linear form, with flashbacks and flashforwards. Rather as in *American Beauty*, Paul's disembodied voice confides in us his last thoughts as we see the scene of his deathbed in hospital, with Jack returning to his family, and understanding that Cristina will have Paul's child.

> How many lives do we live? How many times do we die? They say we all lose twenty-one grams at the exact moment of our death. Everyone. And how much fits into twenty-one grams? How much is lost? When do we lose twenty-one grams? How much goes with them? How much is gained? *How much is gained?* Twenty-one grams. The weight of a stack of five nickels, the weight of a hummingbird, a chocolate bar. How much does twenty-one grams weigh?

When Paul repeats "How much is gained?" we see Cristina who has lost everything, including Paul, now reflecting on the future life in her womb.

The film certainly has transgressional material in it, but also the naturalistic portrayal of bereavement that turns to a fury of grief, even anger at life itself, is dramatized in Cristina's tirade against her father who had apparently taken the death of Cristina's mother so philosophically. "No, no," she cries out against him, "It's a lie. Life does not just go on." The scenario is not just realistic, it falls perhaps in the category of social realism, but without the socialist or politically correct message, and it is of course emotionally intense. Its artistry is of the highest order, a product of postmodern approaches to narrative. And, finally, its critical distance is shown by its non-judgmental approach to the characters, none of whom are morally perfect. But above all it portrays a slice of American life which shows strengths amidst human frailties and errors: it mixes the world of trailer-trash whites with the professional classes of a university lecturer; it mixes moral weakness with moral strength; and it conveys the dramas of ordinary American life including the human wreckage of the automobile accident, the human conundrum of hitech transplant surgery, and the pathos of loves waxing and waning. And ultimately it does what Medved calls for: its creators are celebrants of exactly this American culture, based not on any classical canon or prescriptive Scriptural morality, but of a love for life itself. How much is lost when a life is lost, it asks? How much is gained with a new life, it asks? Life is the value it celebrates.

In *Snow Cake* a quite different question is asked after bereavement in an automobile accident: what happens if the mother is autistic? How is the immediate circle of the bereaved—augmented by the stranger who most closely witnessed the death—going to encompass within their own process a mother who has no idea that it is appropriate to grieve at her loss? Alan Rickman plays Alex, just out of jail on manslaughter charges (he killed the man who ran over his son), who gives a lift to the daughter of autistic mother Linda, played by Sigourney Weaver. Alex's car is hit by a truck; Alex survives but Linda's daughter does not. Alex feels it his duty to offer condolences to Linda, but her behavior is at all times at odds with expectations: she invites him in to put out her garbage.

Whether the film is an accurate portrayal of a person with HFA / AS is a little uncertain, but it must count as a lot more accurate than *I Am Sam* in which an autistic father keeps fighting for the custody of his daughter. The latter film give Sam an implausible depth of feeling for his daughter—given the principal characteristic of autism as the inability to feel for others—while in the former Linda is given perhaps too much indifference to her daughter's death. But *Snow Cake* is nonetheless a valuable exploration of the search for meaning in the face of the meaningless of bereavement by automobile accident. While the male protagonist is English, the female protagonist and the setting is American. Linda as a near-normal autistic is a transgressive figure to the extent that she cannot participate in normal social rituals, and is a slave to other self-imposed and obsessive rituals. Yet the film quietly invites compassion for her, and suggests that American society, even if its social security systems do not match those in Europe, is able to support and tolerate such unusual figures. And Linda's own way of celebrating life is presented to us not the as the object of clinical curiosity, but as of genuine interest. She finds eating snow better than orgasm. So Alex's parting present to her is a "snow cake" left in her refrigerator.

Conclusions

In exploring the theme of "the American madness" on film we have brought to bear a structured criticism which has attempted to avoid the programs of either Left or Right, drawing instead on a Greek model of drama. We saw in connection with *Fight Club* that Paul Watson, though clearly owning the tradition of left-wing critical theory, likewise feels its limitations. He suggests that the tradition created "a critical vocabulary which is unable to capture the genuine sense of helplessness, anomie and pain which attends Jack's narrative and clearly affected the film's audience."[1] Instead he advocates a critical practice that is willing to leave behind pre-programmed theories and address films "more in terms of sentiment." Acknowledging that such a criticism will not have the hinterland of left-wing philosophical theory behind it, he suggests that it will be more ad hoc than programmatic, and that perhaps an appropriate term for such a criticism would be "therapeutic." This might be a useful term if it were not for Lasch's deconstruction of therapy itself as part of the recent American madness: part of the problem as much as the solution. Instead, the five-fold scheme offered here, with its roots in Aristotle, could be called more simply a *dramatic* model of criticism, which allows the recognition that film is first and foremost a dramatic art, and as such is *sui generis*. It does not serve politics, necessarily, and neither does it necessarily serve therapy, even if it is often cathartic.

But the dramatic model of criticism developed here is clearly framed in modern terms that Aristotle could not have understood. The genuine anger in Popper's crucial work *The Open Society and Its Enemies* is partly directed at Plato, Aristotle and Hegel in their defense of slavery of subordinate races. Aristotle required the tragic figure to be well born and wealthy; we have seen that a great strength of contemporary American cinema is in its portrayal of the ordinary citizen, drawn through immigration and the legacy of slavery from all nations in the world. Here is the first point of departure. The second point of departure is that "tragedy" is too limited a form to encompass a cinema that evokes genuine compassion. Hence the term "transgressional cinema" was proposed here to deal with the range of forms that convey the struggle with fate that befalls the ordinary citizen, when behavior moves to the margins of excess. But otherwise Aristotle points us to essential components of our critical method: the plausibility of the scenario, the artistic seriousness of the work, and—though he did not formulate it in this way— critical distance.

This is also a good time to contemplate the difference between the "tragic" figure of Aristotle and the "heroic" figure of Campbell's monomyth, in relation to transgressional cinema. In the first *Rambo* film John Rambo is popularly described as an "all-action hero" but is in fact a tragic figure, brought low by his frailties and errors. Of the protagonists we have considered here perhaps only Clarice Starling fits Campbell's formula for the hero's journey to some degree. Travis Bickle may appear to undergo the hero's journey, but his "redemption"—to cross from Hellenic to Abrahamic metaphor— is dubious and morally squalid. The hero's journey requires encounter with the grotesque of course, and there has been plenty of that in these films: Lecter is grotesque to Starling for example. But in general the encounter with the grotesque in these films has been deeply compromised for the protagonists because they share too many transgressional qualities themselves. We saw that the young Jeffrey Beaumont is recognized by the grotesque Frank as potentially like him—as are all human beings in the contemplation of the id.

But it is Michael Douglas's Nick Curran in *Basic Instinct* who best illustrates the fluid boundaries between the heroic and the tragic in his encounter with Catherine Tramell, the possible serial killer. We commented on the conflicted moral energy which drives Douglas's portrayal of Curran and characters in several other films: he is a good example of Riesman's inner-directed man, plagued by the "dynamo" that animates all such individuals, their self-propelled stance in the world, haunted by the guilt that they have not done enough. In Curran's case the mild, pervasive and motivating inner-directed guilt is topped up by the specific guilt of his shootings in the line of duty that had gone so badly wrong before. *Basic Instinct* can be criticized for its sensationalism, but Douglas's performance epitomizes the unique strengths of the American mind at the borders of sanity / insanity and the heroic / tragic; perhaps his face, animated with the intensity of moral aggression, could even be an *icon* of the American sanity pulled back from the brink.

Sanity's Pathology / Pathology's Sanity

The specific sanities, or greatnesses, of the American mind walk handin-hand with their specific corresponding madnesses. Nothing great has ever been attempted by an individual or culture without throwing up, at the margins, some potential for the pathological; likewise, everything insane also has the germ of something true in it. Hence, in many of the films we have selected to highlight particular aspects of the American madness we can also find telling indicators of the sane, the true, and the good. But we should distinguish sharply between those films that do so knowingly and those that do so only in the negative. In the first category of film, the subject matter, however bleak or despairing, is presented—sometimes in a grotesque exaggeration—in order to serve as a warning or as an indictment, or as the record of some kind of redemptive journey. Other films are made by directors and writers who exhibit in themselves some element of the American madness, and so lack any critical distance from their content. Of the films so far examined a number fall into the latter category (at least to some degree), including: *The X-Files, Seven, Affliction, The Rapture, The Passion of the Christ,* the *Left Behind* trilogy, *Waking Life, What the Bleep, Indigo, Zelig, Zabriskie Point, Fear and Loathing in Las Vegas, Taxi Driver, A.I., Lawnmower Man,* and *In the Cut.*

Films that do show some self-awareness, or present to us an aspect of the American madness as an indictment of that madness, include: *Dr. Strangelove, Rambo: First Blood, The Devil's Advocate, American Beauty, Apocalypse Now, Rain Man, The Truman Show,* and *Pleasantville. Dr. Strangelove* was made by Kubrick explicitly to satirize the American aggression of nuclear war strategy, and so points us to an important element of the American cultural landscape: its anti-war protesters. *Rambo: First Blood,* although its enduring image tends to promote a comic-book American aggression, does in fact remind the American public that every soldier it sends to fight its wars abroad may come home to tell disturbing tales about the reality of that war. *Apocalypse Now* is a film far more determined to equate American foreign policy with unmitigated madness, though the laying down of weapons at the end is little more than filmic symbolism.

The Devil's Advocate and *American Beauty,* though usefully showing for us different aspects of the American madness that lurk beneath the veneer of wealth and success, are actually modern morality tales designed to warn us of excess. In *The Devil's Advocate* the young lawyer—in a profession that represents in the American mind the ultimately unethical pursuit of wealth—is seduced, it seems, by the vast wealth his advocacy can bring him. But the very point of the film is that, having contemplated that wealth, and the price it will exact from him, he turns back from the brink and subordinates his skill to his morals. In *American Beauty* the protagonist is sexually obsessed in a suburban world of apparent sexual license, only to be brought up short at the last minute by the puncturing of the fantasy he is about to consummate. His daughter's young and beautiful friend finally and hesitatingly confesses to him that she is a virgin, despite her continuous display of sexual sophistication. In that moment the middle-aged man sees her not as the object of his fantasy, but more like his own daughter, a schoolchild to whom he effectively has parental obligations—and a need to show parental love. More than that, *American Beauty* is a rhapsodical and gentle subversion of American suburban affluence, not with a nihilistic purpose, but aiming to show that however banal it may become, it hides a continuum of human and natural "beauty." Like *21 Grams* and *Snow Cake* it celebrates life itself, even if it takes death to provoke the longer reflection necessary.

Rain Man is a film that examines two brothers' lives and attitudes, showing how the supposedly successful brother in many ways exhibits the failings of the brother kept in a mental hospital, and how he matures under the challenge of caring for him. Finally, both *The Truman Show* and *Pleasantville* are comedies that target the same suburban dream that *American Beauty* set its sights on. These three films taken together show that America is very capable of questioning the American dream when it runs aground in anodyne superficiality.

Cultural Catharsis and the Uncut Hand

If we accept that some American films intend to warn us through the madness they portray on screen or indict aspects of American behavior that are insane, then these films may be part of the American sanity. On the other hand those films that do not show any critical awareness of the madness they portray can be considered to be part of that madness. This distinction is worth considering in a bit more detail. Watching some of the films discussed in this book can no doubt be an ordeal, and makes pertinent the criticisms from cultural conservatives of either stripe. There is a saying of the Buddha's which seems relevant to this issue of a cultural production that sets out to shock or portray the darker sides of life. He says in the key Buddhist text, the *Dhammapada*: "An uncut hand can handle poison."[2] The Buddha appears to mean by this that a person who is not himself psychologically damaged or wounded can contemplate the dark sides of the human condition without being adversely affected. We might call such a person "sanguine"—one who is cheerfully optimistic, and not prone to gloom and depression. In the Hebraic tradition a comparable sentiment to the Buddha's is: "Yea, though I walk through the valley of the shadow of death, I will fear no evil." (Psalm 23:4)

Hence, although a person may find herself emotionally stirred up by transgressional cinema of the type described here, she will not on the whole succumb to aggression, nihilism, escapism, or any other paranoid state of mind. On the contrary, by engaging with these sometimes extremely dramatic journeys at an emotional level, she may come out the other end in some way *purified*.

Medved says:

> As a nation, we no longer believe that popular culture enriches our lives. Few of us view the show business capital as a magical source of uplifting entertainment, romantic inspiration, or even harmless fun. Instead, tens of millions of Americans now see the entertainment industry as an all-powerful enemy, an alien force that assaults our most cherished values and corrupts our children. The dream factory has become the poison factory.[3]

If Medved is right, that American films are an "alien force" in American culture, then the American madness explored here through film does not really exist in the individuals or collective actions of that nation. It is merely the deranged production of sophisticates who have foisted their filth onto a public somehow incapable of defending itself against it. But Medved has ignored what we have known for nearly three thousand years: the cathartic possibilities in the engagement with stories from the dark side. Every culture has had its ghouls, its bogeymen, its villains, the stories surrounding which are told and retold, first in oral cultures and then in writing, in poems and plays. The Greeks merely refined in their tragedies what was a long-standing custom in the human race since it first gathered around the hearth or tent and told stories. Yes, there are plenty of cultural productions through history that might count as "uplifting entertainment, romantic inspiration, or even harmless fun." But that is not the be-all and end-all of story telling, either in the oral traditions or in the most contemporary of mediums, cinema. All the most enduring stories of old included violence, death, torture, madness— and redemption.

Medved and other cultural conservatives also deny another key element in film production: that these are, at the end of the day, works of art. However commercialized the film industry may be, its creative maestros are determined to ensure that their personal projects see the light of day as much as the formulaic box-office certainties. Francis Ford Coppola took time out between two of the *Godfather* films to make *The Conversation*, a very personal and more European-style *film noir* than the studios were otherwise interested in. Bill Murray insisted on starring in a remake of *The Razor's Edge* between two *Ghostbuster* films, because its spiritual message was close to his heart. (Sadly the film is dire.) And what to say about independent filmmakers like Jim Jarmusch, whose entire oeuvre is the deeply personal vision of a single artist? No, there is a deep artistic and human need to explore the darker sides of life; artists of the twentieth century in particular have excelled in dealing with the transgressional. They have been the lightning rods for our collective anxieties.

Even animals do it. A television nature documentary once featured an infant gorilla brought up by naturalists in a trailer. Its favorite toy, it seems, was a red plastic crocodile, with which it loved to scare itself (crocodiles are the gorilla's only natural predator). One day, when it was fully grown, some (human) friends had been invited over to the trailer and were sitting on the sofa as their hosts prepared tea. The gorilla crept up behind them silently, and then, in what seems a deeply human act, it stretched its arm over them and dangled the red plastic crocodile in their faces. It wanted to scare them, in a friendly sort of way, and chose to use its own "bogeyman," blissfully unaware that to be crept up on by a gorilla is in itself pretty scary. Clearly the gorilla dealt with its deepest fears by confronting the symbol of those fears: human beings simply have a more sophisticated range of methods for doing this.

Having said all this, there is much that Medved and other conservatives say that is valid. While these critics may have lost sight of the cathartic purpose of "difficult" films, they are right to say that many of their makers do just churn out shocking or titillatory images for the sake of it. Western culture is a deeply psychological culture since Freud, and although the appearance of "cod psychology" in films has been lambasted here, it is in the recognition that the work of real psychology is highly valuable. Filmmakers who understand this, whether through study or intuition, use shocking images in their films for a purpose. It is here that film criticism is valuable: not to dismiss the darker sides of cinema as "an alien force that assaults our most cherished values and corrupts our children," but to ask if it is purveyed in a *knowing* manner. Does it dangle the horrific image—the red plastic crocodile—in our faces to titillate, or to help us grapple with our fears and madnesses?

In this context it is good to go back to the Buddha's metaphor, and ask what happens when the *cut* hand handles poison. Even in the time of Sophocles, we may wonder if there was amongst the audience to his play *Oedipus Rex* the odd latent psychopath who was tipped over the edge by its transgresssional images. Could such a person, deeply disturbed by a convincing rendition of the mad Oedipus, rush home from the amphitheatre with sword drawn and kill his father? We may never know, but the question today is important. What happens to that small proportion of contemporary audiences who are far from sanguine in their mental state, who perhaps already find it hard to distinguish reality from fantasy, and who watch, say, *Natural Born Killers*? What happens when a person fails to distinguish the emetic from the nutritive? Critics like Medved are right to pose the question of "copycat" violence, and *Natural Born Killers* is perhaps on the cusp of "knowing" as defined here. The very uncertainty that we have whether this film is genuinely cathartic or merely exploitative helps make the case for a specifically American madness revealed by film. If critics like Medved had their way, such productions would be banned, and in that case we would have to discover the true contours of the American madness through other means. But at the heart of the American sanity is the belief in freedom of expression. It has its roots in Enlightenment thought generally, but also perhaps in Freud's idea of the "talking cure." If a nation can talk to itself in a relatively untrammeled way through its cultural productions, then it is at least partly sane, even if those very productions look at times like "poison."

This book has focused on the extremes in the American mind, but if we pull back from these marginal spaces, we find each time that we are potentially looking at a specific American sanity. For each category of madness there lies a specific strength that marks a greatness in the American mind, a strength that was hinted at as we worked through them and which is worth summarizing here. The phenomena of paranoia and conspiracy theories, while harmful if taken to an extreme, actually demonstrate important aspects of democracy when restrained by rational thought. It is vital in any democracy that official accounts of events are open to challenge, and this constitutionally protected freedom exists in America more than almost any other country. Could a film like *JFK* be made in China today, or even Russia? It is doubtful. If we turn to aggression as the other hallmark of the American madness, then again, if restrained by reason and common humanity, it becomes a dynamic force for progress, a determination to succeed against the odds. It appears so often as frankness, as boldness, as openness. If America does finally accept that global warming is a real threat, its collective energies are more likely to find a solution than those of any other country. The same collective grandeur of vision that put men on the moon is quite capable of solving our more earthly problems. When it comes to the Oedipal and the Freudian, we have pointed out already that the "talking cure" can be a genuine remedy for individual psychological disturbance, and also collectively. Sexual obsession, as painted in some of the films we have examined, is no doubt a path to destruction, but when kept in balance is the source of some of our deepest sanity. The real lesson of the sexual revolution is that repressed sexuality stifles the energies of a person and society, though we also now recognize that an unchecked libido is no better an extreme than its total suppression. When it comes to the Apocalypse, we have taken pains to point out that this represents one of the worst aspects of American religion. By far the majority of American Christians do not succumb to it however, and their genuine and robust faith represents a deeply sane aspect of the American mind. (It is unfortunate that the Islamic world is provided with scant evidence of this in mainstream American culture.) On the question of the legacy of the white man's war on the Native American, we have seen evidence in film that the American mind is much engaged with trying to come to terms with this. When it comes to New Age ideas, one might be legitimately critical of its excesses, but the enthusiastic open-minded spirituality of it is ultimately a great asset to America (if only the conservative religious elements could enter into a proper dialogue with it). The issue of nihilism is one that faces any advanced society, but if not succumbed to is actually a sign of the ability to question conventional values. As to the elevation of the intellect and signs of cultural autism, these are universal aspects of a technologically developed society. The American mind is far too ruddy, too sanguine, to allow this particular madness to overcome it. And finally, when it comes to virtual reality and saccharine fantasy: these extremes merely disfigure at the margins what is undeniably one of America's great contributions to the world: entertainment. The best of American films are original, daring, provocative, and highly entertaining.

The more one understands "the American madness," the more one can see it is a phenomenon at the margins. The point of course is that if Americans, either individually or collectively, are drawn or pushed to those margins, then this is what their insanity looks like. At the same time, the truly American sanity is better understood by what takes place in that marginal world.

How then can any person or nation encourage their friend, America, to pull back from the dark places of its own madness? Firstly, by painting an accurate portrait of it. "Know thyself," said Socrates, and "Be a light unto yourself," said the Buddha. If the portrait here is in the least accurate, it helps America know itself, or at the very least understand how it is seen from the outside; seen, that is, through the medium of its own cinematic productions. And it is through cinema that outsiders have learned about the special place of the Native American in the collective unconscious of white America, which leads one to suggest that there is a particular sanity in the Native American that speaks to the nation as a whole. In Oliver Stone's *U-Turn* the Blind Man tells the white protagonist: "Your lies are old, but you tell 'em well." There is a generosity of spirit here, a forgiveness, a humor, that is emblematic of the Native American. The white American has many sanities, many greatnesses of spirit, but America's indigenous peoples can perhaps teach what will be increasingly a vital lesson for America's very survival: a humility in respect of the natural world, and a recognition of the human as part of a network of relations and not as the armored, aggressive plunderer of Nature.

Obviously no American individual or collective action can ever demonstrate all aspects of the American madness at the same time. This is partly because America is deeply divided between secular and religious communities, which show quite different combinations of the insanities outlined here. The secular mind doesn't succumb to Christian visions of the Apocalypse, and the Christian mind is generally less sexually obsessed at a cultural level, for example. But a true friendship reserves its criticism for times of excess; a true friendship prefers to focus on the sanities of a friend. Hence each weakness in the American mind is shown to be also the counterpoint to some very specific strength, and it is those strengths that we should laud while keeping an eye on the rest. More important still is the necessity to understand American culture as deeply as possible while enjoying its productions. This is because of the genuine necessity to *resist* it as it sweeps across the world. Unless every culture can present its sanities and madnesses to the world with equal voice, we lose what Rabbi Jonathan Sacks calls the "dignity of difference": a cultural conversation between equals.[4] The American madness is *not* the madness of the Chinese, the Indian, the Japanese, or even the French or English; and the American sanity is likewise unique to itself. The generalizations made here about American and other cultures are not meant to create stereotypes, but to celebrate difference.

Filmography

2001: A Space Odyssey, 1968, Stanley Kubrick
21 Grams, 2003, Alejandro González Iñárritu
Altered States, 1980, Ken Russell
Artificial Intelligence: A.I., 2001, Steven Spielberg
Amen, 2002, Costa-Gavras
American Beauty, 1999, Sam Mendes
American Psycho, 2000, Mary Harron
Angel Heart, 1987, Alan Parker
Apocalypse Now, 1979, Francis Ford Coppola
The Apostle, 1997, Robert Duvall
At Play in the Fields of the Lord, 1991, Hector Babenco
Basic Instinct, 1992, Paul Verhoeven
A Beautiful Mind, 2001, Ron Howard
The Birds, 1963, Alfred Hitchcock
The Blair Witch Project, 1999, Daniel Myrick and Eduardo Sánchez
Blue Velvet, 1986, David Lynch
Bonnie and Clyde, 1967, Arthur Penn
Broken Arrow, 1950, Delmer Daves
Buffalo Bill and the Indians, 1976, Robert Altman
Capricorn One, 1978, Peter Hyams
Children of Men, 2006, Alfonso Cuarón
Chinatown, 1974, Roman Polanski
Citizen Kane, 1941, Orson Welles
A Clockwork Orange, 1971, Stanley Kubrick
Conspiracy Theory, 1997, Richard Donner
The Conversation, 1974, Francis Ford Coppola
Crouching Tiger, Hidden Dragon, 2000, Ang Lee
The Crucible, 1996, Nicholas Hytner
Conversations with God, 2006, Stephen Deutsch
Copycat, 1995, Jon Amiel
Dances with Wolves, 1990, Kevin Costner
Daughters of the Dust, 1991, Julie Dash

Dead Man, 1995, Jim Jarmusch
Deliverance, 1972, John Boorman
Demolition Man, 1993, Marco Brambilla
The Devil's Advocate, 1997, Taylor Hackford
Do the Right Thing, 1989, Spike Lee
Dr. Strangelove, 1964, Stanley Kubrick
The Education of Little Tree, 1997, Richard Friedenberg
End of Days, 1999, Peter Hyams
Enemy of the State, 1998, Tony Scott
Eraserhead, 1977, David Lynch
eXistenZ, 1999, David Cronenberg
Extreme Measures, 1996, Michael Apted
Eyes Wide Shut, 1999, Stanley Kubrick
Falling Down, 1993, Joel Schumacher
Fear and Loathing in Las Vegas, 1998, Terry Gilliam
Fight Club, 1999, David Fincher
The Fisher King, 1991, Terry Gilliam
Forbidden Planet, 1956, Fred M. Wilcox
Forrest Gump, 1994, Robert Zemeckis
The Game, 1997, David Fincher
Ghost, 1990, Jerry Zucker
Ghost Dog—the Way of the Samurai, 1999, Jim Jarmusch
The Golden Compass, 2007, Chris Weitz
The Gospel According to St. Matthew, 1964, Pier Paolo Pasolini
Groundhog Day, 1993, Harold Ramis
The Handmaid's Tale, 1990, Volker Schlöndorff
Happiness, 1998, Todd Solondz
Henry: Portrait of a Serial Killer, 1986, John McNaughton
Holy Smoke, 1999, Jane Campion
The Hulk, 2003, Ang Lee
I Am Sam, 2001, Jessie Nelson
I Heart Huckabees, 2004, David O. Russell
In the Cut, 2003, Jane Campion
Indigo, 2003, Stephen Simon
It's a Wonderful Life, 1946, Frank Capra
JFK, 1991, Oliver Stone
Johnny Mnemonic, 1995, Robert Longo
Jungle Fever, 1991, Spike Lee
The Last of His Tribe, 1992, Harry Hook
Last of the Mohicans, 1992, Michael Mann
The Last Supper, 1976, Tomás Gutiérrez Alea
The Late, Great Planet Earth, 1979, Robert Amram

Lawnmower Man, 1992, Brett Leonard
Left Behind, 2000, Vic Sarin
Left Behind II: Tribulation Force, 2002, Bill Corcoran
Left Behind III: World at War, 2005, Craig R. Baxley
Light Sleeper, 1992, Paul Schrader
Little Big Man, 1970, Arthur Penn
Magnolia, 1999, Paul Thomas Anderson
Men In Black, 1997, Barry Sonnenfeld
The Matrix, 1999, Andy Wachowski and Larry Wachowski
The Matrix Reloaded, 2003, Andy Wachowski and Larry Wachowski
The Matrix Revolutions, 2003, Andy Wachowski and Larry Wachowski
Mullholland Dr., 2001, David Lynch
Natural Born Killers, 1994, Oliver Stone
Oedipus Rex, 1967, Pier Paolo Pasolini
Oh God!, 1977, Carl Reiner
The Omega Code, Robert Marcarelli, 1999
One Flew Over the Cuckoo's Nest, 1975, Milos Forman
Open Your Eyes, 1997, Alejandro Amenábar
The Outlaw Josey Wales, 1976, Clint Eastwood
The Passion of the Christ, 2004, Mel Gibson
The People vs. Larry Flint, 1996, Milos Forman
Pleasantville, 1998, Gary Ross
Poltergeist, 1982, Tobe Hooper
Psycho, 1960, Alfred Hitchcock
Rain Man, 1988, Barry Levinson
Rambo: First Blood, 1982, Ted Kotcheff
The Rapture, 1991, Michael Tolkin
The Razor's Edge, 1984, John Byrum
A Scanner Darkly, 2006, Richard Linklater
Schindler's List, 1993, Steven Spielberg
Seven, 1995, David Fincher
Silence of the Lambs, 1991, Jonathan Demme
Smoke Signals, 1998, Chris Eyre
Snow Cake, 2006, Marc Evans
Solaris, 1972, Andrei Tarkovsky
Solaris, 2002, Steven Soderbergh
Soldier, 1998, Paul W.S. Anderson
Southern Comfort, 1981, Walter Hill
Star Wars, 1977, George Lucas
Stir Crazy, 1980, Sidney Poitier
Straw Dogs, 1971, Sam Peckinpah
The Sunchaser, 1996, Michael Cimino
Taxi Driver, 1976, Martin Scorsese

Team America: World Police, 2004, Trey Parker
The Texas Chainsaw Massacre, 1974, Tobe Hooper
The Terminator, 1984, James Cameron
Thunderheart, 1992, Michael Apted
Tron, 1982, Steven Lisberger
The Truman Show, 1998, Peter Weir
Twelve Monkeys, 1995, Terry Gilliam
U-Turn, 1997, Oliver Stone
Vanilla Sky, 2001, Cameron Crowe
Waking Life, 2001, Richard Linklater
Whale Rider, 2002, Niki Caro
What Dreams May Come, 1998, Vincent Ward
What the Bleep Do We Know!?, 2004, William Arntz and Betsy Chasse
Where the Buffalo Roam, 1980, Art Linson
The Wild Bunch, 1969, Sam Peckinpah
Witness, 1985, Peter Weir
World Trade Center, 2006, Oliver Stone
The X-Files, 1998, Rob Bowman
Zabriskie Point, 1970, Michelangelo Antonioni
Zelig, 1983, Woody Allen

Chapter Notes

Preface

1. George Steiner, *The Death of Tragedy* (London: Faber and Faber, 1961), 351.
2. Mike King, *Secularism: the Hidden Origins of Disbelief* (Cambridge: James Clarke, 2007), 82–86.

Introduction

1. Robert Kolker, *A Cinema of Loneliness—Penn, Stone, Kubrick, Scorsese, Spielberg, Altman* (New York: Oxford University Press, 2000), ix.
2. Susan Sontag, *Against Interpretation* (London: Vintage Books, 2001), 7.
3. Harry M. Benshoff and Sean Griffin, *America on Film—Representing Race, Class, Gender, and Sexuality at the Movies* (Oxford: Blackwell, 2004), 7.
4. The three "masters of suspicion" according to Paul Ricoeur are Marx, Nietzsche, and Freud: Paul Ricoeur, *Freud and Philosophy: An Essay on Interpretation* (New Haven, London: Yale University Press, 1970), 32.
5. Ray Pratt, *Projecting Paranoia—Conspiratorial Visions in American Film* (Lawrence, KS: University Press of Kansas, 2001), 31.
6. Christopher Sharrett, "End of Story: The Collapse of Myth in Postmodern Narrative Film," in *The End of Cinema as We Know It—American Film in the Nineties*, ed. Jon Lewis (London: Pluto Press, 2002), 319.
7. Henry A. Giroux and Imre Szeman, "Ikea Boy Fights Back," in *The End of Cinema as We Know It—American Film in the Nineties*, ed. Jon Lewis (London: Pluto Press, 2002), 96.
8. *American Film and Politics from Reagan to Bush Jr*, eds. Philip John Davies and Paul Wells (Manchester and New York: Manchester University Press, 2002), 3.
9. Theodor W. Adorno and Max Horkheimer, *Dialectic of Enlightenment* (London: Verso, 1997), 137.

10. Peter Watson, *A Terrible Beauty: The People and Ideas that Shaped the Modern Mind* (London: Phoenix, 2000), 721.
11. Ibid., 451.
12. Allan Bloom, *The Closing of the American Mind: How Higher Education Has Failed Democracy and Impoverished the Souls of Today's Students* (London: Penguin, 1987), 380.
13. Christopher Lasch, *The Culture of Narcissism: American Life in an Age of Diminishing Expectations* (New York and London: W. W. Norton, 1991), 150.
14. David Martin, *On Secularization—Towards a Revised General Theory* (Aldershot: Ashgate), 2005.
15. Daniel J. Czitrom, *Media and the American Mind—From Morse to McLuhan* (Chapel Hill: University of North Carolina Press, 1982), 191.
16. For an instructive history of this regulation see Stephen Prince, *Classical Film Violence—Designing and Regulating Brutality in Hollywood Cinema, 1930–1968* (New Brunswick, New Jersey: Rutgers University Press, 2003).
17. Prince, *Classical Film Violence*, 252.
18. Michael Medved, *Hollywood vs. America* (New York: HarperCollins, 1993), cover text.
19. Tim LaHaye and David Noebel, *Mind Siege—The Battle for Truth in the New Millennium* (Nashville: Word Publishing, 2000), 184.
20. Medved, *Hollywood vs. America*, 3.
21. Greenville College, *www.greenville.edu/backup/campus/addresses/medved.shtml*, last accessed 23rd August 2007.
22. Medved, *Hollywood vs. America*, xxv.
23. Ibid., 300.
24. Roger Lipsey, *An Art of Our Own—The Spiritual in Twentieth-Century Art* (Boston and Shaftesbury: Shambhala, 1988), 244.
25. Lasch, *The Culture of Narcissism*, 126.
26. Steiner, *The Death of Tragedy*, 4.
27. Friedrich Nietzsche, *Thus Spoke Zarathustra* (London: Penguin Books, 1969), 65.

28. Jean-Paul Sartre, *Saint Genet* (London: Heinemann, 1988).

29. Aristotle, *Poetics* (London: Penguin, 1996), 21.

30. Ibid., 22.

31. Prince, *Classical Film Violence*, 244.

32., Wheeler Winston Dixon, *Visions of the Apocalypse—Spectacles of Destruction in American Cinema* (London and New York: Wallflower Press, 2003), quoted in frontispiece.

33. Lasch, *The Culture of Narcissism*, 33.

Chapter 1

1. Otto Weininger, *Sex and Character: An Investigation of Fundamental Principles*, trans. Ladislaus Löb (Bloomington, IN: Indiana University Press, 2005).

2. Victor J. Seidler, *Shadows of the Shoa—Jewish Identity and Belonging* (Oxford, New York: Berg, 2000), 50.

3. See for example Kenneth McKinnon, "After Mulvey: Male Erotic Objectification" in *The Body's Perilous Pleasures—Dangerous Desires and Contemporary Culture*, ed. Michele Aaron (Edinburgh: Edinburgh University Press, 1999), 13–29.

4. Winston Churchill, *History of the Second World War*, vol. V (Boston: Houghton Mifflin, 1951), 532.

5. Jacques Derrida, *Writing and Difference* (London and New York: Routledge, 1978), 192.

6. Emmanuel Levinas, *Totality and Infinity*, trans. Alphonso Lingis (Pittsburgh, Pennsylvania: Duquesne University Press, 1969).

7. Barbara W. Tuchman, *Bible and Sword: England and Palestine from the Bronze Age to Balfour* (New York: Ballantine Books, 1984), 132.

8. Mel Alexenberg, *The Future of Art in a Digital Age: From Hellenistic to Hebraic Consciousness* (Bristol: Intellect, 2006, p.17).

9. Peter Watson, *A Terrible Beauty*, Chapter 19.

10. Richard Rudgley, *Pagan Resurrection: A Force for Evil or the Future of Western Spirituality?* (London: Century, 2006), 194.

11. Kenneth Sylvan Guthrie, *The Pythagorean Sourcebook and Library* (Grand Rapids: Phanes Press, 1987), 30.

12. Sigmund Freud, *Civilization and Its Discontents* (New York, London: W.W. Norton, 1961), 93.

13. Gerald Corey, *Theory and Practice of Counseling and Psychotherapy* (Belmont: Wadsworth Publishing, 2001), 67.

14. Merlin Stone, *When God was a Woman* (New York: Harcourt, 1976), 21.

15. Leonard Shlain, *The Alphabet Versus the Goddess—The Conflict Between Words and Images* (New York: Penguin / Compass, 1998), 33.

16. For example, aggression in shamanic cultures is more readily played out in the world of the demons: see Mircea Eliade, *Shamanism: Archaic Techniques of Ecstasy*, Bollingen Series 76 (Princeton and Oxford: Princeton University Press, 2004), 509. Another relevant work is Hugh Brody, *The Other Side of Eden—Hunters, Farmers, and the Shaping of the World* (New York: North Point Press, 2000).

17. Henry Chadwick, *The Early Church* (Middlesex: Penguin, 1967), 11.

18. Ibid., 56.

19. Although Augustine is usually credited with bringing the Platonic stream of thought into Christianity, his writings show that he regarded learning as much inferior to piety. See for example St. Augustine , *Confessions*, trans. R. S. Pine-Coffin (Middlesex, England: Penguin, 1986), 154.

20. Michael Grosso, *The Millennium Myth—Love and Death at the End of Time*, Wheaton (Madras, London: Quest Books, 1995), 28.

21. Michael Northcott, *An Angel Directs the Storm—Apocalyptic Religion and American Empire* (London: I.B. Tauris, 2004), 44.

22. Grosso, *The Millennium Myth*, 5.

23. Chadwick, *The Early Church*, 21.

Chapter 2

1. Isaac Kramnick, ed., *The Portable Enlightenment Reader* (London: Penguin, 1995), xix.

2. Philip Callow, *Walt Whitman—From Noon to Starry Night* (London: Allison & Busby, 1992), 323.

3. R. M. Bucke, *Walt Whitman* (Philadelphia, 1883), 42.

4. John Burroughs, *Whitman: A Study* (London 1894), 41.

5. Leonard Quart and Albert Auster, *American Film and Society since 1945* (Westport, Conn., London: Praeger, 2002), 107.

6. Walt Whitman, *Leaves of Grass* (Oxford, New York: Oxford University Press, 1990), 66.

7. See Lawrence's attack on Whitman in D. H. Lawrence, *Studies in Classic American Literature* (London: Penguin, 1977).

8. David Riesman, *The Lonely Crowd* (New Haven and London: Yale University Press, 2001), 24.

9. Bloom, *The Closing of the American Mind*, 145.

10. Sigmund Freud, "On Narcissism: An Introduction," in *The Freud Reader*, ed. Peter Gay (New York: Norton, 1985), 559.

11. Ellen Schrecker, *Many are the Crimes—McCarthyism in America* (Princeton, New Jersey: Princeton University Press, 1998), 330.

12. Riesman, *The Lonely Crowd*, 14.

13. Peter Watson, *A Terrible Beauty*, 663.

14. Ray Pratt, *Projecting Paranoia—Conspiratorial Visions in American Film* (Kansas: University Press of Kansas, 2001), 28.

15. Marita Sturken, *"Affliction—When Paranoid Male Narratives Fail,"* in *The End of Cinema as We Know It—American Film in the Nineties*, ed. Jon Lewis (London: Pluto Press, 2002), 208.

16. Pratt, *Projecting Paranoia*, 20.

17. Northcott, *An Angel Directs the Storm*, 14.

18. Grosso, *The Millennium Myth*, 40–59.

19. Margaret Gullan-Whur, *Within Reason—A Life of Spinoza* (London: Jonathan Cape, 1998), 203.

20. Northcott, *An Angel Directs the Storm*, 15.

21. Carl Elliott and Tod Chambers, eds., *Prozac as a Way of Life (Studies in Social Medicine)*, (Chapel Hill and London: University of North Carolina Press, 2004), 52.

22. Dixon, *Visions of the Apocalypse*, 2.

23. Hal Lindsy, *The Late Great Planet Earth* (Michigan: Zondervan, 1970).

24. Peter Knight, *Conspiracy Culture— American Paranoia from the Kennedy Assassination to The X-files* (London: Routledge, 2001), 2.

25. Richard Hofstadter, *The Paranoid Style in American Politics, and Other Essays* (London: Jonathan Cape, 1966), 3.

26. Knight, *Conspiracy Culture*, 3–5.

27. Hofstadter, *The Paranoid Style in American Politics*, 5.

28. Pratt, *Projecting Paranoia*, 48.

29. Cited in Spencer Selby, *Dark City—The Film Noir*, (Jefferson, N.C., London: McFarland, 1984), 1.

30. Michael L. Stephens, *Film Noir—A Comprehensive, Illustrated Reference to Movies, Terms, and Persons* (Jefferson, N.C.: McFarland, 1995), ix.

31. Nicholas Christopher, *Somewhere in the Night—Film Noir and the American City* (New York: Free Press, 1997).

32. Dana Polan, *Power and Paranoia—History, Narrative and the American Cinema, 1940–1950* (New York: Columbia University Press, 1986), 14.

Chapter 3

1. See for example: David Ray Griffin, *The New Pearl Harbour—Disturbing Questions about the Bush Administration and 9/11* (Northampton, Massachusetts: Olive Branch Press, 2004).

2. David Dunbar and Brad Reagan, *Debunking 9/11Myths—Why Conspiracy Theories Can't Stand up to the Facts* (New York: Hearst Books, 2006), 42.

3. Pratt, *Projecting Paranoia*, 12.

4. Kolker, *A Cinema of Loneliness*, 53.

5. Ibid., 124.

6. Knight, *Conspiracy Culture*, 170.

7. Ibid., 16.

8. Ibid., 53.

9. Pratt, *Projecting Paranoia*, 99.

10. Kolker, *A Cinema of Loneliness*, 126.

11. Ibid., 128.

12. Charles Maland, *"Dr Strangelove (1964): Nightmare Comedy and the Ideology of Liberal Consensus,"* in *Hollywood as Historian: American Film in a Cultural Context*, ed. Peter C. Rollins (Lexington: University Press of Kentucky, 1998), 206.

13. Pratt, *Projecting Paranoia*, 230.

14. Knight, *Conspiracy Culture*, 217.

15. FEMA, *World Trade Center, Building Performance Study*, FEMA report 403, May 2002.

16. Knight, *Conspiracy Culture*, 77.

17. Pratt, *Projecting Paranoia*, 224.

18. Kolker, *A Cinema of Loneliness*, 74.

19. Quart and Auster, *American Film and Society*, 179.

20. Pratt, *Projecting Paranoia*,18.

21. Sturken, *"Affliction—When Paranoid Male Narratives Fail,"* 208.

22. Polan, *Power and Paranoia*, 13.

23. Pratt, *Projecting Paranoia*, 19.

24. Knight, *Conspiracy Culture*, 9.

25. Karl Popper, *The Open Society and Its Enemies, Vol. 2: Hegel and Marx* (London: Routledge, 1973), 95.

26. Whitman, *Leaves of Grass*, 27.

27. Pratt, *Projecting Paranoia*, 8.

28. Ibid., 126.

Chapter 4

1. Lasch, *The Culture of Narcissism*, 117.

2. Quart and Auster, *American Film and Society*, 145.

3. Medved, *Hollywood vs. America*, 229.

4. Pratt, *Projecting Paranoia*, 195.

5. Ibid.

6. John Izod, *Myth, Mind and the Screen—Understanding the Heroes of our Time* (Cambridge: Cambridge University Press,2001), Chapter Six.

7. Medved, *Hollywood vs. America*, 162.

8. Marsha Kinder, "Violence American Style: The Narrative Orchestration of Violent Attractions," in *Violence and American Cinema*, ed. Slocum, J. David (New York, London: Routledge, 2001), 78.

9. Prince, *Classical Film Violence*, 219.

10. Ibid., 245.

Chapter 5

1. E. Ann Kaplan, ed., *Psychoanalysis & Cinema* (New York, London: Routledge, 1990), 10.

2. Peter Watson, *A Terrible Beauty*, 505.

3. Ibid., 759.

4. Nicholas Haeffner, *Alfred Hitchcock* (Harlow: Longman, 2005), 84.

5. Joseph Campbell, *The Hero with a Thousand Faces* (Princeton, New Jersey: Princeton University Press, 1973).

6. Christopher Vogler, *The Writer's Journey—Mythic Structure for Storytellers and Screenwriters*, 2nd edition (London: Pan Books, 1998).

7. Benshoff and Griffin, *America on Film*, 129.

8. Lasch, *The Culture of Narcissism*, 12.

9. Ibid., 178.

10. Sturken, *"Affliction—When Paranoid Male Narratives Fail,"* 209.

Chapter 6

1. Susan Jacoby, *Freethinkers—A History of American Secularism* (New York: Metropolitan Books, 2004), 308.

2. David Boadella, *Wilhelm Reich: The Evolution of his Work* (London: Vision Press, 1973).

3. Quart and Auster, *American Film and Society*, 203.

4. James Schamus, "A Rant," in *The End of Cinema as We Know It—American Film in the Nineties*, ed. Jon Lewis (London: Pluto Press, 2002), 257.

5. Medved, *Hollywood vs. America*, 167.

6. Pratt, *Projecting Paranoia*, 152.

7. Medved, *Hollywood vs. America*, 270.

8. Pratt, *Projecting Paranoia*, 178.

Chapter 7

1. *The Guardian*, 17 July 2004.

2. Jacoby, *Freethinkers*, 118.

3. Mick Broderick, "Heroic Apocalypse: Mad Max, Mythology, Millennium," in *Crisis Cinema—The Apocalyptic Idea in Postmodern Narrative Film*, ed. Christopher Sharrett (Washington: Maisonneuve Press, 1993), 252.

4. Heather Hendershot, "Waiting for the End of the World—Christian Apocalyptic Media at the Turn of the Millennium," in *The End of Cinema as We Know It—American Film in the Nineties*, ed. Jon Lewis (London: Pluto Press, 2002), 333.

5. Northcott, *An Angel Directs the Storm*, 66.

6. Hendershot, "Waiting for the End of the World," 335.

7. Lindsy, *The Late Great Planet Earth*, 176.

8. LaHaye and Noebel, *Mind Siege*, 13.

9. Christopher Sharret, "End of Story—The Collapse of Myth in Postmodern Narrative Film," in *The End of Cinema as We Know It—American Film in the Nineties*, ed. Jon Lewis (London: Pluto Press, 2002), 320.

10. *Crisis Cinema—The Apocalyptic Idea in Postmodern Narrative Film*, ed. Christopher Sharrett (Washington: Maisonneuve Press, 1993), 221.

11. Dixon, *Visions of the Apocalypse*, p.9

12. Ibid., 16.

13. *www.raptureready.com*, last accessed 26th August 2007.

14. *www.raptureready.org/faq/faq65.html*, last accessed 26th August 2007.

15. Medved, *Hollywood vs. America*, 58.

16. Grosso, *The Millennium Myth*, 17.

17. Ibid., 174–175.

18. John Gray, *Black Mass: Apocalyptic Religion and the Death of Utopia* (London: Allen Lane, 2007), 52–53.

19. See for example: Francis Wheen, *Karl Marx* (London: Fourth Estate, 2000), 225–227.

20. *www.operation-exodus.org/Operation-Exodus*, last accessed 26th August 2007.

21. Northcott, *An Angel Directs the Storm*, 163.

22. *www.leftbehind.com/channelfree.asp?pageid=1315&channelID=175*, last accessed 26th August 2007.

23. *www.ala.org/ala/oif/bannedbooksweek/bbw links /100mostfrequently.htm*, last accessed 26th August 2007.

24. Sir James George Frazer, *The Golden Bough—Study in Magic and Religion*, abridged (New York: Touchstone, 1996).

25. Medved, *Hollywood vs. America*, 217–220.
26. William M. Hagen, "*Apocalypse Now* (1979): Joseph Conrad and the Television War," in *Hollywood as Historian: American Film in a Cultural Context*, ed. Peter C. Rollins

(Lexington: University Press of Kentucky,1998), 245.
27. Quart and Auster, *American Film and Society*, 125.
28. Medved, *Hollywood vs. America*, 58.
29. Hendershot, "Waiting for the End of the World," 335.

Chapter 8

1. Benshoff and Griffin, *America on Film*, 98.
2. Medved, *Hollywood vs. America*, 60.
3. See for example: Ake Hultkrantz, *The Religions of the American Indians* (Berkeley: University of California Press, 1979).
4. Jacquelyn Kilpatrick, *Celluloid Indians— Native Americans and Film* (Lincoln and London: University of Nebraska Press, 1999), xv.
5. Ibid., 58.
6. Benshoff and Griffin, *America on Film*, 104.
7. Brenda Murphy, *Congressional Theatre— Dramatizing McCarthyism on Stage, Film and Television* (Cambridge: Cambridge University Press, 1999), 158.
8. Kilpatrick, *Celluloid Indians*, 156.
9. Michael Hilger, *The American Indian in Film* (Metuchen, London: Scarecrow Press, 1986), 164.
10. S. Naifeh and G. W. Smith, *Jackson Pollock—An American Saga* (London: Pimlico, 1992), 337.
11. Frances Stonor Saunder, *Hidden Hands— A Different History of Modernism* (London: Channel 4 Television, 1995), 25–31.
12. John Golding, *Paths to the Absolute— Mondrian, Malevich, Kandinsky, Pollock, Newman, Rothko*, (Princeton, New Jersey: Princeton University Press, 2000), 118.
13. Hilger, *The American Indian in Film*, 140.
14. Kilpatrick, *Celluloid Indians*, 84.
15. Ibid., 147.
16. Kolker, *A Cinema of Loneliness*, 380.
17. C. G. Jung, *Memories, Dreams, Reflections* (London: Fontana, 1993), 276.
18. Eric G. Wilson, *Secret Cinema—Gnostic Vision in Film*, (London: Continuum, 2006), 10.

19. Gregory Salyer, "Poetry Written with Blood: Creating Death in *Dead Man*," in *Imag(in)ing Otherness: Filmic Visions of Living Together*, eds. David Jasper and S. Brent Plate (Atlanta: Scholars Press, 1999), 23.
20. Cited in Kilpatrick, *Celluloid Indians*, 171.
21. Mary Katherine Hall, "Now you are a Killer of White Men: Jim Jarmusch's *Dead Man*, Traditions of Revisionism in the Western," *Journal of Film & Video*, 52 no. 4 (2001): 3.
22. This is the spelling given in: Kilpatrick, *Celluloid Indians*, 171.
23. Dawn Perlmutter, "Postmodern Idolatry: the Media and Violent Acts of Participation," in *Reclaiming the Spiritual in Art: Contemporary Cross-Cultural Perspectives*, eds. Dawn Perlmutter and Debra Koppman (Albany: State University of New York Press, 1999), 135.
24. Benshoff and Griffin, *America on Film*, 105.
25. Dawn Perlmutter and Debra Koppman, eds., *Reclaiming the Spiritual in Art: Contemporary Cross-Cultural Perspectives* (Albany: State University of New York Press, 1999), 135.
26. The term "cod philosophy" is a useful British colloquialism which is not adequately substituted by "pop philosophy" or other similar American phrases—the latter lacks the negative connotation of the former, which may derive from "codswallop" meaning rubbish, derived in turn from fish entrails.
27. Dee Brown, *Bury my Heart at Wounded Knee* (London: Pan Books, 1978), 341.
28. Anthony F. C. Wallace, "Revitalization Movements: Some Theoretical Considerations for Their Comparative Study," *American Anthropologist* 58 no. 2 (1956): 264–81.
29. L. Frank Baum, "The Wounded Knee Editorial," *Aberdeen Saturday Pioneer*, January 3, 1891.
30. Kilpatrick, *Celluloid Indians*, 128.
31. Benshoff and Griffin, *America on Film*, 97.

Chapter 9

1. James Redfield, *The Celestine Prophecy—An Adventure* (New York: Bantam, 1994).
2. Quart and Auster, *American Film and Society*, 99–101.
3. David Tacey, *The Spirituality Revolution— The Emergence of Contemporary Spirituality* (Hove and New York: Brunner-Routledge, 2004), 146.
4. Bloom, *The Closing of the American Mind*, 146.

5. Lasch, *The Culture of Narcissism*, 19.

Chapter 10

1. Bloom, *The Closing of the American Mind*, 155.

2. Paul Watson,. "American cinema, political criticism and pragmatism: a therapeutic reading of *Fight Club* and *Magnolia*," in *American Film and Politics from Reagan to Bush Jr*, eds. Philip John Davies and Paul Wells (Manchester and New York: Manchester University Press, 2002), 18.

3. Alexandra Juhasz, "The Phallus UnFetished: The End of Masculinity As We Know It in Late-1990s 'Feminist' Cinema," in *The End of Cinema as We Know It—American Film in the Nineties*, ed. Jon Lewis (London: Pluto Press, 2002), 213.

4. Giroux and Szeman, "Ikea Boy Fights Back," 97.

5. Lasch, *The Culture of Narcissism*, 11.

6. Pratt, *Projecting Paranoia*, 38.

7. Kolker, *A Cinema of Loneliness*, .

8. Christopher Deacy, *Christologies, Redemption and the Medium Of Film* (Cardiff : University of Wales Press, 2001), 117.

9. Clive Marsh and Gaye Ortiz, eds., *Exploration in Theology and Film—Movies and Meanings* (Oxford: Blackwell, 1997), 63.

10. Kolker, *A Cinema of Loneliness*, 261.

Chapter 11

1. Gary B. Mesibov, Victoria Shea, and Lynn W. Adams, *Understanding Asperger Syndrome and High Functioning Autism* (New York, Boston, Dordrecht, London, Moscow: Kluwer Academic / Plenum Publishers, 2001), 3.

2. Ibid., 6.

3. Eric Schopler and Gary B. Mesibov, eds., *High-functioning Individuals with Autism* (New York and London: Plenum Press, 1992), 23.

4. Mesibov, Shea, and Adams, *Understanding Asperger Syndrome*, 5.

5. Andrew Williams, "60 SECONDS: Gary Numan," *Metro*, November 6, 2006.

6. Jennifer Elder, *Different Like Me: My Book of Autism Heroes* (London and Philadelphia: Jessica Kingsley Publishers, 2006).

7. Hofstadter, *The Paranoid Style in American Politics*, 3.

8. Daniel Goleman, *Emotional Intelligence—Why it Can Matter More Than IQ* (London: Bloomsbury, 1996).

9. Schopler and Mesibov, *High-functioning Individuals with Autism*, 13.

10. Dixon, *Visions of the Apocalypse*, 361.

11. Ibid., 197.

12. Hofstadter, *The Paranoid Style in American Politics*, 4.

Chapter 12

1. Mike King, "Virtual Reality: Give Us a Visual Clue," in *Proceedings of the First Split Screen Conference*, July 1996, Chichester Institute of Higher Education (1997), 180–187.

2. William Irwin, ed., *The Matrix and Philosophy—Welcome to the Desert of the Real* (Chicago and La Salle, Illinois: Open Court, 2002), 2.

3. Catherine Constable, "Baudrillardian Revolutions: Repetition and Radical Intervention in the *Matrix* Trilogy," in *The Matrix trilogy—Cyberpunk Reloaded*, ed. Stacy Gillis (London and New York: Wallflower, 2005), 151.

4. Jean Baudrillard, *Simulacra and Simulation*, trans. Sheila Faria Glaser (Ann Arbor: University of Michigan Press, 1994), 1.

5. Aude Lancelin, "The *Matrix* Decoded: *Le Nouvel Observateur* Interview With Jean Baudrillard," *International Journal of Baudrillard Studies*, Volume 1, Number 2 (2004).

6. Peter B. Lloyd, *Exegesis of the Matrix* (London: Whole-Being Books, 2003), 2.

7. Eric G. Wilson, *Secret Cinema—Gnostic Vision in Film* (London: Continuum, 2006), viii.

8. John Shelton Lawrence, "Fascist Redemption or Democratic Hope?" in *Jacking in to the Matrix Franchise*, eds. Matthew Kapell and William G. Doty (New York, London: Continuum, 2004), 80–96.

9. IMDb user miokey2004, *http://www.imdb.com/title/tt0242653/usercomments*, last accessed 18th March 2008.

10. Pat Mellencamp, "The Zen of Masculinity—Rituals of Heroism in *The Matrix*," in *The End of Cinema as We Know It—American Film in the Nineties*, ed. Jon Lewis (London: Pluto Press, 2002), 91.

11. Stacy Gillis, ed., *The Matrix Trilogy—Cyberpunk Reloaded* (London and New York: Wallflower, 2005), 1.

12. Mellencamp, "The Zen of Masculinity," 83.

13. Michael Brannigan, "There is No Spoon: A Buddhist Mirror," in *The Matrix and Philosophy—Welcome to the Desert of the Real*, ed.

William Irwin (Chicago and La Salle, Illinois: Open Court, 2002), 110.

Chapter 13

1. Walt Whitman, *Specimen Days* (London: The Folio Society, 1979), 118.
2. Ronald W. Clark, *Benjamin Franklin: A Biography* (London: Weidenfeld and Nicholson, 1983), 8.
3. Sam Abrams, *The Neglected Walt Whitman: Vital Texts* (New York, London: Four
Walls Eight Windows, 1993).

Chapter 14

1. Medved, *Hollywood vs. America*, 25.
2. Stephen Simon, *The Force Is With You: Mystical Movie Messages That Inspire Our Lives* (Charlottesville, VA: Hampton Roads, 2002),21.

Conclusions

1. Paul Watson, "American cinema, political criticism," 17.
2. This is a shortening of the translation of

chapter ix, line 124, usually rendered along these lines: "He who has no wound on his hand, may touch poison with his hand," see *The Dhammapada,* trans. Eknath Easwaran (London: Arkana, 1986), 110.
3. Medved, *Hollywood vs. America*, 3.
4. Jonathon Sacks, *The Dignity of Difference— How to Avoid the Clash of Civilisations* (London, New York: Continuum, 2003).

Bibliography

Aaron, Michele (ed.). *The Body's Perilous Pleasures: Dangerous Desires and Contemporary Culture*. Edinburgh: Edinburgh University Press, 1999.

Abrams, Sam. *The Neglected Walt Whitman: Vital Texts*. New York: Four Walls Eight Windows, 1993.

Adorno, Theodor W., and Max Horkheimer. *Dialectic of Enlightenment*. London: Verso, 1997.

Alexenberg, Mel. *The Future of Art in a Digital Age: From Hellenistic to Hebraic Consciousness*. Bristol: Intellect, 2006.

Aristotle. *Poetics*. London: Penguin, 1996.

Augustine (Saint). *Confessions*. Trans. R. S. Pine-Coffin. Middlesex, England: Penguin Books, 1986.

Baudrillard, Jean. *Simulacra and Simulation*. Trans. Sheila Faria Glaser. Ann Arbor: University of Michigan Press, 1994.

Baum, L. Frank. "The Wounded Knee Editorial." *Aberdeen Saturday Pioneer*. January 3, 1891.

Benshoff, Harry M., and Sean Griffin. *America on Film: Representing Race, Class, Gender, and Sexuality at the Movies*. Oxford: Blackwell, 2004.

Bloom, Allan. *The Closing of the American Mind: How Higher Education has Failed Democracy and Impoverished the Souls of Today's Students*. London: Penguin, 1987.

Boadella, David. *Wilhelm Reich: The Evolution of his Work*. London: Vision Press, 1973.

Brannigan, Michael. "There is No Spoon: A Buddhist Mirror." In *The Matrix and Philosophy: Welcome to the Desert of the Real*. Ed. William Irwin. Chicago: Open Court, 2002.

Broderick, Mick. "Heroic Apocalypse: Mad Max, Mythology, Millennium." In *Crisis Cinema: The Apocalyptic Idea in Postmodern Narrative Film*. Ed. Christopher Sharret. Washington: Maisonneuve Press, 1993.

Brody, Hugh. *The Other Side of Eden: Hunters, Farmers, and the Shaping of the World*. New York: North Point Press, 2000.

Brown, Dee. *Bury my Heart at Wounded Knee*. London: Pan Books, 1978.

Bucke, R.M. *Walt Whitman*. Philadelphia, 1883[SS1].

Burroughs, John. *Whitman: A Study*. London, 1894.

Callow, Philip. *Walt Whitman: From Noon to Starry Night*. London: Allison & Busby, 1992.

Campbell, Joseph. *The Hero with a Thousand Faces*. Princeton, New Jersey: Princeton University Press, 1973.

Chadwick, Henry. *The Early Church*. Middlesex: Penguin, 1967.

Christopher, Nicholas. *Somewhere in the Night: Film Noir and the American City*. New York: Free Press, 1997.

Churchill, Winston. *History of the Second World War*. Vol. V. Boston: Houghton Mifflin, 1951.

Clark, Ronald W. *Benjamin Franklin: A Biography*. London: Weidenfeld and Nicholson, 1983.

Constable, Catherine. "Baudrillardian Revolutions: Repetition and Radical Intervention in the *Matrix* Trilogy." In *The Matrix Trilogy: Cyberpunk Reloaded*. Ed. Stacy Gillis. London and New York: Wallflower, 2005.

Corey, Gerald. *Theory and Practice of Counseling and Psychotherapy*. Belmont: Wadsworth Publishing, 2001.

Czitrom, Daniel J. *Media and the American Mind: From Morse to McLuhan*. Chapel Hill: University of North Carolina Press, 1982.

Davies, Philip John, and Paul Wells (Eds.). *American Film and Politics from Reagan to Bush Jr.* Manchester: Manchester University Press, 2002.

Deacy, Christopher. *Christologies, Redemption and the Medium of Film*. Cardiff: University of Wales Press, 2001.

Derrida, Jacques. *Writing and Difference*. London: Routledge, 1978.

The Dhammapada. Trans. Eknath Easwaran. London: Arkana, 1986.

Dixon, Wheeler Winston. "Twenty-Five Reasons Why It's All Over." In *The End of Cinema as We Know It: American Film in the Nineties*. Ed. by Jon Lewis. London: Pluto Press, 2002.

Dunbar, David and Brad Reagan. *Debunking 9/11 Myths: Why Conspiracy Theories Can't Stand up to the Facts.* New York: Hearst Books, 2006.

Elder, Jennifer. *Different Like Me: My Book of Autism Heroes.* London: Jessica Kingsley Publishers, 2006.

Eliade, Mircea. *Shamanism: Archaic Techniques of Ecstasy.* Bollingen Series 76. Princeton and Oxford: Princeton University Press, 2004.

Elliott, Carl, and Tod Chambers (eds.). *Prozac as a Way of Life (Studies in Social Medicine).* Chapel Hill and London: University of North Carolina Press, 2004.

FEMA. *World Trade Center, Building Performance Study.* FEMA report 403, May 2002.

Frazer, Sir James George. *The Golden Bough: Study in Magic and Religion* (Abridged). New York: Touchstone, 1996.

Freud, Sigmund. *Civilization and Its Discontents.* New York: W.W. Norton, 1961.

_____. "On Narcissism: An Introduction." In *The Freud Reader.* Ed. Peter Gay. New York: Norton, 1985.

Frith, Uta (ed.). *Autism and Asperger Syndrome.* Cambridge, England: Cambridge University Press, 1991.

Gillis, Stacy (ed.). *The Matrix Trilogy: Cyberpunk Reloaded.* London: Wallflower, 2005.

Giroux, Henry A., and Imre Szeman. "Ikea Boy Fights Back." In *The End of Cinema as We Know It: American Film in the Nineties.* Ed. Jon Lewis. London: Pluto Press, 2002.

Golding, John. *Paths to the Absolute: Mondrian, Malevich, Kandinsky, Pollock, Newman, Rothko, and Still.* Princeton, New Jersey: Princeton University Press, 2000.

Goleman, Daniel. *Emotional Intelligence: Why It Can Matter More Than IQ.* London: Bloomsbury, 1996.

Gray, John. *Black Mass: Apocalyptic Religion and the Death of Utopia.* London: Allen Lane, 2007.

Griffin, David Ray. *The New Pearl Harbor: Disturbing Questions about the Bush Administration and 9/11.* Northampton, Massachusetts: Olive Branch Press, 2004.

Grosso, Michael. *The Millennium Myth: Love and Death at the End of Time.* Wheaton, Illinois: Quest Books, 1995.

Gullan-Whur, Margaret. *Within Reason: A Life of Spinoza.* London: Jonathan Cape, 1998.

Guthrie, Kenneth Sylvan. *The Pythagorean Sourcebook and Library.* Grand Rapids, Michigan: Phanes Press, 1987.

Haeffner, Nicholas. *Alfred Hitchcock.* Harlow: Longman, 2005.

Hagen, William M. "*Apocalypse Now* (1979): Joseph Conrad and the Television War." In *Hollywood as Historian: American Film in a Cultural Context.* Ed. Peter C. Rollins. Lexington: University Press of Kentucky, 1998.

Hall, Mary Katherine. "Now You Are a Killer of White Men: Jim Jarmusch's *Dead Man,* Traditions of Revisionism in the Western." *Journal of Film & Video.* Winter 2001, Vol. 52, Issue 4.

Hendershot, Heather. "Waiting for the End of the World: Christian Apocalyptic Media at the Turn of the Millennium." In *The End of Cinema as We Know It: American Film in the Nineties.* Ed. Jon Lewis. London: Pluto Press, 2002.

Hilger, Michael. *The American Indian in Film.* Metuchen, New Jersey: Scarecrow Press, 1986.

Hofstadter, Richard. *The Paranoid Style in American Politics, and Other Essays.* London: Jonathan Cape, 1966.

Hultkrantz, Ake. *The Religions of the American Indians.* Berkeley: University of California Press, 1979.

Irwin, William (ed.). *The Matrix and Philosophy: Welcome to the Desert of the Real.* Chicago: Open Court, 2002.

Izod, John. *Myth, Mind and the Screen: Understanding the Heroes of our Time.* Cambridge, England: Cambridge University Press, 2001.

Jacoby, Susan. *Freethinkers: A History of American Secularism.* New York: Metropolitan Books, 2004.

Juhasz, Alexandra. "The Phallus UnFetished: The End of Masculinity As We Know It in Late-1990s 'Feminist' Cinema." In *The End of Cinema as We Know It: American Film in the Nineties.* Ed. Jon Lewis. London: Pluto Press, 2002.

Jung, C. G. *Memories, Dreams, Reflections.* London: Fontana, 1993.

Kaplan, E. Ann (ed). *Psychoanalysis & Cinema.* New York, London: Routledge, 1990.

Kilpatrick, Jacquelyn. *Celluloid Indians: Native Americans and Film.* Lincoln: University of Nebraska Press, 1999.

Kinder, Marsha. "Violence American Style: The Narrative Orchestration of Violent Attractions." In *Violence and American Cinema.* Ed. David J. Slocum. New York: Routledge, 2001.

King, Mike. "Virtual Reality: Give Us a Visual

Clue." In *Proceedings of the First Split Screen Conference*, July 1996, pp. 180–187. Chichester Institute of Higher Education, 1997.

_____. *Secularism: The Hidden Origins of Disbelief.* Cambridge: James Clarke, 2007.

Knight, Peter. *Conspiracy Culture: American Paranoia from the Kennedy Assassination to The X-files.* London: Routledge, 2001.

Kolker, Robert. *A Cinema of Loneliness: Penn, Stone, Kubrick, Scorsese, Spielberg, Altman.* New York: Oxford University Press, 2000.

Kramnick, Isaac (ed.). *The Portable Enlightenment Reader.* London: Penguin, 1995.

LaHaye, Tim, and David Noebel. *Mind Siege: The Battle for Truth in the New Millennium.* Nashville: Word Publishing, 2000.

Lancelin, Aude. "The *Matrix* Decoded: *Le Nouvel Observateur* Interview with Jean Baudrillard." In *International Journal of Baudrillard Studies* Volume 1: Number 2 (2004).

Lasch, Christopher. *The Culture of Narcissism: American Life in an Age of Diminishing Expectations.* New York: W. W. Norton, 1991.

Lawrence, D.H. *Studies in Classic American Literature.* London: Penguin, 1977.

Lawrence, John Shelton. "Fascist Redemption or Democratic Hope?" In *Jacking in to the Matrix Franchise.* Eds. Matthew Kapell and William G. Doty. New York: Continuum, 2004.

Levinas, Emmanuel. *Totality and Infinity.* Trans. Alphonso Lingis. Pittsburgh: Duquesne University Press, 1969.

Lewis, Jon (ed.). *The End of Cinema as We Know It: American Film in the Nineties,* London: Pluto Press, 2002.

Lindsy, Hal. *The Late Great Planet Earth.* Michigan: Zondervan, 1970.

Lipsey, Roger. *An Art of Our Own: The Spiritual in Twentieth-Century Art.* Boston: Shambhala, 1988.

Lloyd, Peter B. *Exegesis of the Matrix.* London: Whole-Being Books, 2003.

Maland, Charles. "*Dr. Strangelove* (1964): Nightmare Comedy and the Ideology of Liberal Consensus." In *Hollywood as Historian: American Film in a Cultural Context.* Ed. Peter C. Rollins. Lexington: University Press of Kentucky, 1998.

Marsh, Clive, and Gaye Ortiz (eds.). *Exploration in Theology and Film: Movies and Meanings.* Oxford: Blackwell, 1997.

Martin, David. *On Secularization: Towards a Revised General Theory.* Aldershot: Ashgate, 2005.

McKinnon, Kenneth. "After Mulvey: Male Erotic Objectification." In *The Body's Perilous Pleasures: Dangerous Desires and Contemporary Culture.* Ed. Michele Aaron. Edinburgh: Edinburgh University Press, 1999.

Medved, Michael. *Hollywood vs. America.* New York: HarperCollins, 1993.

Mellencamp, Pat. "The Zen of Masculinity: Rituals of Heroism in *The Matrix*." In *The End of Cinema as We Know It: American Film in the Nineties.* Ed. Jon Lewis. London: Pluto Press, 2002.

Mesibov, Gary B., Victoria Shea, and Lynn W. Adams. *Understanding Asperger Syndrome and High Functioning Autism.* New York: Kluwer Academic / Plenum Publishers, 2001.

Murphy, Brenda. *Congressional Theatre: Dramatizing McCarthyism on Stage, Film and Television.* Cambridge, England: Cambridge University Press, 1999.

Naifeh, S., and G. W. Smith. *Jackson Pollock: An American Saga.* London: Pimlico, 1992.

Nietzsche, Friedrich. *Thus Spake Zarathustra.* London: Penguin Books, 1969.

Northcott, Michael. *An Angel Directs the Storm: Apocalyptic Religion and American Empire.* London: I.B. Tauris, 2004.

Perlmutter, Dawn. "Postmodern Idolatry: the Media and Violent Acts of Participation." In *Reclaiming the Spiritual in Art: Contemporary Cross-Cultural Perspectives.* Eds. Dawn Perlmutter and Debra Koppman. Albany: State University of New York Press, 1999.

_____, and Debra Koppman (eds.). *Reclaiming the Spiritual in Art: Contemporary Cross- Cultural Perspectives.* Albany: State University of New York Press, 1999.

Polan, Dana. *Power and Paranoia: History, Narrative and the American Cinema, 1940–1950.* New York: Columbia University Press, 1986.

Popper, Karl. *The Open Society and Its Enemies, Vol. 2: Hegel and Marx.* London: Routledge, 1973.

Pratt, Ray. *Projecting Paranoia: Conspiratorial Visions in American Film.* Lawrence: University Press of Kansas, 2001.

Prince, Stephen. *Classical Film Violence: Designing and Regulating Brutality in Hollywood Cinema, 1930–1968.* New Brunswick, New Jersey: Rutgers University Press, 2003.

Quart, Leonard, and Albert Auster. *American Film and Society since 1945.* Westport, Connecticut: Praeger, 2002.

Redfield, James. *The Celestine Prophecy: An Adventure.* New York: Bantam, 1994.

Ricoeur, Paul. *Freud and Philosophy: An Essay on Interpretation.* New Haven: Yale University Press, 1970.

Riesman, David. *The Lonely Crowd.* New Haven: Yale University Press, 2001.

Rudgley, Richard. *Pagan Resurrection: A Force for Evil or the Future of Western Spirituality?* London: Century, 2006.

Sacks, Jonathon. *The Dignity of Difference: How to Avoid the Clash of Civilisations.* London, New York: Continuum, 2003.

Salyer Gregory. "Poetry Written with Blood: Creating Death in *Dead Man.*" In *Imag(in)-ing Otherness: Filmic Visions of Living Together.* Eds. David Jasper and S. Brent Plate. Atlanta: Scholars Press, 1999.

Sartre, Jean-Paul. *Saint Genet.* London: Heinemann, 1988.

Saunder, Frances Stonor. *Hidden Hands: A Different History of Modernism.* London: Channel 4 Television, 1995.

Schamus, James. "A Rant." In *The End of Cinema as We Know It: American Film in the Nineties.* Ed. Jon Lewis. London: Pluto Press, 2002.

Schopler, Eric, and Gary B. Mesibov (eds.). *High-functioning Individuals with Autism.* New York and London: Plenum Press, 1992.

Schrecker, Ellen. *Many Are the Crimes: McCarthyism in America.* Princeton, New Jersey: Princeton University Press, 1998.

Seidler, Victor J. *Shadows of the Shoa: Jewish Identity and Belonging.* New York: Berg, 2000.

Sharret, Christopher. "End of Story: The Collapse of Myth in Postmodern Narrative Film." In *The End of Cinema as We Know It: American Film in the Nineties.* Ed. Jon Lewis. London: Pluto Press, 2002.

_____ (ed.). *Crisis Cinema: The Apocalyptic Idea in Postmodern Narrative Film.* Washington: Maisonneuve Press, 1993.

Shlain, Leonard. *The Alphabet Versus the Goddess: The Conflict Between Words and Images.* New York: Penguin Compass, 1998.

Simon, Stephen. *The Force Is with You: Mystical Movie Messages That Inspire Our Lives.* Charlottesville, VA: Hampton Roads, 2002.

Sontag, Susan. *Against Interpretation.* London: Vintage Books, 2001.

Spencer. *Dark City: The Film Noir.* Jefferson, North Carolina: McFarland, 1984.

Steiner, George. *The Death of Tragedy.* London: Faber and Faber, 1961.

Stephens, Michael L. *Film Noir: A Comprehensive, Illustrated Reference to Movies, Terms, and Persons.* Jefferson, North Carolina: Mc-Farland, 1995.

Stone, Merlin. *When God Was a Woman.* New York: Harcourt, 1976.

Sturken, Marita. *"Affliction*: When Paranoid Male Narratives Fail." In *The End of Cinema as We Know It: American Film in the Nineties.* Ed. Jon Lewis. London: Pluto Press, 2002.

Tacey, David. *The Spirituality Revolution: The Emergence of Contemporary Spirituality.* Hove and New York: Brunner-Routledge, 2004.

Tuchman, Barbara W. *Bible and Sword: England and Palestine from the Bronze Age to Balfour.* New York: Ballantine Books, 1984.

Vogler, Christopher. *The Writer's Journey: Mythic Structure for Storytellers and Screenwriters,* (2nd edition). London: Pan Books, 1998.

Wallace, Anthony F. C. "Revitalization Movements: Some Theoretical Considerations for Their Comparative Study." *American Anthropologist* n.s. 58(2):264–81. 1956.

Watson, Paul. "American cinema, political criticism and pragmatism: a therapeutic reading of *Fight Club* and *Magnolia.*" In *American Film and Politics from Reagan to Bush Jr.* Eds. Philip John Davies and Paul Wells. Manchester: Manchester University Press, 2002.

Watson, Peter. *A Terrible Beauty: The People and Ideas that Shaped the Modern Mind.* London: Phoenix, 2000.

Weininger, Otto. *Sex and Character: An Investigation of Fundamental Principles.* Trans. Ladislaus Löb. Bloomington: Indiana University Press, 2005.

Wheen, Francis. *Karl Marx.* London: Fourth Estate, 2000.

Whitman, Walt. *Leaves of Grass.* Oxford, New York: Oxford University Press, 1990.

_____. *Specimen Days,* London: The Folio Society, 1979.

Williams, Andrew. "60 Seconds: Gary Numan." *Metro,* November 6, 2006.

Wilson, Eric G. *Secret Cinema: Gnostic Vision in Film.* London: Continuum, 2006.

Index

www.ingramcontent.com/pod-product-compliance
Lightning Source LLC
Chambersburg PA
CBHW071318090426
42738CB00012B/2723